CHINESE WOMEN

Past & Present

by

Esther S. Lee Yao
University of Houston
Clear Lake City Campus

Mesquite

Ide House

1983

Published by:
Ide House, Inc.
4631 Harvey Drive
Mesquite, Texas 75150-1609

Of the Ide House series **Woman in history** *this is volume 82.*

Library of Congress Cataloging in Publication Data

Yao, Esther S. Lee (Esther Shu-shin Lee), 1944-
Chinese women, past & present.

(Woman in history, ISSN 0195-9743 ; 82)
Includes   bibliographical   references   and   index.
1. Women--China--History. 2. Women--Taiwan--History.
3. Women--China--Social conditions. 4. Women--Taiwan--
Social conditions. I. Title. II. Title: Chinese women,
past and present. III. Series.
HQ1767.Y36 1983   305.4'0951   83-300
ISBN 0-86663-099-6 (lib. bdg.)
ISBN 0-86663-098-8 (pbk.)

In Memory of My Father

Wei-Chin Lee

Who provided equal educational opportunities to his sons and daughters; who had high expectations of all his children; who made me proud of being a woman.

TABLE OF CONTENTS

Chronological Table of Chinese History

B.C.	Era
2852	Culture Heroes: Fu Hsi: inventor of writing, fishing, trapping. Shen Nung: inventor of agriculture, commerce. Huang-ti.
2357	Sage Kings Yao Shun Yu: founder of Hsia Dynasty
1818	Hsia Dynasty
1766	Shang Dynasty
1115	Western Chou Dynasty
722	Eastern Chou Dynasty
221	Ch'in Dynasty
202	Former Han Dynasty

A.D.	Era
25	Latter Han Dynasty
220	Period of the Three Kingdoms & Wei Dynasty
280	Chin Dynasty
317	Northern & Southern Empire
589	Sui Dynasty
685-705	Reign of Empress Wu
907	Five Dynasties Period
960	Sung Dynasty
1260	Yuan Dynasty
1368	Ming Dynasty
1644	Ch'ing Dynasty
1911	Republic of China
1949	People's Republic of China

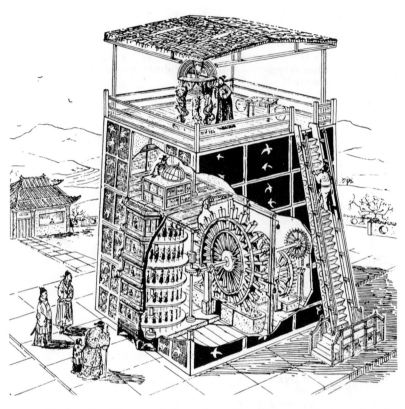

During the T'ang and Sung dynasties Chinese science and technology were far more advanced than European science and technology of the same era. This is best shown in one of the most complicated Chinese scientific-technological and mechanical inventions: the astronomical observatory which dates from approximately 1090 A.D. This instrument used a water-powered clock to rotate the instruments in time with the motion of the stars. A similar invention in the west was not realized until the fourteenth century—and it is only recently that credit for this invention and achievement of this device has been given to China.

PREFACE

Scholars have become interested in studying women of different cultures during the past decade and Chinese women are not excluded. Yet, any examination of the current status of Chinese women requires an historical review of their past lives. Since the days of Marco Polo (1254?-1324?), Chinese women have been surrounded by myth and mystery in the minds of westerners. Over the years many westerners have taken the opportunity to study Chinese history and culture. Yet, understanding an old civilization through a foreign language is difficult and requires the time consuming task of studying lengthy historical records, the diversity of dialects, and knowledge of the changing writing styles of Chinese classical literature. Even if these obstacles are overcome, others remain when women are chosen as a subject for study. Culture refers both to the substantial observable heritage and the imperceptible historical process of human interaction which essentially form the legacy of Chinese women. Although women represent nearly half of the Chinese population, their experience has been ignored by both Chinese and Occidental historians and scholars. Their lives are occasionally revealed in fragmented forms in western literature: either in topics or included as part of Chinese family life.

With so little knowledge of Chinese women's historical background, an attempt to make an interpretation and generalization concerning their present status is a challenge even for a researcher who is a Chinese woman raised and educated in China, and conscious of the inner feelings and underlying problems encountered by Chinese women in the past as well as the present. In addition, my language proficiency permits me to master Chinese classic and modern literature for data collection. With these two advantages I am motivated to present a genuine portrait of Chinese women to the west by tracing the footsteps of my predecessors from antiquity to the contemporary period.

Most of the material used in this book is primarily information written in Chinese. The historical data on Chinese women was collected from the Central Library in Taipei, Taiwan, and several university libraries in Taiwan during the summers of 1979 and 1981. In China, the history of each dynasty has been written by historians from the succeeding dynasty to minimize biased judgement and misinterpretation. As a result, since the Republic was founded in 1911, history has not been officially recorded. The accuracy and integrity of the references published during this period, both in Taiwan and Mainland China, and especially during the power struggle between the Nationalist Party and the Communist Party during World War II is questionable. Since I was raised in Taiwan and witnessed firsthand the reality of women's lives there, my observations and interpretations are far more reliable than those who have either never been there or had only short visits. Unfortunately, since I left Mainland China at the age of 5, I cannot consider the women's situation there as extensively as I can for Taiwan. The coverage I do have is based mainly on my summer trip to China in 1982, available English and Chinese material, and interviews with relatives and friends who recently traveled to the Mainland and also visitors and scholars from the Mainland. My lack of firsthand experience in Mainland China, however, is somewhat balanced by the considerable recognition and admiration women in Mainland China have won from the western world through volumes of publications.

I have been as careful as possible to let the historical material speak for itself. It is an extremely difficult task to explore the intrinsic and extrinsic cultural traits of Chinese women, over a period of more than three thousand years, without personal interpretation. Nevertheless, it is my commitment that the contents of this volume are devoted mainly to the facts based on my review of material instead of my personal judgement on Chinese women's past experiences and present social status.

This book is written for those who are interested in Chinese culture and in the women of China, regardless of their knowledge of Chinese studies or their academic background. Non-sinologists, who are unfamiliar with Chinese historical names and pronounciations may find it difficult to remember some of the information. Basically, the Chinese literature mentioned in this book is both transliterated for sound and translated for meaning. I have employed the Wade-Giles romanization system with the exception of longtime adopted terms and names in quotations. For that reason, I intend to present this book to readers in a very simple and direct form. Those who are interested in gaining more knowledge on the social and economic development of each chronological stage are encouraged to refer to other books on Chinese history.

In conclusion, I sincerely hope that I have achieved my goal in linking Chinese women's past to their present status and helped the readers to more adequately understand Chinese women, both past and present.

—Esther Lee Yao

*University of Houston
  at Clear Lake City*
January 1983

4

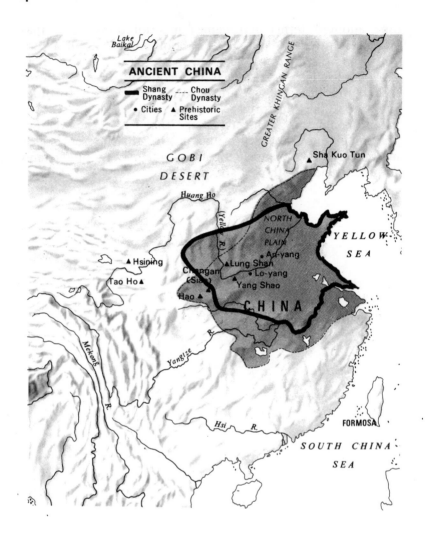

ANCIENT CHINA

Shang Dynasty
Chou Dynasty
• Cities   ▲ Prehistoric Sites

Lake Baikal

GREATER KHINGAN RANGE

GOBI DESERT

Sha Kuo Tun

Huang Ho

NORTH CHINA PLAIN

YELLOW SEA

▲ Hsining

Tao Ho ▲

Chang-an (Sian)

▲Lung Shan

• An-yang

• Lo-yang

Yang Shao

Hao ▲

C H I N A

Mekong R.

Yangtze R.

Hsi R.

FORMOSA

SOUTH CHINA SEA

CHAPTER ONE

Introduction

China is a vast land. People with distinct complexions, religious beliefs, languages, lifestyles, political structures, and ethnic heritages have made Chinese civilization not only enduring but colorful. Chinese women in the various subcultures experience diverse societal roles and status. Their assorted experiences have engendered a variety of observations and interpretations of Chinese women's lives. Any attempt to generalize about all Chinese women would jeopardize honest observation and unbiased judgment. This book focuses on the majority of women in populated regions. I do not emphasize women living in remote areas with separate and distinct social norms and lifestyles, although I have presented a section on women of minority groups briefly at the end of Chapter 6. For example, women on the southwestern boundary of China are responsible for transporting goods on their backs and shoulders along jungle trails and mountain paths. Since they were not confined to the house, their social status was higher than that of women in "civilized" regions. Women in the northern and western provinces rode horseback and were more mobile. The nomadic life in Mongolia afforded women a different perspective on life. Their daily routines and household chores were unlike those of women in the South. Besides the political systems in Mongolia, Tibet, and Sinkiang Provinces differ from the one adopted by the central Communist government, and information concerning the education and employment of women in these semi-autonomous regions has seldom been available to scholars for study.

This book is organized basically in chronological order. Since women's status and roles during the past three thousand years have changed slowly and overlapped at times, I have discussed only the unique transitions occurring in each period. The book is divided into five historical eras: *antiquity* (before 208 B.C.), the *ancient period* (209 B.C.-960 A.D.), the *middle period* (960-1642), the *modern period* (1643-1949), and the *contemporary period* (1949-present). The amount of coverage for each period varies according to the degree of change in women's lives. For example, the Chinese women's movement visible by the end of the 19th century changed women's lives a great deal, especially since it has developed differently under two political regimes. Because of this, the women's movement receives more attention than women's experience in other periods. Two chapters are devoted to Chinese women under the Communists in Mainland China and the Nationalists in Taiwan after 1949 respectively.

Archaeological evidence and ancient writings suggest that prior to the Chou Dynasty (1100-220 B.C.), a matrilineal society existed in which women were highly regarded (Jen, 1925; Creel, 1954; Mou, 1966; Wilhelm, 1970). However, women's status began to deteriorate late in the ancient period, even as Chinese civilization reached a significant economic and cultural peak. A patriarchal clan system instituted in the Chou Dynasty had a detrimental impact on women's social position in subsequent centuries. As the power of the patriarchy increased, women's position in the family declined (Lang, 1968; Gross and Bingham, 1980). Since then, women have been expected to conform to clearly defined social rules determined and enforced by men. The cause for such a drastic reversal of the status of women prior to the Chou Dynasty remains unclear. Based on the available sources, it was found that the social norms and official ceremonial rites described in ancient literature merely reflect the lifestyle of upper-class women and the educated elite; not the common women. Therefore, many missing pieces remain to be found to gain a complete picture of Chinese women in antiquity.

The society that later flourished during the Han and T'ang Dynasties (206 B.C.-907 A.D.), and the emergence of Neo-Confuciasnism in the Sung Dynasty (A.D. 960-1127) further eroded women's dignity and self perception. Cultural influence and social pressure on women confined them within the walls of their homes and induced them to accept the notion of self-sacrifice. As they did so, women began to develop their talents and devote their efforts within the family domain. They languished in the role assigned them and had no inclination to question or challenge it.

Oppressive social practices such as infanticide and footbinding, however, were not to become popular until recent dynasties. Scholars of Chinese women's studies, such as Ch'en Tung-yuan (1926), Olga Lang (1968), Li Chia-fu (1978), and Pao Chia-lin (1979), agree that Chinese women were most repressed, both physically and psychologically, during the Ch'ing Dynasty (1644-1911). Ironically, the door of the Ch'ing Empire was opened to foreigners and allowed westerners a glimpse into the misery of Chinese women's lives. Women's grief and misfortune were often depicted by western novelists and missionaries from their own perspectives and cultural backgrounds. Meanwhile during this period, Chinese men became sympathetic toward the fate of Chinese women and began to oppose this unjust and inhumane treatment of women in the male-dominated Chinese society. They wrote books and articles advocating women's physical freedom and increasing their educational opportunities. The growth of clubs organized by men calling for the return of women's natural foot paralleled the expansion of girl's schools. The revolutionary atmosphere at the end of the Ch'ing Dynasty increased the fervor of the women's movement. Women were encouraged to participate in the revolution for the common cause of saving the nation from the dominance of foreign superpowers. As a result of their active participation and outstanding performance during the revolutionary period of the early 1900s, Chinese women won the right to vote and upon the founding of the republic in 1911, the right to a formal education. However, after that, the women's movement gradually lost strength due to the lack of theoretical foundations and long-term goals as analyzed by P'i (1973).

Even today, women have not completely escaped the deep-rooted thinking of thousands of years. Marriage and motherhood are still highly valued by contemporary Chinese women. Recent decades have brought new opportunities and new roles to women, as well as new problems. Traditional cultural values often conflict with new cultural values. Employment usually requires sending their children to day care centers. Guilt over this and reduced efforts at homemaking frequently affects women's productivity and chances for promotion. Distracted by household problems, they are often regarded as incompetent. Despite their training and intellectual potential, women are still limited by the traditional value systems imposed on them for centuries. Fortunately the influence of such systems is diminishing, and hopefully will soon disappear forever.

Chinese women have been forbidden to pursue goals of their own choosing, discouraged from having a career, segregated from men in their leisure activities, made financially dependent, and treated as if they were ignorant. Nevertheless, their lives were not as pathetic as might be imagined, their homes were their career. They devoted time and effort to the family unit, leaving their husbands in charge of external affairs. Their reward came from the achievements of sons and husbands. They enjoyed making preparations for family anniversaries and the annual festivals, sewing the proper outfits for family members, cooking endless varieties of dishes, arranging play activities for the children, and entertaining friends and relatives. Seasonal festivities and important family events meant women could continuously anticipate celebrations that made their lives more colorful. Their contribution to the household was by no means ignored; their vital role in the family was recognized. Thus, they were not expected to earn a living outside the home; this was considered to be the men's responsibility. In most cases women had their say in the allocation of expenses for family members. Their authority in the family increased with their age. The eldest widow in a family had unchallenged power in decision making. Although most women received no formal education, they were well equipped with negative intelligence and acquired what knowledge they could.

The image most people today have of Chinese women tends to be stereotyped. In one sense, Chinese women have always been strong, both physically and psychologically. The frail women shown in famous ancient Chinese paintings represented the minority: women of the middle- and upperclasses who were free from arduous jobs. Generally, those women who were the models for artists were considered sex objects. However, the formal portraits of women whose husbands were high-ranking officers show sturdy and vigorous Chinese women. Lower-class women working in the fields did not attract much attention from artists and were seldom seen in paintings, particularly those exhibited in museums. According to written material, they were healthy, energetic, and muscular—they had to be in order to perform their daily domestic chores and toil in the field. Psychologically, they were staunch and courageous, neither vanquished by rigid traditional values nor crushed by social norms imposed on them.

Enormous physical hardiness and mental strength turned many women's personal sacrifices into measureless contributions to Chinese history. The deprivation of basic human rights, the depression of their social status, the physical torment of footbinding, and the mental affliction of infanticide and widowhood did not defeat Chinese women, they managed to survive and still be a positive influence to their offspring. In spite of their inferior status in society, some women with a keen intellect and great spiritual sensibility believed that eventually their presence would make an impact on Chinese politics, literature, and education for succeeding generations. Confined to home and deprived of employment, some widows carried on to raise sons who later became famous and held prominent positions in their government. After suffering the loss of baby girls who were victims of infanticide, many women still had the courage and resolution to give birth to another child in hopes of bearing a son.

Nowadays, liberal thinking and western influence have changed the lives of Chinese women to various degrees, whether in Taiwan, Mainland China, or overseas. Some immigration to foreign countries interrupted the cultural experience of overseas Chinese women, their vicissitudes are not encompassed in this book. Moreover, their cultural assimilation in different foreign countries would make the coverage too complicated and difficult. Chinese women who remain in their motherland, either Mainland China or Taiwan, play an important role in this book. They are discussed in Chapters VI and VII respectively. The goal and direction of the women's movement under these two regimes—Nationalist and Communist—reflect their distinct political ideologies, the society in which women's lives have undergone enormous changes and the prospectives of their emancipation.

Since Chinese women have not been equally treated by society in the past and have not been fairly measured by the historian's yardstick, the stories of famous women were given little room in historical records. Liu Hsiang was a pioneer historian completing a book on Chinese women. *Lien Nu Chuan* (*Records of Virtuous Women*) around 29 B.C. Since then, thirteen out of the twenty-five historical volumes for each succeeding dynasty contained the deeds of those women who were judged in their own time to be heroines. Over six hundred women appear in these thirteen historical volumes: *Book of Latter Han, Book of Ch'in, Book of Wei, History of the North, Book of Sui, Book of old Tang, Book of Tang, History of Sung, History of Liao, History of Chin, History of Yuan, History of New Yuan*, and *History of Ming*. They were glorified by historians who selected them basing their choices on the social standards imposed on women at that time. Particularly in the dynasties of Ming and Ch'ing, women were expected to conform to heartless and cruel social standards. To win the historian's praise, women had to sacrifice their lives in order to protect the reputation of their families. When women rebelled against the traditional norms, their unusual behavior could still be recorded by historians, but most likely in a negative manner laced with harsh criticisms. Several empress regents whose contributions to the nation were often overshadowed by the diabolical means they used to achieve power were negatively portrayed by historians. Male historians unfairly condemned these women for their political achievements, basing their criticisms on male egotism. Nevertheless, the stories of famous historical women have been retold constantly in various forms through modern mass media. In order to gain a better understanding of the roles played by women in each era, stories of several renowned women are incorporated in each chapter. Their popularity among the Chinese people and their representativeness of the women of their period are the major criteria for selection. No famous women are included in the last two chapters on women of present day because an objective selection for contemporary famous women would be very difficult. Without the passage of time it is impossible to assess the impact of any woman on the experience of all Chinese women and her contribution to the nation.

Nowadays, Chinese women are still stereotyped as submissive, dependent, and fragile by many westerners, who rarely associate Chinese women's changing outlook with their veiled personality traits of perseverance, adaptability, and self-reliance. I hope that an examination of the history of Chinese women will dispel some of the myths about them, and provide insights into the problems encountered by the current women's movement both in Taiwan and Mainland China.

Oracle bone, dating from 1300 B.C., records the appearance of a new star. Note the pictographic characters.

CHAPTER TWO

Women in Chinese Antiquity
(Before 208 B.C.)

China's ancient civilization during the prehistoric period is very vague. Although the discovery of the skulls of Lantien man (found in 1964), Peking man and upper cave men indicates that as early as 600,000 B.C., inhabitants in China were able to make simple tools and cook food (Chang, 1963, Fawdry, 1977), there were no other objects to reveal anything else to us about the society of that time. The evolution of civilization during this long period between 600,000 and the formation of the Shang Dynasty around 1700 B.C. was basically transmitted to us through legend and folklore (Granet, 1930). The ancient classics written later referring to the period prior to the Shang Dynasty (ca. 1766-1115 B.C.) are also supplemented by legend and folklore. Chinese recorded history began with the archaeological findings of inscriptions on tortoise shells, oracle bones and on stones and bronze excavated from the capital of the Shang, Yin (or Great City Shang). However, most of the evidence reveals findings about the lives of ancient aristocrats but yields very little information about the day-to-day existence of common people—particularly women (Chang, 1963).

The founding of the Chou Dynasty marks a new page in Chinese history. When the Chou conquered the Shang, who were highly civilized, they determined to broaden the horizons of the existing culture. They not only expanded the territory by establishing feudalism but also controlled people's conduct by regulating the interpersonal relationships among rulers, vassals, fathers, sons, brothers, friends and husbands and wives. These two political and social implementations brought China into a new era of social order and induced further advancement of Chinese civilization. Yet, the innovative feudalism was short lived, the growing power of feudal lords eventually led to a divided nation where the king was merely a figurehead. After years of fighting among the feudal lords, seven super powers emerged. Finally from the seven, the Chin counquered all and China became a united nation.

While Chinese people in antiquity were making progress in the use of tools, living conditions, food acquisition, and human relationships, and meeting spiritual needs through art, music, and religion, both men and women's role were also changing. Such supposed changes can be examined based on two periods: prior to and immediately following the Shang Dynasty. Since very little solid information on women prior to the Shang Dynasty is available, most of the material included in this volume is cited from ancient classics written and/or compiled by scholars in later periods. Material on women following the Shang Dynasty is much more concrete and reliable as a result of the archaeological findings early in the 20th century.

Although women in the Shang Dynasty were found to be domestic oriented, patriarchy was not enforced and rigidly imposed on people as it was later on in the Chou Dynasty. People can spot some residual of matriarchy during this period. In fact, some sources support the notion that a matrilineal society existed in the China of remote antiquity before the establishment of the Shang Dynasty (Granet, 1930; Creel, 1954; Lang, 1968; Wilhelm, 1970; and, Wu, 1982).

A. Matrilineal Society in China

The matriarchal stage is viewed traditionally as one of chaotic disorder from its inception. The book, *Spring and Atumn Annals*, informs us that in the ancient era, people co-existed without rulers, and without rules for proper conduct. No differentiation was made between relationships, such as brother/sister, husband/wife, men/women, low class/high class, or young/old. People recognized only their mother, not their father; the primogenitors in the prehistoric period could comprehend only the physical relationship between a mother and her child, not the invisible blood bond between a father and his child (Granet, 1930). Another source, the *Pai Hu Tung*, also indicates: "In the legendary days there was no moral or social order. Men knew only their mother, not their father. When hungry they hunted for food, when replete they threw away what was left. They devoured their food without removing fur or skin, they drank up the blood and wrapped themselves in rushes and skins" (Creel, 1954). Furthermore, the book *Tao Chih Pien*, by Chuang Tzu, refers to the same period as a society where people experienced a changing lifestyle: they built shelters, planted crops, and only recognized the consanguinity with their mother, but not their father. The prominent French sociologist and China scholar, Marcel Granet, also felt that

> It was in fact a time when births were aquired at the sole profit of the wives and when the only re-incarnations were those of maternal ancestors. It was the time when houses and villages belonged to the women. They ruled there, bearing the title of mothers. . . . Thus there was a period when the earth which had been inhabited and claimed had none but female attributes. Organization was then almost entirely matriarchal.[1]

Olga Lang (1968) also pointed out "the basic social unit at the end of the New Stone Age was evidently the matrilineal clan. . . ."[2] Based on the above sources, it is suspected that during that early period, people were free from social structure, such as the tribe, and a polyandrous society was very possible.

Polyandry was thought to be linked to matriarchy (Ts'ai, 1934; and, Ch'en, 1975). In recounting the birth of folklore heroes, the mother's name was mentioned, but not the father's. Based on Tuan Yu-t'sai's *Exegeses on Chu Shen's Dictionary*, the germinal king Yao was conceived after his mother Ch'ing Tu was impregnated by a red dragon.[3] Both *Tzu Hsiu Wu P'ien* of Huay Nan, and Lo Mee's *Lu Sse Yu Pian* recorded that the birth of Yu, the first king of the Hsia Dynasty, was somehow associated with a stone—either his mother became a stone after his birth, or she swallowed a stone to become pregnant. A woman named Chien-ti, a daughter of the tribe Yu-jung, while bathing with her sisters in the Hsuan Chiu Shui, swallowed an egg from a black bird, swallow, or phoenix flying overhead; later she found that she was pregnant and in due time gave birth to a child who later became King Ch'i of the Shang Dynasty (Jen, 1925; Chen, 1926; Chang, 1963; Mau, 1966; and, Li, 1978a). According to the same sources, the founding father of the Chou Dynasty, Hou Chi, was the son of Chiang-yuan who was inspired by giant footprints in the woods. All of the above-mentioned rulers had no inkling as to the identity of their fathers, only their mother's names and the strange conception process were recorded. Thus, it is possible that sexual promiscuity was practiced by women who were the only recognizable parents to be responsible for raising the children.[4]

Although these mythical recordings have no scientific basis, ancient kings most likely used this tactic to dramatize their births and to better control their subjects. For example, the term "Heaven's Son" traditionally referring to Chinese emperors implied the extraordinary birth of ancient Chinese rulers and symbolized the power granted to the rulers from Heaven. In order to convince the vassals of their heavenly domination or supremacy, only their mothers were mentioned. It was inferred that only half of their blood came from heaven and there was no physical evidence to the contrary.

Archaeological findings which reveal the residual matriarchy existing in the Shang society are more concrete and reliable than the above-mentioned folklore to support the notion that matriarchy thrived in this early Chinese society (Creel, 1954). Lo Cheng-yu's *Yin Hsu Books* (Book on the City of Yin) which were based on the unearthed objects in ancient capitals, disclosed that people in the Shang Dynasty showed respect for their dead mothers by honoring them in a special sacrificial ceremony.[5] This posthumous ritual indicates the unique societal status of women at that time. According to Chang's findings, unlike the commoners, the structure of the Shang or Yin royal family is relatively clear where female members were partnered with their male counterparts, such as grandfathers, fathers, husbands and sons.[6] Subsequent dynasties stripped the deceased mothers of this honor by mourning them only as ordinary members of the family.

Furthermore, one of the earliest history books, *Spring and Autumn Annals*, written after the Shang Dynasty, also contains three compelling clues which support the contention that matrilineal society existed prior to the Chou Dynasty. First, until the Spring and Autumn period, women were in charge of regular offerings in a family. Since these rituals were considered major and sacred responsibilities, very often the oldest girl of a family (called Wu Erh) remained unmarried to fulfill this obligation. An offertory rite conducted by a married woman was unacceptable for fear of bringing bad luck to the family. This is believed to be a residue of matriarchy (Jen, 1925; and, Mou, 1966). Social trends reversed sharply as a result of the establishment of the hierarchic clan system in the Chou Dynasty. A patrilineal system was then favored. Men began to conduct offertory rites while women merely assisted.

A second piece of evidence in support of matriarchy is that the definition of brotherhood during the Spring and Autumn period was based upon the mother's surname. Siblings borne by and bearing the name of the same mother, did not necessarily share the same father. The term "brotherhood", referring to people who carried the same maternal surname, was not restricted to one generation. This is also supported by Chang's conclusion on the social structure in the Yin Dynasty.[7] Therefore, uncles were brothers to their nephews, because they all inherited the same surname from the maternal side. Since the mother's surname was vital in determining kinship, the inheritance of kingdom prior to the Chou Dynasty was also arranged according to this relationship. The succession of kinship was based on birth order, passing from the older brother to the younger brother with the oldest son of the youngest brother having the right to ascend the throne (Jen, 1925; and, Mou, 1966). This practice was designed to continue the mother's surname for as long as possible.

The third piece of evidence is that the word "surname" in Chinese has two radicals, or roots: "woman" and "birth". This is an etymological indication that the group or unit which the surname designated was female-centered. While women were entitled to these surnames, men were merely given titles matching their deeds; some lower class men had no title or surname, only first names. Marriage was strictly exogamous to prevent inbreeding; people having the same title as their father's were permitted to marry each other while those having the same surnames as their mothers' were not allowed to do so. Originally there were one hundred ancient surnames derived from five basic sounds.[8] Even the oldest clan names contained the Chinese character of "woman" as one of the radicals. However, very few of these ancient surnames, such as Chiang and Yao, have survived through the years; with the emerging patriarchal power, they have gradually vanished from the pages of history.

B. Marriage and Women's Family Life

Marital customs in China were molded after the emergence of a patriarchal society. Promiscuous matriarchies which thrived in remote primitive societies declined as patriarchy gradually took hold. With changing life styles and greater physical strength, men were eventually able to dominate society in the Chou Dynasty. During the dynasties of Shang and Chou, ceremonial activities essentially centered around the protocol of religious offerings through which men were able to communicate with heaven and/or their ancestors. Less value was placed on marriage, which bonded the relationship between men and women, than men's reverence to their providers and protectors—heaven and ancestors.

The unity of men and women finally metamorphosed into a more rigid and complex wedding ceremony in the late Chou Dynasty. The evolution of marital customs was slow and vague; the three types of marriage, namely capture, purchased, and arranged, paralleled the chronicles of Chinese history and overlapped in light of a different era and geographical location. In the capture marriage, man merely took advantage of his superior strength to possess the woman of his choice, thereby rendering the marriage complete and acceptable. *I Ching* (*Book of Changes*) said of the ancient time: "Upon hearing the neighs of horses, tears would stream down the girl's face, for she realized that this must be the robbers who came to take her for marriage."[9]

The prototype of a wedding ceremony prescribed by *Li Chi* (*Book of Rites*) was reminiscent of the kidnapping style used earlier. *Li Chi* required that the intended groom and his entourage go to the prospective bride's home at dusk to fetch her. A party from the bride's family would then accompany the couple to the home of the groom's family. This ritual assured that while the "capture" marriage allowed a woman to be seized from her home, her family would symbolically come to her rescue.

In a purchased marriage, women were treated more or less as property and slaves, whose only contribution to their husband and his family was the number of children they bore (Chao, 1973). Their function was to produce male offspring to carry on the family name. Once purchased, they became merely their husband's possession with no human rights. They could be traded as an unwanted commodity whenever their husband wished. Like capture marriage, the remanants of purchased marriage could be detected in a formal marital procedure, known as the "Six Proprieties" prescribed in *Li Chi*. Later, in the arranged marriage, which was the prototype of the "Six Proprieties", the groom's family either had to pay a great sum of money or give expensive gifts to the bride's family, the notion of purchase lurking barely out of sight. Purchased marriage was short lived and became unpopular with the establishment of the clan system. The clan system stipulated the precedence of authority, inheritance, and priority of privileges in terms of male seniority within the clan.

Concurrently with the introduction of the clan system, arranged marriage gained prominence by the end of the Chou Dynasty. An arranged marriage had to be accomplished by a matchmaker who acted as go-between for both families. A matchmaker was defined as a person who brought two members of the opposite sex, and different surnames together (Li, 1978a). Later, at one time, the government even resorted to installing an officer to take charge of this affair so that marriage was insured for everyone of marriageable age, regardless of social status (Ch'en, 1975; and, Ch'en, 1977). A marriage without a matchmaker was unacceptable and could be desolved by the husband. If the matched marriage failed, however, the matchmaker was not blamed, since the marriage was supposedly made in heaven, and beyond the control of mere mortals. The ceremony for a matched marriage was at first very simple, and conducted only in certain regions of the nation or within certain social groups (Li, 1978b). Although the "Six Proprieties" for the wedding ceremony were prescribed in *Li Chi*, the observance of such a complicated marital custom was not widely adopted until the end of the East Chou Dynasty.

Before the installment of the "Six Proprieties," boys and girls had adequate social contact and freedom to express affection toward each other. Dating was spontaneous and free from moral obligation, the period of courtship short but full of romance. As mentioned in *Shih Ching* (*Book of Poetry*), a collection of poems, young people were free to date members of the opposite sex after festivities. Again, the *Chou Li* (*Rites of Chou*) states that the second month of spring was a time when men and women could elope without being restricted. Many poems in the *Shih Ching*, such as *Two Souths, North Wind, Yun Wind, Cheng Wind*, and *Ch'en Wind* describe love affairs during this period.

In this era, chastity and virginity were lost causes; women were not expected to be faithful to a dead spouse for the rest of their lives. In fact adultery ran rampant between high class women and noblemen, and was severely criticized by the book *Tso Chuan* (*Commentaries on Spring and Autumn Annals*). According to *I Ching* (*Book of Changes*) there were originally three definitions of women's chastity mainly focusing on women's fidelity which are different from today's meaning: (1) holding the appropriate social or official title, totally separate from the physical connotations; (2) maintaining the husband/wife relationship; and, (3) not being promiscuous (Ch'en, 1977).

By the late Chou Dynasty, the wedding ceremony for an arranged marriage had become both sacred and cumbersome. Marriage, a major endeavor between two persons, was considered having a profound impact on their families and on successive generations. Because of this emphasis on the family, the bride and groom had to pay homage to their ancestors during the wedding ceremony.

The "Six Proprieties" prescribed for the wedding ceremony governed Chinese lifestyle for nearly two thousand years. Connubiality was not recognized until six steps were completed. Each step is explained as follows (Ch'en, 1975; Ch'en, 1971; and, Li, 1978b):

The boy's family could initiate the marriage when he became seventeen and the girl became fourteen years of age. Men and women who remained single until thirty and twenty-one years of age respectively were considered overdue for marriage, and were termed "widowed." The acceptance of a gift from a prospective groom's family was known as *Na Chia* (the first step). With a matchmaker acting as a go-between, the groom's family would send a messenger with a wild goose as a gift of greeting to the prospective bride's family, thereby symbolizing a formal proposal of marriage. Upon receiving the gift, the bride's family wrote down the name and birthday of the young lady and presented it to the messenger; this was the second step, *Wen Ming* (or, name request).

For the third step, *Na Chi*, the groom's family would present the bride's name, birthday, and time of birth to their ancestors' altar for approval. At the front of the altar, the groom's parents would divine for the approval of the spirits of the ancestors. If the result of the divination indicated that the bride's name and birthday were compatible with the groom's, the parents could proceed with the next step.

The young man's family was responsible for the selection of an auspicious wedding date and for the preparation of gifts to be delivered to his future bride's family. This step, *Na Cheng*, was a vital part of the entire procedure, for without it, women were only considered to be concubines, not wives. The value of the gifts for the bride's family depended upon the social status of both families. According to the *Chou Li* (*Rites of Chou*), jade could be given to a prince's bride, and fabric and animal skins to the scholar's, while the common man's bride rated only five ounces of silk. The gifts were delivered by a messenger who was accompanied by a respectable representative of the groom. Following the invitation to wed, the groom's family would inform the bride's family of the wedding date, which was subject to postponement only in the event of a death in either immediate family. Customarily, the bride's parents were consulted as to their choice of a wedding date, a courtesy called *Chin Chi*.

The final stage of the six steps occurred on the wedding day, when both families engaged in preparations for the event. Approaching sunset, the groom's father would give him a wild goose and order him to his intended bride's home. The wedding held at dusk was believed to symbolize the custom of the capture marriage, which occurred during this time. (In fact, the Chinese word for "wedding" originally meant "a ceremony at twilight.") Upon his arrival at the bride's home, the groom was led to the altar of the bride's ancestors. After making his offering and paying his respects, he would drive the bride's carriage for three revolutions of the wheels. Then he would return home in his own carriage before the bride's carriage arrived at his residence. Once the bride had arrived at the groom's home, accompanied by her younger sisters and serving maids, a wedding dinner would be served to the couple in the bridal chamber. The number of women accompanying the bride was in direct accordance with the rank of the bridegroom. In most cases, these women became the groom's concubines in the form of the "sororate" (Lang, 1968). The private nupital dinner for the couple symbolized that they would live and eat together from that time on. Later the bride's entourage arranged the bedding for the newlyweds. After all the helpers had retreated, the groom would remove the foot long hair pin that had bound the bride's hair from the time she was promised to him, blow out the candles in the chamber, and the couple would spend the first evening of their new life together.

However, the status of wife was not granted to the bride until she had fulfilled additional obligations during the first three months of marriage as well as the six steps described above. The day after the wedding, the bride was expected to rise early and greet her parents-in-law. This first greeting was very complicated and included presenting a gift to them, serving them dinner, and in turn, receiving gifts from them. At the end of the first three months, the bride journeyed to her husband's family shrine to give an offering. This visit was meant to inform the groom's ancestors of the status of this new member of the family. If the bride died prior to this ceremony, she was buried in her own family's graveyard as an unmarried woman and was not regarded as a member of the groom's family, so he was not obligated to mourn her. Occasionally, the bride's parents would leave a horse at the groom's stable for this three month period as a gesture of modesty, since the bride was not to presume that she would be liked and accepted by the groom's family. In the event the bride was expelled by the groom, either for poor domestic performance or for a negative evaluation from her in-laws, she would have a way to return home.

Marriage was considered the union of two families and weighed heavily in human relationships. The cumbersome traditions followed by the bride and groom reflected the importance society placed on conjugality. The stability of the marriage was determined by the relationships of all members of the two families, not just the newlyweds. A wife could be repudiated by her husband if she failed to please her in-laws or the marriage was voided completely if a dispute arose between the two families (Li, 1978b).

The married woman's role at home depended upon the social rank of her spouse (Ch'en, 1975). The queen's role was to unify her subjects for the benefit of the country; the duchess' main responsibility was food preparation; noblemen's wives were to keep the household clean; the wives of common men were in charge of cooking, sewing, and cleaning. The prime mission of all married women, regardless of their social status, was to bear a son. One of the greatest crimes against honored ancestors was in not having a son to carry on the family name. Girls who married into middle- and upper-class families devoted their best years to activities centered around their parents-in-law home while women from poor families were required to join the labor force to survive. The social position of the wealthy wife was immediately elevated when her son married, entitling her the same honor and deference she had given to her parents-in-law over the years.

A good daughter-in-law's constant aim was to pay a great deal of respect to her parents-in-law, to obey them as she would her own parents, and to meet their every need. Each morning she would greet them in their living quarters carrying the tools needed for her daily tasks which included starting a fire, helping them wash, and serving them breakfast. The in-laws constantly and continually judged their young daughter-in-law by her abilities and manners. She was under even more pressure to behave well for their favor if there were other daughters-in-law with whom to compete. Strict rules prohibited a daughter-in-law from sighing, coughing, sneezing, or scratching in the presence of her in-laws. She could not leave her room without their permission. Before returning to her husband in the evening, she would arrange the bedding for her in-laws and help them bathe.

Another major duty of the wife was food preparation. She was responsible for the meals served to all members of the family, including her in-laws. The traditional culinary art can be traced back to this period when young wives spent a large part of their time preparing the most tasteful and appealing food possible for the enjoyment and approval of their in-laws. The ancient rituals for food preparation were laborious; details describing the quality of food, types of meat and methods of cooking, seasoning, and serving are found in the book *Li Chi*. The numerous sacred worships and ceremonies throughout the year, which required more elaborate food preparation, took a great deal of time and presented a challenge to the married woman. It was the custom that the eldest son and his wife ate the leftovers from the parent's meal. If the father was deceased, the son ate with his widowed mother and his wife consumed the leftovers alone. Such was the way to express filial piety.

Regardless of socioeconomic status, the parents-in-law were the undisputed heads of the extended family. They ruled with unquestionable authority over their children and daughters-in-law. The in-laws controlled their daughters-in-law to such an extent that the young women were not allowed to own or control personal property or savings. A daughter-in-law had to ask permission from her in-laws to lend or borrow goods. Any gift received by her from a relative had to be relinquished to her in-laws; if the in-laws chose, they could allow her to keep it. Rebellious daughters-in-law who refused to yield to this domineering authority received physical punishment or were expelled from the family.

The relationship between husband and wife under such trying conditions would certainly be apathetic by today's standards. From what we have learned of the ancient lifestyle, it seems that the daughter-in-law, with no private life of her own to spend with husband and children, was nothing more than a slave. The higher a woman's social status, the more she was bound to her in-laws, and the less initimate the relationship with her husband (Lang, 1968; and, Gross & Bingham, 1980). Because it was not socially acceptable for a husband and wife to share hangers, suitcase, bathroom, or well, physical segregation was an additional hardship for the wife. An ancient saying states that marriage meant the

the in-laws procured a daughter-in-law, not that their son gained a wife. To a certain extent this was true, but mostly among the aristocrats who could afford to devote the necessary time required to accomplish the complicated routine.

On the other hand, common people who lived under great financial pressure could not afford these entangled steps in their daily lives. The poor majority of ancient Chinese women were less restricted than upper-class women by the rules described by *Li Chi*. The love between husband and wife is repeatedly expressed in such phrases as "I hope I'll grow old with you" in the *Shih Ching* (*Book of Poetry*). This book includes the laments of many widows and wifes over their husband, such as:[10]

> My husband is away on service,
> And I know not when he will return.
> Where is he now?
> The fowls roost in their holes in the walls,
> And in the evening of the day,
> The goats and cows come down from the hill,
> But my husband is away on service,
> How can I but keep from thinking of him?
>
> My husband is away on service,
> Not for days merely, but for months.
> When will he come back to me?
> The fowls roost on their perches,
> And in the evening of the day,
> The goats and cows come down and home.
> But my husband is away on service;
> Oh if he be but kept from hunger and thirst!

In addition to meeting the demands of in-laws and living with the hardship of physical segregation, a couple's martial relationship was also threatened by the unofficial existence of polygamy (Lang, 1968). Polygamy was probably practiced during the period of capture and purchased marriages, when there were no well-formed social norms to govern the desire for more possessions. This custom occurred mostly among the upper class; the lower class could not afford such luxury. According to Ch'en's analysis (1977), polygamy did not prevail at this time because divorce and remarriage were acceptable; it was easier to change partners than to support an extra one. Under the clan system in the latter part of this era, the relationships among all members of the family and the status of each individual were well defined. There was only one woman who was formally married to the head of the family, and only her children could carry on the family name. Any other women having an affair with her husband was called a concubine, was considered inferior to the wife, and was regarded as a spare. The wife retained her powerful position in the family no matter how many concubines her husband adopted. It was said that during the Hsia Dynasty, the emperor was allowed twelve women, and dukes were permitted nine.[11] By the end of the Chou Dynasty, concubinage had become prevalent among the aristocracy. The emperor, for example, was entitled to one hundred and twenty women with different titles.[12]

A concubine was acquired in one of several ways. First, aristocratic brides were often accompanied to the groom's home by a group of bridesmaids, sometimes including the bride's sisters. These girls were automatically accepted as concubines by the groom. Second, dukes married nine girls simultaneously; one was selected as his wife, the remainder were concubines. Third, men could accept a woman as a concubine if she had failed to qualify as a wife by not completing the six proprieties. Finally, women from purchased or capture marriages were considered concubines.

A concubine's status in the family varied; the highest might be directly under the authority of the wife as her chambermaid while the lowest might be treated as miserably as a slave. Hence, concubines had different titles to distinguish their positions (Ch'en, 1975; and, Ch'en, 1977). Women were assigned nights with the husband in accordance with their title, although a wife shared more nights with him than did the concubines. The marginal status of a concubine could be improved by having male offspring. As to be expected, jealousies and intrigues were bred by putting these women in harem-like seclusion, and in competition for the pleasure and power of one man. However, cooperation between them was generally secured because of the wife's "worldly wisdom" and the concubine's "knowing their place."

Under the clan system, a woman's status in the family

was determined by her relationship with her husband, and by her husband's or her son's social status. Usually, the status of the mother was second only to that of the father, who had absolute authority over the entire family including the life and death of his family members. The dowager of the eldest generation in a family reigned virtually supreme; no one could challenge her perogative. The very lowest status in a family was reserved for a concubine who had borne no son because her nearly hopeless fate could not be reversed by a son's achievements.

The close relationship between a mother and her son is the subject of numerous historical accounts. Behind many eminent men in Chinese history, one is likely to find a self-sacrificing mother who motivated her son to study in order to excel. Likewise, a son's reverence for his parents was observed since filial piety is the chief of Chinese virtues. Such two-way affection was not compulsory, as reflected in the *Shih Ching*:[13]

> *O my father, who begat me!*
> *O my mother, who nourished me!*
> *You indulged me, you fed me,*
> *You held me up, you supported me,*
> *You looked after me, you never left me,*
> *Out and in you bore me in your arms.*
> *If I would return your kindness,*
> *It is like great Heaven, Illimitable.*

The affection for and attachment to one's family is also illustrated by the following excerpt in which the trees symbolize the family:[14]

> *In the low, wet ground is the carambola tree;*
> *Soft and pliant are its branches,*
> *With the glossiness of tender beauty.*
> *I should rejoice to be like you, (O tree), without*
>   *consciousness.*
>
> *In the low, damp grounds is the carambola tree;*
> *Soft and delicate are its flowers,*
> *With the glossiness of tender beauty.*
> *I should rejoice to be like you, (O tree), without*
>   *a family.*
>
> *In the low, damp grounds is the carambola tree;*

Soft and delicate in its fruit,
With the glossiness of tender beauty.
I should rejoice to be like you, (O tree), without
*   a household.*

In ancient China divorce was permitted and applied only to a wife, not to a concubine. Nevertheless, married couples generally stayed together, even though their lives were miserable. During the Spring and Autumn period men were given the privilege of "discharging" their wives for any of seven reasons, which, according to Confucius were: disobedience to her parents-in-law, barrenness, adultery, jealousy, disease, gossiping, and stealing.[15] A woman could, however, retain her status as wife under one of these four circumstances: (1) an empress could not be discharged even if she failed to bear a son for the emperor; (2) a wife whose parents were deceased and had no one to take care of her could not be dismissed; (3) a wife who contributed to her husband's prosperity by sharing the early hardships and struggles with him could not be ousted; and, (4) a wife who was favored by her in-laws but not by her husband had every right to stay.[16] Even when a wife was discharged by her husband, she was returned to her parent's home in her husband's carriage, with both parties maintaining as courteous a relationship as possible until the wife left the family.

Women's marital rights were better protected during this period than their successors in the Han and Tang Dynasties. Women were not completely helpless, if their natal families were powerful. A wife was supposed to be treated with respect, and if her husband failed to do this she could complain to her family, then her father or her brother would take action to punish the husband (Creel, 1954). Women who were widowed or expelled by their husband could easily remarry. Many well-known historical figures, including Confucius' daughter-in-law, remarried after the death of their spouse (Li, 1978b). Women's chastity was not enforced by society at this time. Furthermore, their marriage was guaranteed by the four above-mentioned conditions under which wives could retain their major role in the family. In the subsequent dynasties, such protection gradually diminished.

C. Women's Status in the Society

The existence of matriarchy in prehistoric Chinese society left its mark on the social status of women until the end of the Chou Dynasty. As discussed earlier, Chinese women in antiquity had an exalted position, playing a major role in ancestral worship and solemn religious ceremonies. Even in the Shang Dynasty, Creel concluded that the position of women of the upper-classes was good (1954). For example, former queens sacrificed also, independently as well as in company with their husbands. And ancestors were not the only deities to whom the Shang offered sacrifices. Among the other powers mentioned, the feminine element was not lacking, such as the "Dragon Woman," the "Eastern Mother" the "Western Mother," and the "Queen Earth"

Shang artisans produced bronze vessels by a casting process as sophisticated as any ever devised. This three-legged wine cup was used in religious ceremonies by the earliest emperors. The swallow on the lid was their emblem.

Even in the Eastern Chou Dynasty, a few old customs were still observed. When envoys carried gifts to a ruler, they usually included gifts for his wife as well. On many occasions high-ranking women were greatly respected by their country-men. For instance, as recorded in the *Spring and Autumn Annals*, when the wife of Duke Chuang arrived in town, all officials had to travel to the countryside to greet her (Mou, 1966). One other remnant of matriarchy in the East Chou

Dynasty was the avuncular political system. While fuedalism was prevalent the power frequently transferred from a woman's brother to her son in order to carry on the family name on the maternal side. The brother's son was not eligible for succession because he carried his mother's surname and was considered an outsider. Thus, an uncle and nephew bearing the same last name formed close political ties. In subsequent dynasties where patriarchy was well established, the aftermath of the avuncular system often led to a power struggle between a ruler's distaff and spear sides. The rule of queen mothers in Chinese history reflects the influence of matriarchy.[17]

The social status of women rapidly deteriorated after the establishment of the clan system in the Chou Dynasty. Women at different levels of the social ladder experienced varying degrees of physical restriction; the higher their status, the more complicated the social norms they were to observe and the less personal freedom they had. According to the writings of *Kung Yang Chuan*, upper-class women were no longer allowed to take a trip unless it was to attend the funeral of their parents. If a woman's husband was a high-ranking officer, an annual trip to visit her family was permitted, but only if the journey did not extend beyond the territory of the feudal state. If a woman came from a neighboring state or nation, she could never again visit her family.[18] A married woman supposedly resided with her husband and could not return to her parents' home (*Kuei*, in Chinese) unless she was expelled from her husband's family and sent back to her parents (*De Kuei*, in Chinese). *Kuei*, meaning "return", and *De Kuei*, meaning "big return" are still used today though in a slightly different form.

Although their position in society was weakened by the clan system, women continued to exert political power. Many admirable queens, from the Hsia through the Chou Dynasties contributed greatly to the strength and stability of kingdoms (Hsu, 1913; and, Yang, 1960). They not only possessed good temperments as models for their subjects, but also assisted their kings in managing domestic affairs. Queen Chiang, wife of King Hsuan in the Chou Dynasty, was praiseworthy for an appeal she made to the King. King

Hsuan had inherited the throne from a tyrant. One morning, in order to entice the King to wake early to continue his work of rebuilding the nation, Queen Chiang removed her hair decorations and dressed as a sinner. She blamed herself for the King's tardiness and asked for retribution. After that, the King worked tirelessly night and day to restore his country. His industriousness resulted in the most famous restoration of the Chou Dynasty.

On the other side of the coin, some famous women, such as Mei Hsi of the Hsai Dynasty, Tan Chi of the Shang Dynasty, Pao Szu of the Chou Dynasty, and Li Chi of the Chin Dynasty, were held responsible for the fall of their dynasties (Pott, 1903; Hsu, 1913; and, Shu, 1924). Chinese kings raided surrounding states, captured foreign beauties, and placed them in the palaces for the pleasure of the kings, their enemies and captors. These women used their attractiveness to lure the kings into acts of cruelty and inhumanity. The kings built magnificent palaces to please their beautiful captives who so distracted the kings that they neglected their responsibilities. Invaders and rebel forces ultimately destroyed these kingdoms. It is interesting to note that this same chain of events was repeated in four consecutive dynasties. One could consider that these women used this contrivance to retaliate for the demolition of their homeland, and so should be praised, rather than cursed for their efforts. Similar stories were replayed later by politicans who used women as pawns to defeat their enemies (Hibbert, 1938).

The social status of women under the clan system is implied by the meanings of the words used for husbands and wives. The term "emperor" means "Heaven's Son," indicating that the Emperor's power emcompassed the entire universe. The term for "empress" means "after" or "later", perhaps inferring that the empress was after the emperor in all respects, including knowledge, intellectual capacity, and rank in the social order. The term used by commoners for husband means supporting, suggesting that husbands must support, lead, and teach their wives. In a classical dictionary, *Shuo wen Chieh-tzu*, "women" (*fu*), means "married females" and suggests serving the husband. The word *fu* is composed of two radicals: "women" and "broom", symbolizing that married women should keep the household clean.

The social positions assigned to men and women can be summarized in this poem about the birth of a child:[19]

> Sons shall be born to him—
> They will be put to sleep on couches;
> They will be clothed in robes;
> They will have sceptres to play with;
> Their cry will be loud.
> [Hereafter] they will be resplendent with red
>   knee-covers.
> The [future] king, the princes of the land.
>
> Daughters shall be born to him—
> They will be put to sleep on the ground;
> They will be clothed with wrappers;
> They will have tiles to play with.
> It will be theirs neither to do wrong nor
>   to do good.
> Only about the liquor and the food will
>   they have to think,
> And to cause no sorrow to their parents.

Women's contribution to the society did not begin at home. How did these ancient women live in a matrilineal society? Did they spend their time hunting? Or did they spend their time caring for home and children? The literature regarding these questions is scarce and vague. Perhaps the most reliable source for answers to these questions is the *Chou Li* (*Rites of Chou*) which contains works of different authors without sufficient background information. Although scholars have different opinions regarding the reliability of this book, it provides our curious eyes a peek into the lives of women of prehistoric times (Hsu, 1954).

Hunting and fishing were the earliest methods of survival. As hunting tools improved, the hunting ground was extended and the hunted changed from small creatures to large animals. When women were physically restricted from engaging in strenuous activity by menstruation and pregnancy, they withdrew from the hunting ground leaving it to the men. It may have been during one of these times when women remained stationary that someone accidentally discovered the use of seeds for farming. In so doing, life became less mobile and the rewards more reliable. The *Li Chi* (*Book of Rites*) records that men offered animal skins during sacred ceremonies while women presented plants. Women conducted business in the market place, a major difference when one considers that their successors were prevented from going outside their own homes. Women profited by selling vegetables from their own gardens because produce was preservable and dependable. They also sold cloth made from silk. The love affair of women with silk and mulberry has often been heralded in Chinese legends. Lei Tsu, the wife of the first Chinese emperor, Huang-ti, was believed to be the first to cultivate silkworms for the making of silk. Numerous poems describe women's work on silkworm farms. Raising silkworms and spinning hemp and yarn were considered suitable tasks for women, while the men took over the farming.[20] Then, women were forced to turn their talents to strictly domestic areas, such as sewing, cooking, preserving meats, and preparing offerings of libation to the gods and to ancestors (Lang, 1968; and, Li, 1978a).

When women retreated from outside physical activities, their lives underwent tremendous change. Their main concern and interest then focused on domestic affairs and interpersonal relationships; they were no longer expected to engage in business deals with outsiders in the open market. If the family had adequate helpers to work the fields, they were even exempt from that chore. Their lifestyle and routine activities contrasted with that of women of less affluence who had to work hard in the fields to support their families.

Changing from outside the home to inside gradually molded women to their domestic role that they were groomed for from childhood. Informal training was well laid out for them by the end of this period. Until the age of seven, girls and boys played, ate, and were taught together. Once they reached the age of seven, they were separated and received different educations. Girls had to avoid seeing boys, except at funerals and at offerings, and they were not allowed to share a well, bathroom, bedding, or clothing. After reaching the age of ten, girls were forced to stay inside the house and learn to be submissive and to weave; they were not permitted to leave the house or engage in any business outside the house. Instead, they learned the necessary housekeeping skills and proper manners for women. By the time that they were fourteen they were trained to serve their parents as they would be required to serve their future in-laws. Every day, young girls rose early and dressed properly to greet their parents and helped to serve their breakfast. Daughters were expected to sit straight, listen quietly, and refrain from looking around, smiling freely, and loitering. Coughing, sighing, yawning, squinting, stretching, spitting, or blowing the nose were also prohibited. They were also required to help prepare food during religious offerings and were eligible for betrothal only after they had begun menstruating.

Social conduct for young Chinese women of antiquity (before 208 B.C.) changed drastically. In a matriarchal society, the oldest daughter in the family usually remained unmarried to fulfill her responsibility in sacred ceremonies as the head of the family, consequently incest and adultery became common.[21] *Spring and Autumn Annals* strongly criticized these phenomena. Several historians attributed natural disasters of the times to incest among duchesses and their brothers and brothers-in-law. Up to the end of the Chou Dynasty, women still had free choice in their marital decisions; widows could remarry as they wished and premarital sexual relationships were evident.[22] Occasionally, aristocratic lords who resented their sisters' affairs with lower-class men even killed the men to end the relationship.[23] The following excerpt from the *Shih Ching Book of Poetry* shows that social contacts between men and women at that time was not restricted by place:[24]

> *The Chen and Wei*
> *Now present their broad sheets of water.*
> *Ladies and gentlemen*
> *Are carrying flowers of valerian.*
> *A lady says, "Have you been to see?"*
> *A gentleman replies, "I have been.*
> *But let us go again to see.*
> *Beyond the Wei,*
> *The ground is large and fit for pleasure."*
> *So the gentlemen and ladies*
> *Make sport together,*
> *Presenting one another with small peonies.*

Then there is the perennial anxiety of the unmarried woman who sees youth slipping away from her: [25]

Dropping are the fruits from the plum-tree;
There are only seven-tenths of them left.
For the gentlemen who seek me,
Now is the fortunate time!

Dropping are the fruits from the plum-tree;
There are but three-tenths of them left.
For the gentlemen who seek me,
Now is the time!

Dropped are the fruits from the plum-tree;
In my shallow basket I have collected them.
Would the gentlemen who seek me
Only speak about it!

During this period of sexual freedom, moralists began to advocate a new code of ethics.[26] The chapter on marriage in *Pai Hu Tung* declared that boys and girls could not marry without parental approval of the matchmaker's choice; this safeguard was to prevent sexual promiscuity. One of the major purposes of the *Spring and Autumn Annals* was to regulate conduct by establishing a system of morality. Confucius, the leading advocate of this movement, traveled extensively to preach his philosophy and five moral principles. Since then, Chinese women began their long journey of various sufferings in numerous ways as presented in the following chapters. Nevertheless, folklore or legends on some women in this period have been told and retold for centuries. They will share part of the book as shown below.

D. Women in Mythology

Records on the well-known women in Chinese antiquity are ambiguous because they were registered based on oral history before the invention of the Chinese written language. The following stories might convey a partial image of Chinese women of antiquity who exhibited traits which enabled them to have an impact on Chinese civilization.

According to legend, the birth place of Chinese civilization is along the Yellow River where people lived as savages in caves. Men and women had no other distinction except physical differences. When Fu Hsi expanded his power and became the tribal chief, his wife Nu Kuo counseled him a great deal. At that time the marital scheme was introduced and the name system was installed to insure proper social order (Hsu, 1913). Nu Kuo, one of the fifteen tribal chiefs before Huang-ti, the first Chinese emperor, succeeded her husband as chief after his death. After executing the rebellious Kung Kung, who led an uprising against her, Nu Kuo consolidated the tribe. The creation of musical instruments and formation of Chinese music can also be traced to Nu Kuo's efforts. In mythology, Nu Kuo was the heroine who put the rainbow in the sky with five colors of stones to save her people. It was said that one day the sky was half bright and half dark due to the fight between the water god and the fire god. It looked as though the dark half would break away from the sky. To hold the sky together, Nu Kuo melted stones of five colors into a paste and then placed the colorful paste in the cracks, forming a five-color curvilinear belt in the sky called a rainbow. As Hsu pointed out (1913), it was not an easy task for someone to unite primitive dwellers in this remote period of Chinese history, and Nu Kuo must have been an extraordinary person.

As previously mentioned, Lei Tsu was believed to be the first person to cultivate silkworms for clothing (Hsu, 1913). Her discovery was a turning point with respect to wearing apparel. She taught people to raise silkworms with mulberry and to process the silk into fabric at home. Widespread production of silk then enabled people to have decent attire. A dress code was later inaugerated regulating the color, materials and style of apparel for males and females of different social classes.

Countless stories reveal that beautiful women were linked to the demise of kingdoms or dynasties, they were used as political pawns to conspire against kings and aristocrats (Shu, 1924; and, Hibbert, 1938). Hsi Shih, an illustrious beauty, was presented as a gift to Duke Wu, who invaded her country Yueh during the period of Spring and Autumn. Hsi Shih had been well trained in dance, art, and literature. It was said that during the one-year training period, she had fallen in love with Fan Li, a young lord in her native land. But since she had been ordered to entice Duke Wu into neglecting his duties, Hsi Shih left her lover and native land for Wu. Duke Wu built a palace for her where they vacationed all year.

Then, years later, after becoming indolent and losing his zeal for training his troops, Duke Wu was defeated by Yueh, Hsi Shih's mother country. Hsi Shih's guilt over Duke Wu's death was so deep that she decided to commit suicide while the palace was under attack by Yueh soldiers. It is said that at that critical moment, Fan Li, who had plotted the invasion, arrived to save her (Ma, 1979). By today's standards, Hsi Shih would be considered a spy, sent by her defeated country on a mission. Because of her efforts and personal sacrifice, her country was restored (Hsu, 1913).

Chinese historians recorded few incidents involving women in the army during this era. However, Duke Wu organized and trained female troops as part of his efforts to amass military power and to conquer surrounding countries. When Sun Tzu, the chief commander for army training, assured him that women could be trained to fight, Duke Wu chose 180 women from his court, with two of his favorite concubines heading the group. They all dressed up, lined up, and when the drum played, the concubine leading the right wing started to laugh. The left wing concubine also giggled when the drum played for her team. Sun Tzu ordered them both to be beheaded, but the Duke intervened. Then Sun Tzu responded, "I have been assigned by you as commander-in-Chief; I have authority over these troops" (Hsu, 1913). The two women were then executed, and there were no further problems. Later this well-trained women's army proved it could indeed withstand a regimentation of strict rules and strenuous marching (Hsu, 1913).

Mencius, who was influenced greatly by his determined mother, is honored as the second sage to Confucius. His widowed mother was particularly famous for the three relocations undertaken for the sake of her son's education (Hsu, 1913; Lang, 1968; and, Liu, 1978). When Mencius was young, he lived next to a cemetary where many people buried their dead and brought sacrificial offerings. He imitated the procedures for burial and offerings, and enjoyed the dramatic play so much that it worried his mother. Because she did not want her son to engage in this type of business in the future, she decided to move. Later, she found that the new residence was also not satisfactory because it was so close to the market that young Mencius copied what people did, including killing a pig for sale and bargaining over the price. She moved again, this time determined to provide a better living environment for her son. Her hope was finally realized when she found a place next to a school, where Mencius developed his interest in learning. One day he returned home early, saying there was nothing to do in school. His mother took a pair of scissors and, cutting off the threads on the spinning wheel, said, "All I have worked for is worth nothing now. Dropping out of school will lead you nowhere, just like my broken threads which became worthless. Only knowledge will make you wise and valuable to society."[27] Mencius was so moved that he studied harder than ever. At that time, scholars enjoyed the highest social ranking. Mencius' mother set high goals for her son and worked hard to educate him. Her determination and perseverance won her a great deal of respect, and set an example for many Chinese women to follow throughout Chinese history.

Conclusion

Information regarding Chinese women's lives in the prehistoric period was mainly inferred from folklore, legend, and archaeological findings. The archaeological remains of the Shang and Chou Dynasties unearthed in the 19th and 20th centuries provide a better picture of women's role and status in ancient Chinese society. Based on the materials reviewed, the role and social status of women changed drastically as a result of the transition from matriarchy to patriarchy during this period. Such change could attribute to the changes in economic conditions, social structure, and the establishment of bureaucratic absolutism over this time span. By the end of this era, women were deprived of outside activities, including political, religious, and business events and devoted their entire life to the domestic arena. However, their declining position mainly reflected those changes in their physical restriction from outside engagement and job assignment. Basically, they were still respected as individual human beings and egalitarianism between men and women was more or less accepted in the areas of morality and family life.

NOTES

[1] Marcel Granet, *Chinese civilization* (London: Kegan Paul, Trench, Trubner and Co., Ltd., 1930), pp. 171-172.

[2] Olga Lang, *Chinese family and society* (New York: Archon Books, 1968), p. 328.

[3] Jen Ta-jung, "Archaeological search of matriarchy in Chinese antiquity," *East Magazine*, vol. 32, no. 1 (1935), pp. 74-75.

[4] *Ibid..*; see also Jen, *op. cit.*, p. 76; and, Ts'ai Hsien-jung, "The beginning of polygamy in China," *Journal of New Social Science*, vol. 1, no. 2 (1934), p. 187.

[5] Pao Chia-lin, *Readings in Chinese women's history* (Taipei, Taiwan: Mu T'ung Publishing Co., 1979), pp. 7-8.

[6] Chang Kwang-Chih, *The archaeology of ancient China* (New Haven: Yale University Press, 1963), p. 168.

[7] *Ibid.*

[8] Wu K. C., *The Chinese heritage* (New York: Crown Publishers, 1982), p. 22.

[9] Ch'en Ku-yuan, *History of Chinese marriage* (Taipei, Taiwan: Commerce Publishing Co., 1975), pp. 78-80; see also Ch'en Tung-yuan, *History of the life of Chinese women* (Taipei, Taiwan: Commerce Publishing Co., 1977), pp. 22-23; and, also, Li Ch'ia-fu, *Lives of ancient Chinese women* (Taipei, Taiwan: Li Min Publishing Co., 1978), p. 2.

[10] James Legge, *The sacred books of the East* (Oxford: Clarendon Press, 1885), vol. 4, pp. 112-113.

[11] Ch'en Tung-yuan, *History of the life of Chinese women* (Taipei, Taiwan: Commerce Publishing Co., 1977), p. 34.

[12] *Ibid., op. cit.*, p. 35; see also, Ch'en Ku-yuan, *op. cit.*, p. 63-65.

[13] James Legge, *op. cit.*, vol. 20, p. 365.

[14] *Ibid., op. cit.*, vol. 4, p. 140.

[15] Lang, *op. cit.*, p. 40; see also, Li, *op. cit.*, pp. 87-88.

[16] Lang, *op. cit.*, p. 41; see also, Li, *op. cit.*., p. 88.

[17] Yang Liang-sheng, "Female rulers in Imperial China," *Harvard Journal of Asiatic Studies*, vol. 23 (1960-1961), p. 51.

[18] Mou Hsun, "Kung Yang's evidence of matriarchy in the Spring and Autumn period," *Hsin Ya Hsueh Po*, vol. 1, no. 1 (1966), pp. 381-421.

[19] Legge, *op. cit.*, vol. 10, pp. 56-58.

[20] Lang, *op. cit.*, pp. 42-43; see also, Hsu Cho-yun, "Women's responsibilities in antiquity based on the *Rites of Chou*," *Mainland Magazine*, vol. 13, no. 12 (1954), pp. 202-203.

[21] Mou, *op. cit.*, pp. 391-400.

[22] Mou, *op. cit.*, p. 397.

[23] Mou, *op. cit.*, p. 394.

[24] Legge, vol. 4, pp. 30-31.

[25] *Ibid.*, p. 141.

[26] Ch'en Tung-yuan, *op. cit.*, pp. 24-28; see also, Mou, *op. cit.*, pp. 381-421.

[27] Liu Tzu-ch'ing, *Critical biographies of famous women in Chinese history* (Taipei, Taiwan: Li Min Publishing Co., 1978), p. 4.

Buddha, Lao-tzu, and Confucius were three of the great leaders of East Asian thought. In this Japanese painting from the Kano period (1336-1558) they are depicted conversing together. Although the three philosophers were not contemporaries, their discussion symbolically represents the interaction of the three philosophical schools.

CHAPTER THREE

Ancient Period
(Han Dynasty to Five Dynasty Period: 209 B.C.-960 A.D.)

The Chou Dynasty actually consisted of two separate periods: the first, Western Chou, had a national government and lasted from 1115-722 B.C.; the following, Eastern Chou, with many feudal states fighting one another, survived for nearly five more centuries: until 249 B.C. Eastern Chou was further divided into two overlapping stages: the Spring and Autumn period (722-481 B.C.), and the Warring States period (403-211 B.C.).

Toward the end of the unstable Eastern Chou many philosophers, such as Confucius, Mo Tzu, Lao Tzu, Mencius, Chuang Tzu, and Han Fei, introduced various doctrines in the hope of achieving stability among the fighting states and thereby bring peace on earth to alleviate human suffering. This was called the period of the Hundred Schools (511-233 B.C.). Many of them journeyed around the feudal states to persuade feudal lords to adopt their ideologies. Most of them, however, including Confucius and Mencius, were not successful. By utilizing legalistic practices that emphasized a strong centralization of power, regimentation of its people, and aggressive warfare, the feudal state of Ch'in annexed her surrounding states and became a superpower in the latter years of the Chou Dynasty. Under King Ch'in's vigorous leadership, Ch'in swallowed up the last six superpowers and formed a united kingdom. In 221 B.C., King Ch'in was proclaimed the First Exalted Emperor of the Ch'in (*Ch'in Shih-huang-ti*). This marks the beginning of the Chinese Imperial Age.

Under the influence of a legalistic prime minister, Li Szu, the emperor standardized laws, customs, dress codes, measurements, and the written language, and constructed highway systems and the renowned Great Wall. He was considered a cruel and inhuman emperor because he inflicted heavy taxes, relocated laborers for construction, standardized social behavior, and abolished the feudal system. This misuse of force, along with the vigorous expansion of Chinese territory and the energetic reconstruction of the nation, eventually contributed to the early demise of the Ch'in Dynasty, ending a domination which lasted only sixteen years. Although he lacked the traits of a good emperor (such as kindness and compassion for his subjects), the profound impact of Ch'in's accomplishments on Chinese civilization was incalculable.

The Chinese entered a new age after the overthrow of the Ch'in Dynasty. The new emperor of the Han Dynasty abolished the legalistic theories which ruled the country during the Ch'in Dynasty, and converted the nation to another teaching: Confucianism. As the nation united and power was centralized, the Emperor of Han had a better chance to practice Confucianism and to bring peace and prosperity to the people.

A. *Economically Flourishing Society*

According to the beliefs of Confucius, peace and prosperity of a nation were the prerequisites for the moral training of her people. After acquiring these two elements for both nation and people, the final product was a sage who possessed the most acute and refined moral sense possible. Ideally, this sage would be selected as the emperor. Since hereditary rulership had been accepted, the sage took a position as counselor to the emperor. With these Confucian thoughts in mind, the succeeding Chinese dynasties engaged in tremendous economic development and regulated people's conduct through moral education.

In reality, several factors contributed to the stimulation of economic growth in the beginning of the Han Dynasty. First, agrarian crises followed the downfall of the Ch'in Dynasty and created severe social disorder. Plagues and destruction of farmland during the rebellion against the Ch'in Dynasty reduced farm production to such an extent that it created a grain shortage and an increase in inflation. Wars and uprisings robbed the people of many resources, leaving them in poverty. Furthermore, the troubles of the northern frontier with foreign neighbors continued after the erection of the Han Dynasty. In order to alleviate the burden on the people and to increase national productivity, the government had to institute several measures which included reducing land tax, minimizing government expenditures, valuing the five grains, making proper use of natural resources, degrading merchants' social status, concentrating on agricultural development, and exchanging grains for high ranks. Consequently, the nation recovered, the population increased, the treasury was filled, and granaries were stocked. Although such economic recovery was at one time hindered by Emperor Wu's ambitious undertakings in military expansion and national construction, overall, the economic condition since Han showed continuous improvement.

As a result of the new monarchy, social system, and economic policy inaugerated in the Han Dynasty, two phenomena were closely related to the fate of women and their influence on the country. These were the emergence of a new class system, and strictly exogamous royal marriage. The feudal system, abolished by the Ch'in Dynasty, was replaced by a new caste system in the Han Dynasty. Eminent officials who had made conspicious contributions to the country were promoted. Rich farmers who traded their surplus grains to frontier troops in exchange for official positions, had the opportunity for appointment to a new status. During the later socially and politically confusing period of the Wei and Ch'in Dynasties, society once again favored the growth of a new aristocracy which was not only powerful in politics but also in the economy. Particularly in the Ch'in Dynasty, some large and wealthy families profited from the turmoil and unrest in the land and gained possession of large estates. Their extravagant lives included raising thousands of beautiful women for sexual pleasure and entertainment (this will be discussed in detail in a later section).

The second phenomenon affecting women was the fact that families related to the emperor by marriage rose to great power and carried considerable influence. Since marriage within an aristocratic family was forbidden in the Chou Dynasty, a feudal lord had to marry his children to another feudal family that carried a different surname. When the bride left her native land and became a princess of another state, her political tie and contact with or backup from her own family ended. She was considered a loyal member of the new family for life. Sometimes she was caught in warfare between her mother state and her husband's state, yet her family background had little influence on her husband's devotion and responsibility to his state. Now, with the destruction of the feudal system, the sovereign family was obliged to select brides from their own subjects. This introduced a new and dangerous element into politics; after the wedding, the position of the consort family was exalted. These new upstarts rapidly grabed power in the court, along with accumulating great wealth, before the death of the empress. When a new empress ascended the throne, a new consort family replaced the old one. In many instances, at the death of the emperor, the empress would exercise the power of the regency, and forthwith the whole imperial authority would pass into the hands of her family, thus casting aside the young emperor who had just succeeded to the throne. The ambition of some members of the consort family led to several insurrections between the Han and Tang Dynasties (Yang, 1960; Crespigny, 1975; and, Holmgren, 1978).

While the standard of living had been improved as a result of progressive economic policy and trades with foreign countries, man's covetousness was not satisfied. Along with the creation and appreciation of fine arts which added another dimension of the life of the rich, women gradually became sexual objects for the pleasure of man.

B. Signs of Decadence

The decline of the status of women was a slow process, unfolding within an economically flourishing society. In the Han Dynasty, remarriage for women was still common (Tung, 1934; Ch'en, 1977; Li, 1978a; and, Nieh, 1979). The government's intention to publicize women's proper behavior was imperceptibly infused to women's marital decision. Those authoritative figures in the family (such as parents, in-laws, and husbands) raised a higher expectation of women and strengthened their dominance on women's marital choice in accordance to the deeds of glorified women. Chu Mai-chen's wife divorced him due to his poor life and married another man. Later, Chu was very kind and gracious to the couple when he became an eminent official.[1] Chiao Chung-chin's wife did not please her parents-in-law and was ordered to return to her parent's home. Upon her return, state and county officials sent matchmakers to her house with a marriage proposal.[2] These stories indicate that divorce carried no social stigma for women in the Former Han Dynasty. Another frequently mentioned case is that of T'sai Yi's daughter, Wen Chi, a young widow. She stayed with her parents during the Hsing Ping Rebellion, until she was captured by northern invaders and presented to their king, Tso Hsien-wong, as a concubine During her twelve years on foreign soil she bore the king two sons. Since she had no brothers to carry on her father's name, she was ransomed by the Chinese ruler, Ts'ao Ts'ao, who was concerned about the continuation of the Ts'ai family. Wen Chi then married Tung Szu; she was not condemned for marrying twice or for having children of mixed blood.[3]

In fact, prior to this period, there were clues signifying women's declining status; governmental policy was one of them. During the Warring States period, the population in China was decreasing due to constant warfare among the feudal states. To replace heavy casualties, some feudal lords, such as Kou Chien of the Yueh state, encouraged people to have children, either legitimately or illegitimately; thus, sexual morality receded.[4] When Ch'in Shih-huang-ti conquered the final six states and formed a centralized government, he became aware of the declining moral standard and attempted to rectify it. His stone inscription addressing proper manners for both men and women was found in the Mount Tai, Ho-shih Gate, and Huichi. He built an altar, called Ch'ing Tai, for a widow named Pa Ch'in in memory of her deeds. This was the first glorification of a virtuous woman by official proclamation.[5]

The Han Dynasty was the turning point for the formation of social order and the beginning of rewarding women's proper conduct. Although many philosophical doctrines were introduced by prominent philosophers during the Eastern Chou Dynasty, none were adopted by feudal lords as the foundation on which to reorganize either their social structure or political system. When legalists failed to prevent the downfall of the Ch'in Dynasty, other ideologies were considered by the first emperor of the Han Dynasty. He regulated music and rites which were based mainly on the Ch'in

46

system. Later, Emperor Wu recruited wise men to spell out explicit criteria for conduct and standards for social norms (Fitzgerald, 1958). Both male and female were expected to follow certain rules for their roles of father, mother, husband, wife, son, or daughter. People could no longer claim they were uninformed. In 58 B.C. and 11 A.D., two virtuous women were awarded clothes and grains.[6] Women used to be reminded of what was considered socially acceptable conduct in the Ch'in Dynasty, and in this period they were even motivated by materialistic gains to act properly. This ploy to bribe women was continuously used later on in history.

Women's declining status was further manifested as a result of more rigid social norms imposed on them after the Han Dynasty. Around 480 A.D., the North Dynasty constructed a monastery in Tang Chou for childless widows who were expected to remain unmarried.[7] In the Sui Dynasty, an emperor's decree indicated that widows whose husbands held one of the nine official ranks, and concubines whose master held a rank higher than the fifth, were not permitted to remarry.[8] Now women were not merely encouraged to have and maintain proper conduct (for which they were rewarded), but they were also forced into a specific mold of virtue—to be faithful to their dead husband. The scope of women's virtues was broadened beyond their competence in domestic affairs and desirable personality for maintaining a good relationship with all family members.

Sung printed book. A page from the *Fa-yuan chu-lin* ("Forest of Pearls in the Garden of the Law"). The book was compiled by the Buddhist monk and scholar Tao-Shih in 688. It was printed in 1124, fully three centuries earlier than the Gutenberg Bible.

The society began to erect inconsistant moral standards for men and women; the latter had to conform to higher social expectations than did the former. Consequently, women no longer played an equal role with men at home; they were inferior to men and both internal and external affairs were restricted morally as well as physically.

Between the Han and Tang Dynasties there was a three hundred year long period of frequent upheavals and continuous social destruction which further downgraded the prestige of women. Women were devalued and treated as property when the practice of home prostitution started during this period. Women who lost their husbands or entire families during this time of social unrest had to make a living for survival. As a result of physical confinement from childhood and a lack of the necessary interaction with the outside world, they were unable to confront the challenge to compete with men in employment. It was most difficult for a berift single women to survive in a male dominated society without support and protection from relatives. Meanwhile, those upstarts who had profited from social turmoil and had taken advantage of the unstable economic conditions recruited beautiful women for domestic entertainment. Women who were attractive but had no means for survival were pushed into home prostitution. Besides being beautiful as a prerequisite, they were also trained in music, dance, art and literature to please their master and his guests, both physically and spiritually. They were different from concubines who were formally accepted by the head of the family and had an assigned position in the family. The home prostitute's sole responsibility was entertaining her master and his company on demand. In addition to the two best well-known home prostitute-raisers, Wong Kai and Shih Chung, Chen Tungyuan (1977) also excerpted 18 additional rich people's lavish lives with thousands of home prostitutes. The treatment of home prostitutes was nearly inhuman; their master could do anything to them he wished. Wong Kai even ordered the death of a prostitute who played her flute too softly.[9]

Along with the prevailing trend of sexually abusing women, men pressed for more artifical beauty from them. Before the Han Dynasty women seldom wore any make-up. The standards for beauty then focused on a natural complexion and a healthy body.[10] But, with economic growth and influence from the west, women in this age became more concerned about their hairstyle, make-up, earrings, clothing, and footwear. The basic function of clothing was no longer for protection; women gradually favored a more sophisticated and extravagant style. Details about women's make-up and customs wil be discussed in section F.

Arranged marriages, which emphasized the social background of both bride and bridegroom, generated several problems, including female infanticide and those discussed in section D. In an economically flourishing era, unlike their predecessors in ancient times, parents had to prepare a dowry for their daughters. To comply with such a social trend, many poor parents who foresaw the upcoming shortage of financial resources for their daughter's dowry simply put baby girls to death. In addition, parents realized that all the efforts and resources for raising girls would be eventually profited from by the groom's family because the girls could become a valuable laborer for their in-laws. Thus, infanticide began. Girls were not just inferior to boys in society, they were even beginning to loose their right to live (additional discussion on the development of infanticide is presented in Chapter Four, below, since it became more prevalent during the Sung and Ming dynasties).

C. Women's Education

The deterioration of women's social status was partially attributed to literature written in the Han Dynasty. Two volumes, written by Liu Hsiang in the Former Han Dynasty, and Pan Chao in the Latter Han Dynasty advocated proper manners for women. These recommendations became the traditional teachings for Chinese women. The book *Lieh Nu Chuan* (*Records of Virtuous Women*) recording the lives of virtuous women was completed by Liu Hsiang around 29 B.C.. It was said that Liu wrote his book to admonish people due to the declining moral standards in the court. The seven discovered chapters of *Lieh Nu Chuan* focus on motherhood, wisdom, kindness, faithfulness, righteousness, discernment, and purity. However, Liu Hsiang did not expect women to possess all of these virtues—he even praised women who had only one of these qualities.[11]

More than one hundred years later, a female historian, Pan Ch'ao, wrote a book entitled *Nu Chieh* (*Admonition to Women*) which consisted of seven chapters dealing with humility, reverence, concentration, submission, manners, and relationships with husband and in-laws.[12] Subsequently published literature for women's education more or less followed the blueprint of the two books *Lieh Nu Chuan* and *Nu Chieh*.

Although women's behavior was governed by the rites and etiquette prescribed in the Chou Dynasty, women were not systematically or specifically taught about proper behavior until the publication of the two aforementioned books. Both (especially *Nu Chieh*) spelled out the details of women's proper conduct and moral training which became a yoke on women's shoulders for nearly two thousand years.[13] Excerpts from *Nu Chieh* are translated as follows:

> —*Women are inferior because they were placed under the beds since they were three days old, while boys were placed on the beds.* (Chapter 1)

> —*It was right for husbands to have concubines, but it was evil for women to marry twice. Total submission to husbands and to God was expected* (Chapter 2)

> —*Tenderness and frailty were desirable traits for women to exhibit* (Chapter 3)

> —*A wife should be in a passive position for her husband's affection. To argue with him was improper; she should quietly discuss and rationalize with him, even if he were wrong* (Chapter 3)

> —*Women had to be submissive to their in-laws and to please them for the sake of their husbands* (Chapter 6)

Pan Ch'ao emphasized that women should consider that marriage was a great favor granted to them by their husbands, even if they were disliked or later deserted by their husbands.[14] She believed that all youngsters should be taught before they were fifteen years of age; for boys, knowledge and conduct were important; for girls, learning to serve their husbands was the major goal of education. Because of Pan Ch'ao's advocacy for women's education, some empresses and princesses were exposed to reading when they were only five or six years old.[15] *Nu Hsun* (*Teachings for Women*), a book similar to *Nu Chieh*, was published around two hundred years later. This book was purportedly authored by Ts'ai Yi, a high-ranking officer in the Wei Dynasty. Later, in the T'ang Dynasty, another work, entitled *Nu Tse* (*Principles for Women*), by Empress Chiang Sun, was released to the public (around 630 A.D.). This book consisted of thirty volumes depicting the virtues of historical female figures.

The most popular book for women in the T'ang Dynasty was *Nu Lun Yu* (*Analects for Women*), written by Sung Jo Hua. Its twelve chapters dealt with self-discipline, study, etiquette, morning chores, relationships with in-laws, husband, children, friends, household management, humility and chastity. It was very easy for young girls to memorize since there were rhyming words throughout the book. This book was even more explicit and detailed about conduct than were other books. Excerpts from the chapters of *Nu Lun Yu* on the wife's relationship with the husband and on chastity are translated as follows:

> *Treating husband as her master. . . Marriage is made in previous life. . . . Considering husband as heaven with a great deal of righteousness. . . . Conjugality is made of husband's strength and wife's frailty. . . . Listening attentively to husband's words. . . . Advising husband of his wrong doings. . . . Keeping husband's itinerary while he is on a trip. . . . Longing for him if he has not returned at dusk. . . . Warming food and waiting for his knock at the door . . . . Serving the husband around the clock when he is ill. . . . Seeking all sorts of medicine to cure him . . . . Hoping he will have a long life. . . . Accepting the blame and keeping quiet while he is in anger. . . . Clothing him with adequate material and serving him with proper food . . . .*

Due to the great influence of this book, women were even more restricted than before. However, during this period they still had the opportunity to learn basic skills such as reading and poetry, and were not totally deprived of intellectual pursuits.

D. Social Caste in the Wei and Chen Dynasties (219 A.D. - 587 A.D.)

Following the considerably stable Han Dynasty the rise of a new aristocratic spirit fermented during the Wei and Ch'in Dynasties and influenced Chinese women in two aspects: marital custom and women's jealousy. During this time Chinese people experienced continuous wars which created a series of short-lived dynasties and led to tremendous economic loss throughout the nation. Businessmen and powerful families took advantage of the warfare by exploiting consumers, they transported goods for higher profits and controlled the necessities to monopolize prices. Those who had political, social, and economic power formed a new aristocracy which had been evolved for procuring a suitable class of officials. This official aristocracy constituted nine grades. Gradually, the breach between aristocracy and bourgeoisie became wider as power passed entirely into those of the landed nobility and a man of the people could never rise above the lower grades. Even among the aristocracy themselves, different ranks were sharply distinguished, such as "ancient families", "family of the second class", "latter-day families", and "ennobled families" (Fitzgerald, 1958).

Such a caste system was so well guarded that marriage between nobility and bourgeoisie was stigmatized as shameful.[16]   In the South-North Dynasty, which followed the Ch'in Dynasty, Wong Yuan, a high-ranking officer, was accused by Shen Yueh of marrying his daughter to a common man.[17]   Shen Yueh believed such a practice would prompt more marriages across social classes and eventually lead to the destruction of the social system. Thus, Shen Yueh proposed that Wong Yuan be fired and thrown into prison. Later, in 462 A.D., the emperor of the North Wei Dynasty promulgated that it was against the law for aristocracy and ranking officials to contract a marriage with the bourgeoisie.[18]   Fifteen years later, the emperor again ruled that marriage across social ranks was prohibited.[19]

The consequences of such a restrictive marriage practice were more negative than positive. Since properly-matched marriages were highly valued, both the bride's and the groom's families attempted to impress the public by an extravagant, often wasteful, wedding. Even the poor tended to follow this pattern, exhausting their financial resources for their children's marriage. As a result, many parents chose to wait until they were more prosperous, rather than to offer a hasty, meager wedding to their offspring. The result of such postponements was an increasing number of bachelors; even the emperor's endeavor to provide festivities for single men and women to have social contact did not hurry the marriages. By 573 A.D., the emperor of the North Chou even decreed that boys over fifteen and girls over thirteen must marry, and marriage was not to be arranged based on the amount of property of both families, plus weddings were to be economical.[20] On the contrary, early marriages were common among the rich and within the royal family. The parental desire for class-matched marriage was so strong that even the unborn did not escape its influence. To preserve the wealth and friendship of two families, some couples would arrange the betrothal with each other soon after the wives became pregnant.[21] If both babies turned out to be the same sex, the parents could become godparents to one another's baby. Since the social class and wealth of both families were considered when choosing marital partners, some parents who could not afford a dowry for their daughters were forced to kill their baby girls early enough to alleviate this pressure; otherwise, marital chances for these unfortunate infant girls were slim. Although a wedding for a son was costly, the parents would benefit by gaining the help of a daughter-in-law in the household after the wedding day. In most cases, the bride's dowry would be kept by her parents-in-law, not by her. Thus, it stands to reason that parents favored girls less than they did boys.

Jealousy in married women was inevitable because the affection of their husbands was constantly threatened by his adoption of concubines and engaging in extramarital affairs with prostitutes. It seemed the higher the education and socioeconomic status of the husband, the less happiness the wife could expect from the marriage. Under these stressful situations in which husbands had initimate relationships with many women, wives often yielded to feelings of jealousy and hatred towards these other women. However, traditional teachings prohibited them from showing their jealousy.

During the Wei and Ch'in Dynasties, women became less restricted by such classical teachings; they reverted to various means within their power to express their jealousy, such as keeping close supervision on their husbands, putting them in jail, and killing the concubines after the husband's death.[22] Hsieh An, a prime minister in the East Ch'in Dynasty, planned to adopt one of his prostitutes as a concubine. Unfortunately, his wife Liu kept her eyes on him constantly. Liu's sons, brothers, and nephews all recognized Hsieh An's desire and tried to persuade Liu to yield to it. They told Liu that two women in ancient times were praised for not being jealous and were respected as virtuous women. Liu knew that they wanted to prod her into making a concession, and she asked "Who wrote the poem?" When they answered, "Duke of Chou," Liu retorted, "Duke of Chou was a man. If the poem had been written by the Duchess of Chou, it would have been recorded differently."[23] Some princesses were so jealous of their husband's concubines that they appealed to the emperor to punish their husbands by sentencing them to imprisonment or death. When Emperor Sung's sixth daughter, Princess Lin Chuan, discovered her husband had a lover, she complained to the emperor. Her husband was then arrested and later executed.[24] Retaliation directed against a husband's concubines after his death was usually quite cruel. It is possible that only the most heartbreaking, extraordinary stories were recorded. For example, upon the death of her husband, Empress Lu, the first Empress of the Hun Dynasty, gradually killed his favorite concubine, Mme. Chi.[25] First she shaved off Mme. Chi's hair, then enslaved her in a mill with a heavy chain on her neck. Later, Mme. Chi's arms and legs were amputated, her eyes were punctured, her ears were burned, and her voice was lost due to the administration of drugs. It was said that even Queen Mother Lu's own son, the new emperor, became very sick after he visited the tortured woman.[26]

After the Wei and Ch'in Dynasties, women were found to be more jealous than ever. Both Li (1978b) and Chen (1926) believed that this trait grew in intensity as women were more suppressed and mistreated by men. In the T'ang Dynasty, the jealousy of a woman named Liu was reported.[27] At that time, it was common for concubines to be given to prominent generals as a reward from the emperor. Liu's husband accepted two concubines from the emperor, with Liu's consent. Because they were a gift from the emperor, Liu dared not reject them. Secretly, she put a drug on the two women's heads which caused them to become bald. When the emperor learned of Liu's actions, he called her to the court and gave her a jug of wine to drink, telling her, "This is poisoned wine, but if you promise not to be jealous anymore you may disregard it." Liu accepted the jar and bowed to the emperor, saying, "My husband and I were both humble people without a social rank before. His accomplishment was the result of our struggles. Now he has a high ranking position and beautiful women from your Majesty, I would rather die." She drank the wine and fell into a sleep. The wine was not poisoned, but flavored with vinegar; the emperor had merely wanted to scare her. This incident gave rise to the old saying, "a jealous woman is a vinegar drinker."

Many stories of jealous women are recorded throughout Chinese history. Male historians often considered these women to be cruel, irrational, and inhuman. Yet, women found that expressing their jealousy helped them to maintain some degree of emotional balance and to cope with the suppression under which they lived. When women were gradually liberated from traditional bondage in the early 1900s, jealous women were no longer a topic or an issue for historian's critiques.

E. The T'ang Legal Codes

To assert greater power on his people, the emperor of T'ang issued a set of laws that was considered the first well-written legal code in Chinese history (Welhelm, 1970). These legal codes prescribed the responsibilities of the state on many things which were previously considered private matters, such as revenge killings and family affairs. Although the books of *Li Chi* (*Book of Rites*), *Tso Chuan* (*Commentaries on Spring and Autumn Annals*), *Chou Li* (*Rites of Chou*), and others spelled out the social norms for proper conduct, the enforcement of these rules was pretty loose and more or less like social sanction with little consistancy. With the effect of the T'ang Codes, women were confronted with the state's power on their life and role in society. However, social crimes which affected women were not broadly covered by the Tang Codes. The verdicts for adultery and rape outside the family were more specifically stated after the Tang Dynasty.

The Hsing Pu (Ministry of Punishment) had jurisdiction over the courts administrating the penal code. The lightest punishment was flogging, which could be fatal if heavily inflicted. The next lightest punishments were (a) banishment for three years to another part of the offender's native province, and (b) banishment for life—a lifetime to be spent on the frontier. The death penalty (the most severe punishment) was usually handed down for a crime against the royal family.

Legal codes became more detailed and specific as time went on. In this section only those codes pertaining to marriage and women will be discussed. For example, the word "betrothal" possessed different meanings before and after the T'ang Dynasty. Among the aristocracy in the Chou Dynasty, a bride had to be promised to the groom's family by her father. The father's consent to the marital proposal was not required by legal codes, but implied betrothal. In the T'ang Dynasty the word "betrothal" was the legal term used for an engagement. Other family elders could substitute for the father and make the decision if both parents were deceased. The consent of the parents and guardians could overrule the wishes of either the bride or groom. The marriage was clearly decided by the elders, not the young couple. A betrothal was legally binding and could not be voided later, even if either party was found to be handicapped. The betrothed girl became a legal member of her fiancee's family; she was immune from governmental punishment of her family for any wrong doing of her father against the emperor. In ancient times, when a father committed a serious crime, his whole family or clan could be put to death. Even distant relatives did not escape punishment for the most severe offenses against the rulers.

Another rule concerning marriage was legally implemented in the T'ang Dynasty, which had been informally observed since the Chou Dynasty. This rule stated that marriage within a clan, where the bride and groom bore the same surname, was socially unacceptable; yet there was some exceptions in ancient times. In the T'ang Dynasty, marriage rested by law on a strictly exogamous basis to prevent inbreeding. Violators were placed in labor camps for two years and the marriage suspended. Yet, the adoption of boys must be carried out between two families having the same surname, although this rule did not apply to the adoption of girls.

Little sexual discrimination existed against women in terms of the sentencing based on the T'ang Codes. For example, the Codes elucidate the penalty for both husband and wife abusers. For having inflicted physical injury, the abuser would receive a punishment ranging from flogging to heavy labor. If the abuse resulted in the death of a spouse, the abuser was executed, either by hanging or by beheading. The T'ang Codes were less rigid as compared to the later Ming Laws which prescribed hanging for a woman who had disabled her husband by beating him. But, a husband would receive only one hundred lashes if he had beaten his wife to death after she had engaged in a verbal confrontation with his parents.

The relationship between daughter-in-law and parents-in-law was reinforced by *Li Chi* prior to the T'ang Dynasty.[28] Parents-in-law had unquestionable authority to terminate the marital bond of a young couple, even if against their son's will. Their uncontested familial status was further insured and protected by the T'ang Codes (Ch'ao, 1973). For instance, either a wife or a concubine had to serve a three year sentence for rebuking her husband's parents or grandparents. The death penalty was given for beating elderly in-laws. On the other hand, daughters-in-law were also shielded by the law to a certain extent. The elderly in-laws would receive one hundred lashes for beating their daughter-in-law if it resulted in physical injury; and they would be jailed for three years if the beating proved fatal. Such rulings also applied to widows, remarried women, and their former in-laws, until the new civil laws proclaimed by the Republic took effect in the early 1900s.

The legal status of concubines was even lower than wives (Ch'ao, 1973). Since concubinage was frequently a part of family life in old Chinese society, a man usually accepted a young concubine in his old age and the concubine was expected to bear many children, especially sons. Unlike the battered wives, concubines had few legal safeguards. A man who injured his concubine was given only a warning. If the abuse led to her death, the abuser received either a flogging or a second degree punishment. On the contrary, if a concubine physically mistreated her master, she was given an irrevocable death sentence.

Divorce has been denoted in different Chinese terms, all referring essentially to the same thing—invalidation of a marital relationship. There are basically three types of divorce: (1) divorce by mutual agreement; (2) forced divorce; and, (3) divorce by petition (Ch'ao, 1973; Ch'en, 1975). Cancelling a marital tie when mutually agreeable to both parties was common in Chinese history, and legal channels were provided for such an appeal. Forced divorce was determined by the government, not by an individual. If the parties involved refused to dissolve the marriage, they were punished according to legal codes. There were five conditions under which a forced divorce could be carried out, as described by the T'ang Codes: (1) if a husband battered his wife's parents or grandparents, or killed his wife's maternal grandparents, uncles, cousins, or siblings; (2) if killings occurred among the immediate relatives of both husband and wife; (3) if a wife scolded or battered her husband's parents or grandparents, or injured the husband's maternal grandparents, uncles, cousins, or siblings; (4) if there was adultery between husband and mother-in-law or between a wife and members of the husband's family; and, (5) if a wife plotted to murder her husband.[29]

Equality of the divorce laws was clearly not practiced since the decree of the T'ang Codes. Except for the second item mentioned above, the rest of the code was designed to protect men's rights, with women's rights denied even with respect to petitioning for divorce. A petition could be made by either party, if one party did not agree to the divorce, the judge decided the case based on the laws. Since the beginning of the Chou Dynasty, a wife could be expelled from the family for seven reasons, in accordance with *Li Chi*. The reasons were: (1) disobedience to parents-in-law, (2) barrenness, (3) adultery, (4) jealousy, (5) incurable disease, (6) excessive talking, and (7) thievery. Although these precedents had been followed through several dynasties, no legal codes were used to enforce them until the T'ang Dynasty.

Women's rights to inheritance as pronounced by the T'ang Codes were minimal. Males—including sons born to concubines if there were no other sons in the family—were considered the carriers of the family surname. As such, they were entitled to share any inherited property. If there was no son in the family, one-third of the inheritance was shared by married daughter(s) and the remaining portion of the inheritance was divided among the unmarried daughter(s).[30]

Titles granted to women were mainly dependent on their husband's achievements and contributions to the emperor. It is believed that this practice did not begin until the Ch'in or Han Dynasties.[31] In the T'ang Dynasty, women were granted proper titles according to the rank of their husband or sons. These titles could be passed on to their descendants. Along with their titles, women were given estates which normally were less than half of the acreage granted to men.

F. Women's Costumes and Fashions

When women became more restricted by legal codes and were treated unequally with men, their costumes and fashions also underwent a certain degree of change. In antiquity, the Chinese people covered their bodies with leaves on warm days, and used animal skins to stay warm in the winter. Fu Hsi, one of the cultural heroes, is believed to have been the inventor of writing, fishing, trapping, and linen clothing. By the time Emperor Huang-ti united the country, records show that dress codes were spelled out.[32] With the availability of linen and silk, the purpose of clothing was no longer limited to body protection; attractiveness was also considered. Thus, the styles became more complicated and extravagant. For example, the portion covering the top part of the body was called *Yi*, the bottom part called *Shang*, the front part *Chin*, and the back part *Chun*. An outfit without a hem was classified as a rag. The top part, Yi, was to have an opening on the right hand side, since an opening on the left was only found among barbarians. A person's social status was easily discerned by the color and texture of his or her attire. Silk cloth and the color yellow predominated in the clothing of the aristocrats. Royal women's clothing was more complex with respect to design and function; there were fashions for various occasions, such as for sacrificial ceremonies, religious worships, social receptions, and night clothes. Men usually wore different colors for Yi and Shang, while women had the same color for both parts. The styles for women's wearing apparel were generally simple.

Changes in women's fashion were detected during the Warring States in the late Chou Dynasty, when the barbarian tribal men of Hu and Hsien Pei invaded China. One of their characteristics was an extra foot long sleeves, worn by both men and women. When the oppression from the emperor of Ch'in ended, people were free to experiment with different types of garments (in the Han Dynasty). Women began wearing long dresses; short dresses were considered out-of-date, even for maids and female slaves, and thus were dressed in silk outfits when presented in the slave market. The dress color was still determined by the rank of a woman's husband. Some colors were even prohibited from use by certain groups of people. For instance, since businessmen were considered to have the lowest position on the social ladder, they were not permitted to wear mixed colors, and were restricted to wearing only orange or light green.

Women's fashions were drastically modified during the unstable 300 year period of the Wei, Chin, North and South Dynasties (Fu, 1974; and, Li, 1978a). Due to warfare and social turmoil, many women who were forced to engage in prostitution or who were adopted as concubines formed a subculture in the society. To gain men's favor, prostitutes and concubines dressed in novel ways; special embroidered designs and the production of new types of fabric stimulated women's desire for fashions that were geared to men's tastes and pleasures. Although royal women were still governed by certain colors and styles, they made slight changes as a result of foreign Hus influence; for example, sleeves were narrowed and hunting shoes were replaced by colorful boots. They could wear a hat with a net covered with jewelry while riding outside; in the past they had to keep their entire body covered to avoid public exposure. Later, women were allowed to dress in what looked like a man's hunting outfit. Lower necklines were also believed to have been influenced by the Hus. Since then, fashions, hairstyles, and the use of cosmetics gradually became affordable, permanent elements of feminine culture.

Skirts, panties, and bras were introduced during this period.[33] Skirts became popular in the T'ang Dynasty and women began wearing various styles, especially red ones. The type of panties worn in ancient times was quite different from present day styles. In fact, long underwear for both males and females was worn with an underskirt called *Ju K'u*; it was very loose, with an opening from the front to the back. Later in the Han Dynasty, women in the imperial court began to tie the Ju K'u with yarn around their waist to hold it together. The short panties for underwear became popular after the founding of the Republic in the early 1900s. There is a short story about how the first bra came into use in ancient China. It was said that Emperor T'ang Ming Huang's favorite concubine, Yang Kwei-fei, had an affair with his general, An Lu-shan. One day her breast was scratched by An Lu-shan. To cover up the scratch, she put a piece of embroidered silk over her breast when Emperor T'ang Ming Huang visited her. This piece of clothing filled with floral embroidery was called *K'e Tzu*, and it is believed to be the earliest bra.

Items for footwear can be traced back to the period of antiquity. The different terms used for footwear depended on the social rank of the person wearing the shoes. Names were given to a variety of styles made of a wide selection of materials including silk, linen, and leather. Usually people went barefoot inside the house. It was a definite rule to take off one's shoes while visiting the emperor. If there were a pair of shoes displayed outside a house, a visitor was to obtain permission from the people inside before entering. Socks were not worn until the Han Dynasty, and were used in the beginning more or less as a wrapper to protect the feet. Socks for both men and women became widespread in the T'ang Dynasty. Due to the influence of foreign Hus, boots of leather or silk became popular with both sexes. Later, wooden and leather slippers replaced the boots. Slippers worn by brides were especially elegant, and were often printed or laminated with colorful designs. Generally speaking, women's footwear changed from a loose, comfortable style to a tight, narrow style. Petite, delicate feet came to be favored by men; this eventually led to the practice of footbinding in the following dynasties.[34]

Hair and body were highly valued by the Chinese people because they believed that they were an inheritance from parents and thus could not be abused. Both boys and girls had long hair; their hair was arranged according to sex; boys used a cap to hold the bun, while girls used a pin to hold theirs. In antiquity the type of hats for men varied according to their feudal rank. The type of hair ornaments for women was a symbol of their social status as well; concubines were not allowed to have any hair accessories. For the affluent, jade, ivory, precious stone, crystal, gold, and silk could be used to adorn the hair. The design of each ornament varied. Common women who could not afford expensive jewelry used wooden hair pins.

Basically there were three hair styles in the T'ang Dynasty: high bun, low bun, and natural bun. Since an abundance of dark hair was considered beautiful, women used wigs to make their bun look more full.

Decorative items, such as necklaces, bracelets, rings, and earrings were also important to women. It is believed that necklaces made of pearl and jade were originally imported from East India. Wearing earrings was thought to symbolize an aristocratic woman's refusal to listen to gossip since the ornaments were attached to her ears.

Earrings became a required item for court women in the Han Dynasty. There were two types of earrings during that period: one was similar to a piece of jade attached to the ears to serve the purpose of blocking out gossip, and the other was a longer styling which hung from the ears. Both types required the ear to be pierced—a practice which dated back to the distant Chou Dynasty.[35]

The simplest cosmetic method to beautify a woman consisted of using rouge and white facial powder. In the earlier days, women knew that a certain creamy substance from plants could be used on their faces to obtain smooth appearing skin. The white facial powder was made of vanilla and starch. The use of different shades of this powder possibly started after the Han Dynasty. Women of the court also used facial powder to condition their complexion. In the T'ang Dynasty the use of facial powder, lip cream, hair cream, and perfume in the imperial court alone cost a million dollars per year.[36]

The shape of the eyebrow was totally artificial.[37] Women shaved off their natural brows and drew them according to fashion; more than ten types of eyebrows were popular in the Five Dynasty era.

Wearing make-up was so widespread among women of the court that only widows—during their mourning period—were not required to wear any. Ordinarily, women had to apply lip cream, rouge, white facial powder, black eye cream, and hair cream to complete their toilette. Cosmetics were as profitable a business in the ancient era as they are today, with exceptional profit coming in the area of face powder.

No one is certain who invented face powder. The substance for face powder came mainly from ground rice; its consistency, however, was not uniform. Like the name brands in today's market, there were many "brands" (or types) produced in ancient society. Some of the brands had a special fragrance, while some served a particular purpose (such as eliminating freckles).

Rouge was introduced to Chinese women by merchants who came from the western part of the present Chinese territory. It was first used to color women's cheeks during the Three Kingdoms era. Rouge, like lip color, was made from a substance found in a particular flower (a detailed procedure for the the production of rouge can be found in Li's book, 1978a).

G. Famous Women Recorded in History

In order to provide a better picture of Chinese women to the reader, the biographies of several well-known Chinese women in Chinese history have been chosen for inclusion in this section. The extraordinary deeds of Chinese women have been recorded by Chinese historians in every generation since the publication of Liu Hsiang's *Lieh Nu Chuan* (*Records of Virtuous Women*) in the late Former Han Dynasty. Among the twenty-five volumes of history that exist for each dynasty following the Han Dynasty, thirteen register over six hundred stories on the conduct of women. However, since several volumes simply repeated stories previously recorded, the actual number of historical volumes dealing with Chinese women is ten.

The women who are portrayed in these volumes represent different social classes and demonstrate virtues which were highly valued during their particular lifetime. Most of these women were queens, princesses, duchesses, widows, or courageous, dutiful women. More upper-class women, such as empresses and the wives of rulers, are described in the earlier volumes; more ordinary women, such as widows, self-sacrficing or destroyed women are listed in later volumes: especially after the *Book of T'ang.* By today's standards, the behavior and action of many of these so-called virtuous, righteous, moral women might be considered either foolish or senseless. For example, in order to demonstrate their faithfulness to dead husbands, women had to abandon their young children and commit suicide, or inflict pain and injury to a part of their body, disabling themselves, in an expression of their mourning.

The stories of famous women selected for this section depict those women who lived during the period 209 B.C. to 960 A.D. The outstanding backgrounds and accomplishments of these women reflect their influence on their nation and on subsequent generations. Women's chastity and self-destructive behavior which has been recorded by their historians is not emphasized here. Two of the six women selected for inclusion in this book played an important and unusual role in the Chinese political arena: in fact, they ruled the Chinese nation for a time. Male historians, who usually exhibit a negative or biased attitude toward female rulers, had more criticism than praise for these women.

Empress Lu was the first Empress of the Han Dynasty. She was the wife of Emperor Kao Tsu. Emperor Kao Tsu was the first commoner to establish an empire in China. He married Lu when he was but a low-ranking county officer, then known by the name of Liu Pang. Liu Pang's primary duty at that time was to transport the draftees to the frontier military camps and to the construction sites of the Great Wall in the northern states. Lu ran the entire household and served her in-laws while her husband was frequently away from home. Later she helped him to organize army deserters and runaway draftees into a revolt against the Emperor

Ch'in II. After five years of fighting other insurgents, Liu Pang triumphed and ascended the throne. He became the founding father of the great Han Empire, an empire which lasted more than four hundred years. The marital relationship between this royal couple deteriorated as the emperor adopted more and more concubines (who were also known as "Madames"). The best known story about Empress Lu, as described earlier in this chapter, was her cruel treatment of one of her husband's favorite concubines. Lu's resourcefulness, boldness, and decisiveness were traits which enabled her to avert several attempted coups while her husband was fighting or inspecting troops in other parts of the nation.[38] Her greatest significance was that she was able to maintain control of the country for fifteen years after the death of her husband. The three young emperors installed as rulers during these years were mere figureheads since Empress Dowager Lu asserted her power in every respect (she even selected relatives from her own family to be the princes stationed in various geographical locations!). Her dream to have her family continue ruling the empire was shattered immediately following her death. The elderly Han loyalists eventually terminated the Lu family and annointed the son of another favorite concubine of the late Emperor Kao Tsu.

Some historians viewed Empress Dowager Lu's rule as an insurrection, and condemn her interference in governmental affairs. However, some of her policies and accomplishments were quite impressive and deserve praise. For instance, she constructed high walls to protect the capital city, Chang An; she reduced taxes from four-tenths of the people's income to one-fifteenth; she lessened corporal punishment for those under ten and above seventy years of age; she established good relations with neighboring countries and insured peace in the western territory. As Liu comments, "Empress Lu was an unusual woman who, with minimum learning, was able to rule a country which had to be rebuilt after the Ch'in suppression and destruction. Her leadership and management skills were shown by the stable and affluent society enjoyed by her subjects."[39]

Many famous Chinese women were outstanding in areas

other than politics. One of these women was Pan Ch'ao who had a splendid family background. Her two older brothers made prominent achievements in Chinese history: Pan Ku was the author of *Ch'ien Han Shu* (*Book of the Former Han Dynasty*), and Pan Ch'ao was a hero in the expansion of the western territory of the Han Empire. Due to her family's influence, Pan Ch'ao was exposed to volumes of books and was able to pursue more learning than ordinary girls of her period (a learning she maintained even after she became a widow after forty years of marriage!)

One of Pan Ch'ao's most important contributions was helping the completion of the *Ch'ien Han Shu*. Her brother, Pan Ku, was originally responsible for this laborious writing project. Prior to the conclusion of the volume, Pan Ku was accused of a political conspiracy, was put in prison, and there died. Emperor Ho then instructed Pan Ch'ao to continue the project, which ultimately contained eight charts and ten astronomics. (Because Pan Ch'ao studied and researched day and night in the Tung Kuan Imperial Library, she began her contact with the court women who were greatly influenced by her philosophy.) An equally noteworthy work by Pan Ch'ao was *Nu Chieh* (*Admonition to Women*). *Nu Chieh* was written mainly to exhort her unmarried daughters to be good wives and daughters-in-law. She may not have intended to advocate these qualities for all women, and was probably concerned merely about her own unmarried daughters—nevertheless, this book became the model for other forthcoming women's books used to educate women in the ways demanded by men.

Pan Ch'ao was not only an author, but was also a teacher to the queen and other imperial personages.[40] For a time she was even involved in governmental affairs. Empress Dowager Teng advised the teenaged emperor after the death of her husband, Emperor Ho. She frequently consulted Pan Ch'ao for advice in decision making. Pan Ch'ao did not misuse or abuse this privilege by attempting to influence policy, organize her supporters, or accept bribery—instead she worked for the good of all people.

Because Pan Ch'ao was highly honored and respected by Emperor Ho, a petition for her brother Pan Ch'ao's return from the western territory was granted. Pan Ch'ao had been stationed in the western territory for thirty years, during which time he was highly successful at preventing neighboring foreigners from creating a disturbance. He had submitted his resignation three years before his sister's request—when he was nearly seventy years old and in poor health. The emperor refused to accept his resignation. Then Pan Ch'ao presented a heart-rending appeal to Emperor Ho, who was finally moved and granted her request. Only one month after his arrival in the capital, Pan Ch'ao died of a chronic illness. Since the Chinese believed that dying in one's native land was a blessing and would give his after-spirit a permanent place to rest, Pan Ch'ao's favor to her brother carried even more importance. As a woman, her scholarship and impeccable record as a court politician made her one of the most highly reputed characters in Chinese history.

The deeds of famous women are not always commensurate with their age and experience. Hsun Kuan was a mere teenager who had been recognized and remembered by people throughout Chinese history. Born in the Chin Dynasty, her boldness was recorded in both the *Chin Shu* (*Book of the Chin Dynasty*), and *Shih Chi* (*Book of History*). Numerous courageous, fearless women are chronicled with Hsun Kuan in the *Chin Shu*; it is possible that women had to be valorous due to the constant threat of revolts (during this warring period, women were trained to be able to fight alongside of their husbands on the front lines).

Hsun Kuan was the daughter of Commander General Hsuan Sung, who was stationed in Wan during the West Chin Dynasty.[41] When the city was attacked and surrounded for days by the troops of Tu Tseng, Hsun Sung's troops ran out of supplies and suffered great casualties. Commander General Hsun was forced to send his thirteen year old daughter, Hsun Kuan, out of the tightly encircled city to a distant city for help. Disguised as a boy, she and a dozen men broke through the surrounding enemy lines during the night. They traveled a winding mountain trail to reach Hsiang Yang, where her father's former comrade, Shih Lan, was stationed. General Shih Lan was so impressed with the fearless young lady that he promised to save the people in Wan. Since he was concerned about his own limits of strength, he instructed

Hsun Kuan to request support from another general, Chou Fang in Chin Chou. Hsun Kaun wrote a letter requesting aid for her father, and presented it to General Chou in person. Because of her determination and bravery, General Chou sent his son and troops with Hsun Kuan back to Hsiang Yang, and then personally joined Shih Lan's armed forces already heading for Wan. When the revolting troops heard that Shih Lan was leading two divisions to rescue the city, they fled and the city was delivered from destruction. Though only thirteen, Hsun Kuan had not been afraid to accept her father's order and was proud to accomplish her mission. (This is the only part of Hsun Kuan's life mentioned by historians. Evidently they were convinced that this worthy action deserved recognition in Chinese history above any other part of her life.)

Wong Ch'ao-Chun was another brave woman whose decision to marry a foreign ruler made possible a lengthy period of peace along the northwestern Chinese border.[42] She was the most reputed among the hundreds of concubines of the Emperor Yuan, but was never called by the emperor until the eve of her departure to the foreign country. Emperor Yuan had a habit of selecting beauties for the night on the basis of viewing pictures painted by palace artists. The chief artist, Mao Yen-shou, demanded bribes from those women who wanted to be called by the emperor, but who did not possess the necessary quality of beauty the emperor demanded. Upon receiving a large bribe, Mao would create a painting of his own version of a beautiful woman. Wong Ch'ao-Chun resented this practice and never stooped to bribe Mao to paint a flattering picture of her; she thought her striking beauty was sufficient to win the emperor's attention. What she did not know was that the portrait of her presented to the emperor had been distorted by the vindictive Mao.

As a result of endless waiting and frustration, Wong Ch'ao-Chun finally volunteered to be considered as the bride of Hu Han Hsieh, the king of Hsiung Nu, a neighboring nation northwest of China. To maintain peace along this northwestern border, many previous emperors of the Han Dynasty sent court women to the kings of the foreign nations as concubines. When Hu Han Hsieh made the long journey to China to pay his respects and tributes to Emperor Yuan, his desire was to request a beauty of his own from the Chinese emperor. Naturally, Emperor Yuan was delighted to offer the pick of his court. When Wong Ch'ao-Chun's wish was granted and she was presented in front of the emperor to his foreign dignitary, the two heads of state had different reactions. The Emperor was at once dazzled by her beauty and filled with regret at the terrible mistake that had kept her from him; he wished her for his own, but it was too late. Hu Han Hsieh was surprised at his good fortune and immediately chose her to be his queen. When Emperor Yuan learned the reason that he had never summoned Wong, he ordered the imperial chief artist Mao Yen-shou and his staff beheaded.

Ch'ao-Chun left China with her husband in 33 B.C. and never returned to her motherland again. The lifestyle in the nothern land was quite different from where Wong Ch'ao-Chun was born and raised. She not only had to adjust to a different climate, language, type of food, daily life routine, and social structure, but she was also expected to maintain a peaceful relationship between China and Hsiung Nu. After Hu Han Hsieh's death, she married his oldest son from a previous marriage—in accordance with the custom of Hsiung Nu. Although this marriage was against her will and cultural background, she accepted it.

Wong Ch'ao-Chun played an influential role during her second husband's regime. Her most notable contribution was the maintenance of a peaceful border for the development and expansion of the Han Dynasty. Ch'ao-Chun was respected for her courage and personal sacrifice for the sake of her country. She was also renowned for her instrument playing (P'i P'a), and poetry writing.

Queen Ch'ang Sun's story was not as dramatic as that of other female figures. She was honored and praised for her meekness and humility.[43] Raised in a prominent family, she learned to read Chinese classics at a young age. At thirteen she married Li Shih-ming—who later became Emperor T'ai Tsung of the T'ang Dynasty. Complying with the traditional teachings for women, she always acted properly and thereby won the heart of her husband. She was exalted to the rank of Queen after Tai Tsung, the second son of

Emperor Kao Tsung, seized power following a political confrontation with his brothers.

Queen Ch'ang Sun maintained a simple, frugal lifestyle which influencd her children, and court politics. She assisted the Emperor in numerous ways and won his respect—yet never abused her prerogatives. When the emperor planned to promote her brother, a longtime friend of the Emperor, to prime minister, she objected vigorously. She convinced the Emperor to retain those honest and loyal wisemen in the court. She resented political interference from a queen's family—such as Empress Lu's, which eventually led to power struggles in the court.

The reign of Emperor T'ai Tsung, called the Administration of Chen Kuan, was applauded by historians as one of the most stable and prosperous periods in Chinese history. Queen Chang Sun's contribution to the Emperor's success was incalculable.

Not only was her political acumen incalculable, but her personal modesty was also noteworthy: a modesty especially apparent when she was suffering from a fatal disease at the age of 36. Her son, the crown prince, proposed to the Emperor that he grant amnesty to criminals in order to eliminate the reputed source of the attack of her illness. The Emperor agreed to grant the amnesty, but Queen Ch'ang Sun insisted that he retract the order because she placed the interest of her country above her life. (In addition to setting this courageous example for court women to follow, Queen Ch'ang Sun authored a thirty volume treatise, *Nu Tse* (*Principles for Women*), which reviewed the conduct of early virtuous Chinese women, offering their life stories as additional examples for court women to follow. Her thirty volume treatise later became a part of the collection used for the education of Chinese women.)

In contrast to Queen Ch'ang Sun's humility, Empress Wu Tse T'ien was criticized by historians for demonstrating the same traits and qualifications for which successful male rulers were traditionally praised.[44] Nevertheless, she was the only crowned female ruler in Chinese history. Many empresses, such as Lu and Teng of the Han Dynasty, assisted the young emperors in managing the government by practicing what was called "reigning from behind the curtain," since women were not allowed to hold face-to-face conferences with men, female surrogate rulers had to sit behind a semi-transparent screen to conduct business. Unlike her predecessors, Tse T'ien inaugerated her own dynasty, named Chou, after she had assisted three emperors for over twenty years. Calling herself the "Holy Emperor," her self-proclaimed sovereignty lasted fifteen years (690-705 A.D.). On the eve of her death at the age of 83, she reinstalled her son as the Emperor of T'ang, and invalidated her title as the Holy Emperor of Chou.

Wu Tse T'ien's intelligence and leadership were first manifested when she was called to the palace to comfort the widowed Emperor T'ai Tsung after the death of Queen Chang Sun. Because of her beauty and talents in literature, she was selected as the "talented" to entertain the emperor in art and literature; she was only fourteen years old at that time. According to regulations, upon the death of the emperor, she was forced, along with the other imperial women, to retreat to a Buddhist nunnery and become a nun. However, at age 27, she refused to accept this imposed lifelong widowhood, and waited for an opportunity to leave the temple. Her dream came true when she was recalled to the court after the new Emperor Kao Tsung had met her at the nunnery while attending his father's fifth annual memorial service. One year later, in 655 A.D., Wu Tse T'ien plotted successfully to eliminate the empress and the emperor's favorite concubines and became empress. When Emperor Kao Tsung began suffering from poor health, Wu Tse T'ien took charge of the state's business for him. Aided by her background in Chinese classics, her performance was truly outstanding, and she earned Emperor Kao Tsung's trust and confidence. Shortly after the death of Emperor Kao Tsung and the succession of her son, Chung Tsung, the Empress Dowager Wu Tse T'ien replaced her son with another prince as emperor. Once again, she created the opportunity to act in a decision-making capacity. Following another six years of "reigning from behind the curtain," she erected a new dynasty, named Chou, and became the only female ruler to head a dynasty in Chinese history.

As expected, the installation of a new dynasty invited a great deal of opposition and disturbance throughout the nation—particularly since the ruler was a woman. Yet, with her discerning judgment and intelligence, she was able to subdue the rebellious forces against her. Since loyalty to the emperor of a dynasty was stressed by Confucianism and strongly held by Chinese intellectuals, many older high-ranking officers were forced to either stiffle their criticism, or face persecution under her administration.

Even though the private life of Wu Tse T'ien was dramatized by story writers and even criticized by historians, her ability to manage governmental affairs for forty years was unquestionable. Her fairness and tactics in governing court officials should not be distorted or overlooked. In addition to her ambitiousness, aggressiveness, and decisiveness, she was a reasonable and open-minded person willing to accept criticism and suggestions. A woman who had been suppressed by traditional teachings and social norms, Wu Tse T'ien must have possessed extraordinary qualities to achieve her goals in Chinese politics. Furthermore, she had to confront numerous obstacles and challenges that arose during her administration simply because of her sex.

In the final years of her reign, her two favorite young men, who were brothers, dominated the court affairs which caused conflict with her expelled son, the former Emperor Chung Tsung. When Wu Tse T'ien was dying, Chung Tsung was escorted back to the palace and reinstated in power by the loyalists who had earlier killed the young brothers who were the old empress' favorites. Wu Tse T'ien then ended the Dynasty of Chou in 705 A.D., and allowed her son to restore the throne of the T'ang Dynasty.

It is hoped that the preceeding section provides readers with different facets of Chinese women in this era and that some of the personality traits possessed by those chosen women will generate a certain degree of positive impact on today's Chinese women. Based on the deeds of these above-mentioned women, one can conclude that court women played an important role in Chinese politics and that women were less restricted by society in developing their potential. Thus women were able to make contributions in literature and governmental affairs. Meanwhile, their stories have served as either an admonition or as a dose of encouragement for women in succeeding generations.

Conclusion

Decadence of women's status was slowly becoming evident as the China Empire was gradualy established and expanded by the rulers during this stage in Chinese history. First, government began restraining women's conduct and their roles in society. The T'ang Codes, the first well-written Chinese laws, further spelled out women's legal rights in which more egalitarianism for both sexes was detected than the social norms proclaimed in the succeeding dynasties. At least women were neither deprived of intellectual pursuits, nor totally prohibited from divorce and remarriage. However, at times, the social climate and customs were not in favor of women's rights. The beginning of raising home prostitutes and offering dowries had downgraded women's position in the family. Compared to the declining social status experienced by women in the previous period, women in this era found that in addition to inheriting the existing lower social status, they countered the social force which reinforced a greater breach between men's and women's position in the family.

NOTES

[1] Li Ch'ia-fu, *Lives of ancient Chinese women* (Taipei, Taiwan: Li Min Publishing Co., 1978), p. 105.

[2] *Ibid.*

[3] *Ibid.*, p. 106; see also Ch'en Tung-yuan, *History of the life of Chinese women* (Taipei, Taiwan: Commerce Publishing Co., 1977), pp. 56-57.

[4] Ch'en, *op. cit.*, p. 42.

[5] *Ibid.*, p. 43; see also Ch'en Ku-yuan, *History of Chinese marriage* (Taipei, Taiwan: Commerce Publishing Co., 1975), p. 183.

[6]Ch'en Tung-yuan, *op. cit.*, pp. 43-45.

[7]*Ibid.*, p. 84.

[8]*Ibid.*, p. 88.

[9]*Ibid.*, p. 68.

[10]Li Ch'ia-fu, *Chinese ancient women* (Taipei, Taiwan: Li Min Publishing Co., 1978), p. 75.

[11]Ch'en Tung-yuan, *op. cit.*, p. 47.

[12]Liu Naite, "China's first woman historian," *Women of China* (April, 1980), pp. 40-41; see also Nancy Lee Swann, *Pan Ch'ao: Foremost Scholar of China* (New York: Century Co., 1932), pp. 82-90; and, see also, Ch'en Tung-yuan, *op. cit.*, p. 46.

[13]Ch'en Tung-yuan, *op. cit.*, pp. 47-48.

[14]*Ibid.*, pp. 49-50.

[15]*Ibid.*, p. 54.

[16]Ch'en Ku-yuan, *op. cit.*, pp. 30-33.

[17]*Ibid.*; see also Ch'en Tung-yuan, *op. cit.*, p. 63.

[18]*Ibid..*, p. 64.

[19]*Ibid..*

[20]*Ibid.*, p. 65.

[21]*Ibid.*, p. 66.

[22]Li, *Chinese ancient women*, p. 30.

[23]Li, *Lives of ancient Chinese women*, p. 77.

[24]Li, *Chinese ancient women*, p. 34.

[25]*Ibid.*, p. 49; see also Liu Tzu-ch'ing, *Critical biographies of famous women in Chinese history* (Taipei, Taiwan: Lin Min Publishing Co., 1978), pp. 60-79.

[26]*Ibid.*, p. 76.

[27]Li, *Chinese ancient women*, pp. 35-36.

74

[28]Li, *Lives of ancient Chinese women*, pp. 37-45; see also Ch'en Ku-yuan, *op. cit.*, pp. 199-201.

[29]Ch'ao Feng-chieh, *Legal position of Chinese women* (Taipei, Taiwan: Shih Huo Publishing Co., 1973), pp. 52-53.

[30]*Ibid.*, pp. 73-74.

[31]*Ibid.*, pp. 114-115.

[32]Li, *Chinese ancient women*, p. 125.

[33]*Ibid.*, pp. 133-135.

[34]*Ibid.*, p. 150.

[35]*Ibid.*, pp. 116-122.

[36]*Ibid.*, pp. 103-104.

[37]Fu Le-ch'eng, "Women's lives in the T'ang Dynasty," *Shih-huo Magazine* IV.1-2 (1974), pp. 3-4.

[38]Liu Tzu-ch'ing, *op. cit.*, pp. 60-74.

[39]*Ibid.*, p. 77.

[40]Liu Naihe, *op. cit.*, pp. 40-41; see also, Liu Tzu-ch'ing, *op. cit.*, p. 122.

[41]*Ibid.*, pp. 151-153; see also, Hsu T'ien-hsiao, *New history of Chinese women* (Shanghai: Shen Chou Publishing Co., 1913), p. 62.

[42]Li, *Chinese ancient women*, pp. 183-198; see also, Shu Jiong, *The most famous beauty of China* (New York: D. Appleton and Co., 1924), p. 168.

[43]Hsu, *op. cit.*, p. 89; see also, Liu Tzu-ch'ing, *op. cit.*, pp. 178-181.

[44]Hsu, *op. cit.*, pp. 91-92; see also, Liu Tzu-ch'ing, *op. cit.*, pp. 185-192; and, Yang Liansheng, "Female rulers in Imperial China," *Harvard Journal of Asiatic Studies* XXIII (1960), p. 51; and, also, Li, *Chinese ancient women*, pp. 41-58.

CHAPTER FOUR

Middle Period
(Sung Dynasty to Ming Dynasty: 959-1642 A.D.)

The Sung Dynasty (960-1280 A.D.) marks the turning point for Chinese women's status in society. Chastity, female infanticide, footbinding, and the perception of women as sex objects began to prevail as social trends—trends which extended over the next seven centuries and finally climaxed in the Ch'ing Dynasty (1644-1911). Prior to this period, although women were circumscribed by traditional norms and social behavior that stressed virtue and proper conduct at home in order to maintain patriarchal authority within a family unit, they were physically free from impairment caused by social pressure: that is, they had the right to live and to walk on their natural feet. They were even allowed to remarry after the death of their husbands. Less fortunate than their predecessors, women in the Sung Dynasty and successive dynasties were not only restrained by traditional moral standards for women, but also physically confined by bound feet. Worse yet, the very right to life was denied by female infanticide which was socially acceptable and suicide or physical disfigurement for continence was encouraged by family members.

A. The Impact of Neo-Confucianism on Women

These drastic changes did not occur simultaneously with the founding of the Sung Dynasty; most likely, women's further suffering stemmed from Neo-Confucianism which actually developed nearly fifty years after the installation of the new dynasty.[1] Neo-Confucianism, sometimes considered a revival or renaissance of Chinese cultural heritages, generated a great impact on logic and philosophy which in turn penetrated literature, arts, and people's daily existence. In particular, it brought misery to women's lives in the subsequent dynasties.

Neo-Confucianist scholars who can be clustered into three developmental stages of Confucianist doctrine (Table 1)

Table 1*

Neo-Confucian Scholars in the Sung Dynasty

Stage I		Stage II		Stage III	
Year of Birth	Name	Year of Birth	Name	Year of Birth	Name
960	Erection of Sung Dynasty	1017	Chou Tun-yi	1032	Cheng-Hao
		1019	Sze-Ma Kuang	1033	Cheng Yi
989	Fan Chung-yen	1020	Chang Tsai, Su Sung	1045	Yu Tso, Huang Ting-chien
993	Hu Yuan				
1007	Ou-Yang Hsiu	1021	Wong An-shih		
1008	Su Tze-mei				
1009	Su Hsun, Li Kou			1053	Young Shih
1011	Shao Yung			1072	Lo Ts'ung-yen
				1088	Li Tun
				1130	Chu Hsi

possessed different attitudes toward women. In the first period, scholars expected less of women. For instance, Fan Chung-yen was a reformer who assisted the Emperor of the Sung Dynasty in reestablishing the social systems following the collapse of the Five Dynasties (907-960 A.D.). His mother married into the Chu family after the death of his father. He was adopted by the Chus and named Chu Shuo. He resumed his natural father's family name when he became successful in politics. Later, he arranged the marriage of his widowed daughter-in-law to his widowed student Wong Tao. He never denounced remarried women; on the contrary, he ruled that the expenses of remarriage for widows should be taken care of by the government. Later, Hu Yuan was more demanding on the virtue of women. He believed that it was

*Source: Adapted from Chen Tung-yuan, *History of the Life of Chinese women* (Taipei, Taiwan: Commerce Publishing Co., 1977), pp. 130-132.

suitable for daughters to marry into superior families but that sons should marry women from inferior families. The rationale behind this thinking was that inferior young wives would be more obedient and work harder to please the haughty family figures of "superior" homes.

An almost imperceptible change was seen during the second stage as diversity among scholars' viewpoints emerged. First, as discussed in Sze-Ma Kuang's book, *Chia Fan* (*Family Morality*), little girls were required to study *Hsiao Ching* (*Classic of Filial Piety*), *Lun-Yu* (*Analects*), *Nu Chieh* (*Admonition to Women*), and *Lieh Nu Chuan* (*Records of Virtuous Women*), by the age of seven—but were not given opportunities to learn or enjoy poetry—as did females in previous dynasties—because poetry writing was believed not to be a learning experience to facilitate women's virtues. Moreover, he condemned divorce and expected women to be absolutely submissive to their husbands, with no talking back. Both Chou Tun-yi and Chang Tsai were pioneers in formulating Neo-Confucianism by combining Buddhism, Taoism, Confucianism, and the traditional thinking from books such as *Ta Hsueh* (*Great Learning*), *Li Chi* (*Book of Rites*), and *I Ching* (*Book of Changes*). As a result, women were not favored by their belief.

Wong An-shih was a reformer and was considered a liberal philosopher when he arranged a divorce for his daughter-in-law who was mistreated by his son.[2] Now the deterioration of women's fate could be detected.

In the last stage, and the longest period, when Neo-Confucianism became more mature, more demands were placed on women. The theories argued by the rationalists, Cheng Hao and Cheng Yi, emanated from the varied schools of thought. The so-called Two Chengs perpetuated the rationale delineated by thinker Chou Tun-yi in the previous phase which, influenced by Buddhism, emphasized the primacy of the mind and the importance of mental cultivation. After that, Neo-Confucianism was well-conceived and structured. Change Hao and Cheng Yi vigorously advocated Neo-Confucianism at the expense of women's livelihood.[3] In *Chin-Szu Lu* (*Reflection on Things at Hand*), Cheng Hao postulated that it was better for women to die of starvation than to repudiate chastity. He also recommended the double moral standard for men and women in his book *Hsin-li Ta Chuan* (*Philosophy of Nature and Principle in its Completeness*). This book suggested that men be allowed to divorce their wives and that a widower should remarry for the sake of his aging parents who required a daughter-in-laws services, but Cheng Hao did not permit women to do the same. After four generations of teaching, Neo-Confucianism was detailed by Chu Hsi at the end of the Sung Dynasty. In reality, society was not complying completely with the newly shaped Neo-Confucianism; exceptional cases of remarriage among divorced and widowed women were still found in various social classes, including the royal families. However, its influence was reflected by the book *The Geneology of the Chang Lineage* which clearly described proper manners for women and their roles at home as demanded by this period. Examples of sex segregation, physical constraint, and female "inferiority" are found throughout this book.

B. Female Chastity

The Neo-Confucianism that developed in the Sung Dynasty continued to play a vital role in women's declining status: they

Heavy Porcelaneous vase with simple design. Sung Dynasty (960–1279).

were overwhelmingly afflicted by male tyranny which flourished in the succeeding dynasties. Women were cruelly discriminated against by the dual or conflicting moral standards set for men and women in the marital arena. Men could abuse their regal male rights while women had to conform rigidly to the unreasonable moral code forced on them by men.

The rapid assimilation of Mongolian rulers into Chinese culture led to the full blossoming of forced female chastity in the coming Ming and Ch'ing Dynasties. Widows were expected to be sexually abstinent and were forbidden to remarry—even a princess was not excepted from this expectation.[4] In the preceeding Sung Dynasty (960-1280 A.D.), there was only one princess out of more than 80 who was granted the freedom to remarry, while even earlier, in the T'ang Dynasty (618-907 A.D.) there were 27 princessess out of a total of 211 princesses who were granted this freedom.[5]

Women who were disowned by their husbands due to unfaithfulness and disobedience were deprived of employment, bearing remorse and disgrace for life. Since most of these women had no means of earning a living because of their total dependence on men, suicide was often their only alternative. Unfortunately, such an act was gradually favored by society and encouraged by the family as a symbol of chastity. In the Ming Dynasty the most common practices associated with continence, reflecting the injustice done to women, were death and disfigurement. Women who committed suicide for the sake of chastity were classified as *lieh nu*, while those disfigured women were called *chieh fu*. Both *lieh nu* and *chieh fu* would bring fame and benefits to the family. Very often the decision was made by the family, which instantly grabbed the chance to glorify the family name—giving the widow no choice but to die. The statistics on women sacrificed for chastity, including those who maintained their body purity by death and those who willed to remain celibate by physical impairment, are derived from the histories of the Chou Dynasty down to the Ch'ing Dynasty, as shown in Table 2. These figures embody almost the entire Chinese recorded history. The comparison of recorded sacrificed women in different dynasties shows that chastity was increasingly imposed on women as time went by. Since the collected data was only available until 1725, most of the women in the Ch'ing Dynasty were not included. Tung (1937) believed that the trend of women sacrificing their lives continued to increase in numbers and reached a peak in the Ch'ing Dynasty.[6]

Based on the figures in Table 2, Tung concluded that the Sung Dynasty was the turning point for the emphasis on female chastity—which was manifested to such an extent that young women and their parents complied with the social

80

model without any hesitation.[7]   During the Han and T'ang
Dynasty marital arrangement was conducted in a purchasing

Table 2*

Cases of Female Chastity: Chou to Ch'ing Dynasties
(1100 B.C. to 1725 A.D.)

Dynasty	Number of Cases by Death	Number of Cases by Disfigurement
Chou (1100-421 B.C.)	7	6
Ch'in (221-206 B.C.)	19	1
Han (206 B.C.-221 A.D.)	35	22
Wei, Chin, Norther & Southern (221-589 A.D.)	29	29
Sui, Tang, Wu Tai (589-960)	34	34
Sung (960-1280)	150	152
Yuan (1280-1368)	383	359
Ming (1368-1644)	8688	27141
Ch'ing (1644-1725)	2841	9482

---

manner—the marriage was only valid following the wedding
ceremony. Contrary to such practice, betrothal in the Sung
Dynasty was considered a contract which became effective
immediately after the agreement; the wedding was a mere
formality. Therefore, a betrothed girl was expected to fulfill
all moral obligations as a wife to her husband and as a
daughter-in-law to her husband's parents. If her fiance died
prior to the wedding, she was required to move to the
in-laws' house and maintain her widowed status for the rest
of her lifetime.

Table 3 indicates the most popular ways of dying for
chastity employed by women during the Yuan and Ming
Dynasties. Like Table 2, the data in Table 3 was compiled
from recorded cases in history. Undoubtedly many chaste
women have been overlooked by historians; however, these
figures reveal the social trends and the worthlessness of
women's lives based on the type of sacrifices and the increas-

---

*Source: Tung Chia-tsun, "The statistics of sacrificed women,"
Contemporary History III.2 (1937), pp. 1-5.

Table 3*
Recorded Methods of Sacrifice in the Sung & Yuan Dynasties

Method Used	Sung Dynasty (960-1280 A.D.)	Yuan Dynasty (1280-1368 A.D.)
A. Suicide		
1. Drowning	40	103
2. Hanging	18	90
3. Starvation	4	14
4. Jumping off a cliff	4	15
5. Burning	0	11
6. Other	5	61
B. Killed		
1. Stabbed	37	48
2. Beheaded	0	6
3. Split, drawn & quartered	4	2
4. Other	2	20

ing number of cases. Physical injuries, including amputation of arms, hands, fingers, ears and noses, signified their widowed status which further prevented them from remarriage and also earned fame and fortune for their families.

The main reinforcement of such zealous practices came from governmental policy.[7] Beginning in 1367, the families of sacrificed widows were exempted by law from governmental service. Shrines and monuments to the dead widows, whether from sacrifice or suicide, were erected by local officials to promote this social practice. Well-known cases of sacrificed widows who employed unusual methods of self-destruction were documented in volumes of books by historians in each dynasty. Because of public recognition through governmental rewards and historical literature, widows and their families were induced to continue and elaborate this cruel and inhumane custom.

The prevalence of female chastity gave rise to a new social insitution in the Ming Dynasty that became well formalized in the Ch'ing Dynasty. Local fame-seeking officers and wealthy rural gentry established a "Shrine of Chastity" to

*Source: Tung Chia-tsun, "The Statistics of Sacrificed Women," *Contemporary History* III.2 (1937), p. 5.

help financially disabled widows and to prevent them from remarrying (Kao, 1935). Economically, a widow had little or no chance to become independent; remarriage was forbidden and an actual threat to their lives if they did. Thus, this welfare-type institution took care of the material needs of widows as well as their young children. However, widows who took refuge in the shrines were most likely confined in that area forever and were not even allowed to have visits by male relatives. The size of public and private shrines varied from accommodating 30 women up to several hundred women. The "Shrine of Chastity" was later changed to "Refugee Centers" in 1929; the institution gradually disappeared during the 1930s and 1940s.

The stress on virginity was another form of forced chastity. Like widows being denied the right to remarry, young single girls were totally prohibited from premarital sex. The growing desire for virgins emerged gradually during the Sung Dynasty when widows who remarried were referred to as "the reopening of an old store".[9] At that time it was not uncommon for men over sixty to buy a virgin concubine. Some of the methods applied to test a woman's virginity were anything but reliable. Frequently a bride who, rightly or wrongly, was found not to be a virgin on the wedding night was forced to return to her parents' home the next morning. Afterwards her chances of getting married again became exceedingly slim; her alternatives were to either be a concubine or to be sold into prostitution. Even if she were reluctantly accepted by her husband, the marriage was considered to be already in trouble, and most likely her husband would despise her forever—a further indication of an unfair moral standard imposed on women—even at the expense of one's fate.

C. Concubines and Prostitutes

Monogamy was merely a theoretical term referring to the marital pattern of the majority of the Chinese population; in reality, polygamy had been practiced since the Chou Dynasty. Men were given the privilege of having concubines, in addition to the "official" wife who legally held the highest status among all women in the same household. Her leading position granted her power in decision making and commanding the respect of the concubines. A much more restrictive legal code on concubinage, promulgated in the Ming Dynasty, regulated that: (1) princes were permitted to select up to ten concubines; (2) royal family members could have two concubines if no son was born by age 25, and two more if no son was born by age 30; (3) army generals were allowed to have two concubines if there was no son in the family by age 30, and one more if no son was born by age 35; (4) marshalls could take their first concubine at age 30, and an additional one at age 35 if no son was born; (5) commoners could have one concubine if no son was born by age 40. The penalty for violation of the law was 40 paddlings, although enforcement of the law sometimes varied with location.[10] Superficially, this law was good inasmuch as it limited male covetousness; in truth it put the blame for a woman's barrenness on the woman, while exonerating the man and leaving him free from all responsibility. Worse than that, legalized concubinage encouraged open trading of concubines. Consequently, women were valued as a commodity instead of as an individual. Several hundred poor families in Yangchou specialized in preparing and selling their daughters as concubines.[11] Matchmakers visited the town regularly to recruit qualified young girls. Those selected were given a hair-pin to wear and a contract was written by the girls' parents spelling out the amount of gold, jewelry and clothing required in exchange for their daughters.

The relationship among husband, wife, and concubines was both delicate and complicated. Several conditions are given to illustrate the interactions among these three parties. If a wife had sons and was widely respected, her position in the family would be less affected by her husband's acquisition of a concubine even though a newly adopted concubine would create a stormy atmosphere in the family. The wife's relationship with the concubine was determined by her husband's affection and respect for her; the husband had the authority to balance the power between the two women. Dominating or influential concubines often invited the wife's jealousy. After the death of the husband, a depraved or malevolent concubine most likely would confront retaliation from the dead man's widow; physical abuse was a

popular means of revenge.[12]   In other cases, a wife could be
more clever than a concubine, enabling her to manipulate the
latter to attain her goals. This was particularly true when a
wife was infertile and yearned for a son borne by a concubine. A wife could legally adopt a concubine's son, who later
would be qualified for inheritance as a "number one son."
The complexity of the power struggle among household
women varied based on the number of concubines. For example, due to the large number of concubines, princesses,
and female officers, the imperial court was a place where a
great deal of jealousy, hatred, malice, antagonism, and human
tragedy existed.

The practice of prostitution in Chinese history was
basically introduced and dominated by the social and intellectual elite of the upper class. According to Ch'en Tung-
yuan's search it is believed that prostitution started in the
Han Dynasty when Emperor Wu hired women to satisfy the
sexual needs of his soldiers.[13]   Later, prostitutes who had the
talent to learn singing and dancing were recruited by wealthy
families to entertain house guests. Keeping prostitutes became popular and socially acceptable among prestigious families during the South-North Dynasty.[14]   The number and
quality of household prostitutes were determined by social
status: those in the low caste were deprived of having home
prostitutes. By the T'ang Dynasty official prostitutes were
made available to high ranking officers.[15]
During the Sung Dynasty the evolution of prostitution
was nearly complete. There were so-called official prostitutes, household prostitutes, army prostitutes, front-line
prostitutes, and monasterial prostitutes.[16]   The role of
official prostitutes was to entertain high-ranking officers with
song, dance, and poetry. Sometimes, they would be chosen
as concubines. Nanking was the capital of official prostitutes
and in the Ming Dynasty numerous official prostitutes were
assigned to a sixteen story building designed especially for
them.[17]   Household prostitutes were usually purchased by
the rich to amuse friends of the family. Wong Chen in the
East Chin Dynasty used to own three hundred beautiful
prostitutes.[18] This glamorous kind of life, however, was not
widespread in the Sung Dynasty due to the movement of

Neo-Confucianism. The sexual desires of soldiers were well tended to by their superiors who provided prostitutes during their training sessions. It is believed that such a practice was launched during the Han Dynasty while young people were being drafted.[19] Mobile prostitutes were called when the armies were on the road or at the frontline. These women were normally recruited from the local districts and were dismissed after the military maneuver was over. Monasterial prostitutes nested around monasteries to attract customers from both inside and outside the religious houses.

For centuries cities like Ch'angan, Loyang, Yangchou, and Nanking were capitals of commercial prostitution. A visitor in Yangchou described the road leading to a residence crowded with five to six hundred sullen-faced prostitutes resentful of the strong competition in the business.[20] The annual classic examination for civil service held in major cities brought more business to prostitutes in the fall. In their contact with prostitutes, contestants often found not only sexual pleasure, but spiritual satisfaction not provided by wives who lacked the knowledge to enjoy poetry and music.

Engaging in sexual activities was merely a part of the Chinese prostitutes' role in business. They were classified into five major groups according to their special talents which attracted different types of patrons: dancing, singing, playing musical instruments, writing poetry, and serving and drinking during meals. Some prostitutes—both private and official— were even drafted to participate in a parade held annually prior to spring. They dressed up in unusual blouses, capes, hair pieces, earrings, and other accessories. Less affluent prostitutes who were unable to afford such attire for the occasion had to borrow from others. They often were the objects of teasing from the spectators and were even called upon to engage in business before the conclusion of the parade.[21]

In a sense, Chinese prostitutes lived a better life than women of poor families who were deprived socially, economically, and educationally. Most prostitutes inhabited urban areas and experienced better economic conditions and opportunities than their sisters in rural areas. They were often the ones to start a new fashion in hairdos, jewelry, dress, etc. For women from poor families, this way of making a living might grant them economic betterment and lead them to an advancement on the social ladder. At least they were fed by their owners—who kept them free from starvation. Business contacts with middle- or upper-class men might bing them the opportunity to become a concubine (who was better protected by a male-dominated society). Official and household courtesans who were well trained in music and writing poetry received a better education than the average person.

Regardless of the economic gains and/or educational opportunities, prostitutes were not positively regarded by the general public. This negative public attitude was associated with the background of the prostitutes. Generally speaking, prostitutes were beggars' children who faced starvation; or, prostitutes were victims of rape coming from poor households (if a family failed to cover up the assault by use of money or power, the marital prospects of the girl were doomed); or, prostitutes were young girls enticed by materialistic attractions. Victims from the first two categories were given no other alternative than to be sold to a "female guardian" for sexual service. With no education or skills to earn a living, they had to accept this fate. Some prostitutes were quite successful and became wealthy enough to form their own business. After the age of thirty they received little attention from society; not much has been recorded of their later life. The more fortunate ones became concubines or headed a group of young prostitutes to continue the business, while ill-fated prostitutes had to charge less or go to low-class areas to survive. Unfortunately, their wretched backgrounds and miserable experiences did not win public mercy; people not only looked down upon them but also cursed their "evil doings," particularly during the Sung Dynasty.

During this period society was placed in a moral dilemna; prostitution was openly promoted and facilitated by government as well as by private citizens, yet the morality of prostitutes was vigorously attacked and condemned by the general public. Worse than that, the problems of prostitutes and their outlook on life received no concern or sympathy from society. Such social phenomena further downgraded women's status and disregarded their dignity as an individual.

D. Domestic Education and Employment

During this status-declining period, women's educational opportunities depended mainly on their family backgrounds. Children from the middle and upper classes had more exposure to Chinese classics and scholastic stimulation than children from the lower class. In order to later function as a manager of the household, girls were taught basic vocabulary and mathematical operations. Few were fortunate enough to learn poetry writing and to study classical literature. Szu-Ma Kuang, in the Sung Dynasty, suggested that seven year old girls ought to start memorizing *Lun Yu* (*Analects*) and *Hsiao Ching* (*Classic of Filial Piety*). By the age of nine, girls were expected to interpret these two volumes and other related books. Nevertheless, Szu-Ma Kuang strongly opposed girls' learning how to write poetry inasmuch as poetry composition was often associated with prostitutes and prostitution.

The volumes of classical literature for women were expanded in the Ming Dynasty. The book *Nei Hsun* (*Internal Rules*), written by Empress Yuan Hsiao Wen around 1403 A.D., contained twenty chapters with special emphasis on interpersonal relationships at court. The submissiveness of women was once again addressed in her book. Some of the principles could be applied to common citizens as well as the royal family. Furthermore, in addition to *Nei Hsun*, Empress Yuan Hsia Wen edited *Ku Chin Lieh Nu Chuan* (*History of Virtuous Women*), recorded by previous dynasties. The popularity of these two volumes further nourished the idea of chastity; women were motivated to give up their lives for historical recognition. Liu Kuang wrote *Kwai Fan* (*Norms for Girls*), which was more popular than *Nei Hsun* due to its attractive illustrations and simple style. This book reached many women from various social classes and inspired several well-known heroines. Another book entitled *Wen Mu Hsun* (*Mother's Admonition*) was released at the end of the Ming Dynasty. It contained some unique points which were considered quite liberal at that time. The author, Mrs. Wen, felt that a widow had the right to make her own decision about whether or not to remarry. In a conservative vein, however, she advised widows to keep themselves occupied with household chores all day long if they choose to remain unmarried.

She also warned of the awkward position of being a step-mother who was often the scapegoat in family conflicts, as well as being the subject of gossips. She feared that even a fair officer would fail to make acceptable judgments to all on matters involving family discord. Mrs. Wen objected to formal education for girls because she claimed that women needed only a limited vocabulary related to housekeeping.[22] These books, all of which had a profound impact on women's education, discouraged women from furthering their pursuit of learning opportunities—even at home. Later, the popular saying "ignorance is a virtue" was conceived under such a social climate in the Ch'ing Dynasty.[23] Since then, the social acceptance of ignorant women was widespread for more than three hundred years. Girls talented in poetry writing were portrayed by novelists either as unfaithful or as dying in their teens.[24] The famous novels *Hsi Hsiang Chi* (*The Tale of the West Chamber*), and *Fan Chiao Lu* (*Record of Burning Pepper*) implied that women's knowledge of reading and writing poetry contributed to their infidelity and tragedy. These two books convinced readers that only un-educated women could live up to the vital goal of women's lives, that of being loyal to their husband. Dullness and stupidity, the traits desired by men in women, induced total female subservience to men. Being brainwashed by such social expectations, women adjusted very well to their forced lifestyle by developing their talents in handicrafts and other domestic skills; their intellectual stimulation was replaced by artistic work. Usually they were content with their ac-complishments around the house and devoted their time to husband and children.

Women who had to seek a living outside the home were much more independent from their husbands and unable to enjoy their role as full-time wife and mother. Yet such struggles were not always accompanied by disadvantages; the work environment served as a natural classroom, the interaction with other people became a valuable lesson and the required independence prepared them better for widow-hood and/or desertion. Because of the social contact with various types of people, they were more knowledgeable than those women who had a more fortunate financial back-ground. In addition to an enriched mental outlook they often experienced fewer physical restrictions. In order to perform on the job, they could not afford to have their feet bound, be frail in body, or be confined within the courtyard. In a sense, these financially deprived women had more freedom in the areas of mental stimulation and physical mobility.

Working women were found in areas such as business, light industry, and agriculture. Based on obtainable documents, domestic and commercial services, small businesses, entertainment and prostitution were most prevalent among female wage earners.[25] Young girls from the lower or lower-middle classes were often hired by middle and upper class families to be pages, cooks, sitters, wet nurses, seamstresses, dancers, and companions for playing checkers and performing puppet shows. Some of the girls were trained from childhood to execute a particular task. Cooks usually received the best pay but were considered the lowest grade of employee—receiving little respect from their peers. A middle-woman called *Ya Sao* served as a personnel agent between employers and employees, such as recruiting waitresses for restaurants. Since personnel agents had to negotiate with the girls and their prospective employers, Ya Sao dominated the job market for female workers.

Aside from domestic services, women also worked in stores and shops. It was not uncommon to see female owners of tea shops, seafood stores, drug stores, candy stores, handicraft shops, hat and hairpiece shops, etc. Very often they were able to manufacture and/or process the food or merchandise they sold; thus their business was sufficiently independent and self-reliant. It is conceivable that some female owners were the sole bread winners for their families after the death of their husbands.

Women in entertainment required both skill and beauty. Basically, there were two groups depending upon the location of the performances.[26] Mobile groups traveled from town to town and performed on the streets where they could rally a small crowd. Performances on permanent sites were held in taverns, restaurants, and guest houses. The contents of the programs included dancing, singing, and acrobatic acts.

Prostitution was the most popular and easiest source of income for young women who unfortunately were either involuntarily ensnared by middlemen or voluntarily engaged in this business due to family bankruptcy or death of the family breadwinner. The backgrounds of prostitutes, including their previous socioeconomic status, their skills in writing poetry, dance, and the arts, varied greatly. The heterogeneity of this group fostered diverse stereotypes of women involved in prostitution, depending on the particular needs of society during certain historical periods. The earnings of prostitutes were mainly determined by the class of their customers, which was usually associated with the status of pimps. Prostitutes from a large "institution" had a better chance of reaping more profit than those that were available to peddlers, workers, and the poor or disadvantaged bachelors. In addition, prostitutes in wealthy families and those affiliated with big operations were entitled to much greater materialistic compensation than common women. Luxurious living conditions were the main attraction for young girls to enter this occupation.

In summary, Chinese women's contribution to the labor force varied depending upon the demand and developmental stage of their time. Women in antiquity were agriculturally oriented, but were later forced into domestic spheres as men became less mobile and began farming and animal raising in their place. Although ancient women's jobs were associated with weaving, sewing, and sericulture (cultivation of silkworms), employment in these areas was not seen until the economic system was gradually established in China. Due to the economic demand of the society, lower class women in the Sung Dynasty were given more opportunities to work outside the home as wage earners. Even though women in all occupations required certain skills and encountered a great deal of hardship, at least only those determined and persistent women could earn a living on a regular full-time basis. This could be the launching of the female labor force which has swelled rapidly during the past decades.

E. Infanticide of Female Babies

Unfortunately women's employment and contribution to society was not recognized and valued at this time; ironically, their lives were threatened as a result of the growing popularity of infanticide. Such a brutal practice can be traced back to early Chinese history. The earliest recorded evidence of infanticide, reported by *Tso Chuan* (*Commentaries on Spring and Autumn Annals*), was the case of an abandoned baby girl found under a dike.[27] Later, in his article (the sixth chapter), Han Fei Tzu referred to the social trend of congratulations for baby boys and death for baby girls as savage.[28] However, the social preference for boys continued and became even more widespread in the Han Dynasty. As a result of the emphasis on materialistic living, people (especially the poor) became quite realistic about their financial obligations; unlike baby boys, baby girls were an economic liability because parents needed to provide dowries for their marriage. Since the bride's status in her husband's family depended on the amount of dowry brought over, her parents customarily stretched their resources to an extreme. To avoid the burden of a dowry in later years, termination of the life of a baby girl was considered to be the best answer for many parents. The book *Yuan Shih Chig Fan* (*The Family Norms of Yuan*) of the South-North Dynasty reveals that in a wealthy family a maid was sent to the room of a laboring concubine to be ready for the merciless killing of a newborn—if it was a girl. The mother had no choice in this cruel family rule for her only function was to bear a son.

Infanticide was extremely prevalent in the Sung Dynasty—being greatly influenced by the philosophy of Neo-Confucianism which denied women basic human rights, including the right to live.[29] For unknown reasons a limited number of children per family (two boys and one girl) was once advocated, and to avoid going above that number, women were encouraged to abort the unborn; abortion was available for most women in Hunan and Hupei.[30] Perhaps control of a population explosion was then a social issue; still it reflected definite sexual discrimination against baby girls. The book *Su Tung Po Chi* (*Collections of Su Tung Po*) indicates that the common method used for infanticide in the Sung Dynasty was by putting the newborn girl baby into cold water.[31] This method was called "water baby". The mother's heart was broken when she heard her baby's first screams gradually die away. People in the coastal provinces drowned unwanted baby girls in the ocean, while the residents who lived inland dumped innocent baby girls into lakes or out houses, deserted them in the woods, or strangled or stabbed them to death. Still, not all people favored such a cruel and brutal practice; opponents Yu Wei and Lo Ch'in-Jo were both local officials who tried to alter the social tone by regulating the number of infanticide cases each year; yet their preaching against such an inhumane practice was only effective in their immediate areas and failed to generate a greater force in reaching more people.[32] During that period infanticide was regional—some areas were immune from such savagery. The regions with prevalent female infanticide were Fukien, Kiangsi, Szechwan, Anhwei, Yunnan, and Hakka.

The overall low status of women determined and perceived by the male-dominated society was the crucial factor contributing to such vicious social phenomena (Li, 1935; Ch'en, 1977; and, Li, 1978a). Because of their inferior and "worthless" position, women were the first to be sacrificed and/or eliminated whenever and wherever the situation required. They were frequently the victims of wars, famine, and overloaded taxation. They were the first to be abandoned, sold, or killed by their parents during those crises. Infanticide was also applied to female children born out of wedlock—if the pregnancy had not been terminated by abortion—because of the disgraceful extramarital relationship of the parents. Male illegitimates faced a different fate and were usually saved and adopted by relatives.

Financial liability to parents also played a vital role in the practice of female infanticide. The bride's parents were expected to contribute both an able-bodied worker and a spectacular dowry for the wedding—with no return for their efforts. This giving of everything to the groom's family commonly provoked resentment toward daughters, and parents were understandably apprehensive about their financial obligations. An old story tells that a woman even starved her two young daughters to death after she saw an extravagant procession carrying a huge dowry past her window.[33] On the other hand, a son could win a woman who became an asset by performing domestic tasks and was loyal to his family forever. Consequently, people with good sense of investment learned to rear fewer girls than boys; an old Chinese saying explains the attitude of parents who preferred boys to girls: "A married daughter is like water spilling out from the bucket." Infanticide reached its peak in the Ch'ing Dynasty and was epidempic throughout the nation. It was abolished by the government after the founding of the Republic. However, abandoned girls were still found roaming on the streets and were admitted to orphanages until the 1930s.

Nowadays, parental attitudes toward girls have rapidly changed. Modern Chinese women are more independent than their predecessors due to educational advancement and employment opportunities. Meanwhile, their status at home and in society has been greatly promoted: they are better treated by parents because they are no longer considered a liability to the family. On the contrary, daughters are often an asset to many retired parents whose sons and daughters-in-law are reluctant to stay with them in order to maintain their own nuclear family with more privacy and less interferance from the elderly.

F. Footbinding

Beside infanticide, footbinding was another unfair and inhumane social practice against Chinese women; one was to exterminate baby girls, the other was to mistreat those who survived.

An examination of the development of footbinding could erase or eliminate some of the misconceptions shared by many people. Scholars have different theories regarding the beginning of footbinding. Based on several sources (Chia, 1924; Levy, 1966; Li and Chang, 1975; Ch'en, 1977; and, Li, 1978a), the Emperor Li of South T'ang in the Five Dynasties (907-960 A.D.) is believed to be the originator of such a cruel fashion for women. He designed a special kind of shoe for his favorite concubine to wear during her dance. According to *Ta T'ang Hsin Yu* (*New Book of the Great T'ang*) women from the middle and upper classes in the previous dynasty were accustomed to wearing their husbands shoes for fun.[34] If their feet were bound their husbands' shoes evidently could not fit their feet. The poems written by Tu Mei and Han Wo also indicated that the size of women's feet were about six inches—which was twice the size of women's bound feet in subsequent dynasties. Following Emperor Li's invention for court dancers, upper-class women tried to use bandages to wrap their feet into a pointed shape, and wore specially desiged narrow shoes to restrain the movement of the foot and bend it into the shape of a new moon (Ch'en, 1977; and, Li, 1978a).

Although footbinding was not prevalent prior to the Sung Dynasty, the size of women's feet certainly began shrinking. A poem written by Su Tzu Chan mentioned an inspection of a bound foot that fit in one's palm.[35] When Yuan conquered China, footbinding became even more widespread and the size of the foot was reduced to three inches.[36] (The Yuans originated from Mongolia and perceived themselves as inferior to the Hans in culture. Although they were the rulers of China, they rapidly assimilated themselves into the Chinese mainstream and willingly adopted the Chinese lifestyle, fashion trends, and social norms.) From the musical operas which reflected an unique art form during the Yuan Dynasty, audiences could easily delineate the development of footbinding during this period, including the promotion of three-inch "golden lotuses" (a style of footbinding) and its advantages to people who raised girls. A girl's foot size became one of the major criteria to be evaluated by matchmakers when arranging marriages.

Nevertheless, footbinding was only circumscribed in some regions and for certain groups of women in different ages of history.[37] It was mainly seen in wealthy families and was not known in the Southeast region of China during the Sung Dynasty.[38] Ordinary girls were not qualified to conform with the "fashion" for they had to engage in various laborious jobs. Footbinding, therefore, became a symbol of social status. This trend gradually spread from the northern states of the south and from the inland to the coastal provinces. The beauty of footbinding was most cultivated in the Ming palace where various styles of footwear were introduced. At that time people considered footbinding a basic privilege (human right) for most of the people except beggars. Since beggars were believed to be vulgar people, their sons were deprived of learning, and their daughters were not allowed to have their feet bound.

Things worsened for women in the Ch'ing Dynasty. Like the Mongolian-originated Yuan Dynasty, the Manchus, considered as foreigners, were unsuccessful in abolishing foot-binding. On the contrary, Manchu women even imitated their Han counterparts. Social pressure coerced women, both Manchu and Han, into the unnatural and hurtful physical restraint. Only in a few places, like Tibet, Hsin Chiang, Chinghai, and Yunnan, were women lucky enough to remain unfettered. The adoration of footbinding came to a climax under Manchu rule, as analyzed in the next chapter.

The painful process of footbinding won little sym-pathetic attention. By the age of four or five, girls began to bundle their feet daily for a period of time—gradually in-creasing the length of time until it reached 24 hours a day. The wrapping was so designed to eventually prevent any growth of the foot. Children received corporal punishment if they were caught unfolding their binding for temporary re-lief. In order to make the bones soft enough to form the desirable shape and appropriate size, prolonged soaking and smoking in hot water and herb liquid were required. Soaking and smoking often contributed to bleeding and erosion of skin and muscle. Infection caused by this process, and the tied furl of a broken foot, produced great pain. Yet, the final product—soft, tiny feet—was often the theme of poetry. As expected, poets praised and enjoyed the "sexy" and jade-like artifact. Sympathizer Chu Jo-shui, in the Sung Dynasty, op-posed this cruel exercise at home in his writing *Chiao Ch'i Chi (Odor of Feet)*.[39] He questioned the value and purpose of footbinding. Unfortunately, response to his viewpoint was extremely scarce.

Initially, the purpose of footbinding was to please men who liked to see women walking and dancing in a frail manner. Since Chinese women were financially dependent on their spouses or their lovers, they had to comply with such painful demands. Later, men discovered that women could be confined within the family courtyard by this phys-ical handicap and were convinced that women's unfaithful conduct could thus be stopped. Some women were so handi-capped that they had to rely on a maid's help to move around the house—or they had to walk leaning against a wall. Chia (1924) offered another reason for footbinding—which was to emphasize sex differences and reinforce feminity.[40] He pointed out that footbinding was considered part of the proper clothing for women at that time which could manifest their sexual charms. It became more evident than ever before that women were only sexual objects for men's pleasure and could only be sexy within the limits set by men. Such conflicting demands made by society generated greater psychological suffering than physical mistreatment of Chinese women.

G. Famous Women

Chinese women were able to continue to play the roles assigned to them by the male-dominated society. Under extreme social deprivation and restriction, some women even made unique contributions to Chinese culture and history by developing their potential. These women, whose deeds were systematically recorded by historians, frequently responded to the social morality imposed on them. Faithful widows and unmarried women dying for chastity dominated the historical scene in the Yuan Dynasty, while outstanding women during the Sung and Ming Dynasties were noted for more diverse actions in the areas of literature, politics, and military service. In this section several prominent women will be introduced to readers to illustrate the multiple roles played by Chinese women.

Li Ch'ing-chao, the most famous poetess in Chinese history (Chen, 1926; Liu, 1978; and, Hong, 1980), was born in 1081 A.D. Raised in a very prominent, culturally oriented family, she was given the opportunity to learn reading and writing. She became the daughter-in-law of a former prime minister and enjoyed writing poetry with her husband, Ch'ao Min-chuan, for over twenty years. She created a style of her own and has been held in high esteem by the literati through the centuries. Her works distinguish themselves by their high artistic quality. She was skilled in creating a perfect image of conception by giving rein to her imagination or using novel metaphors. The rigid style of her poetry was exquisite and radiant. Her most charming and captivating poems depicted her intimate marital relationship with Ch'ao Min-chan. At times her brilliant poems overshadowed her husband's ordinary works. One day Ch'ao Min-chan presented a friend,

Lu Ta-fu, with a poem he cogitated over three days and nights without interruption, in which he had blended some of Li Ch'ing-chao's verses. After reciting the poem several times, Lu Ta-fu picked out the three most refined and elegant verses—which turned out to be excerpts from Li Ch'ing-chao's poem.

Li's literary career can be divided into two stages, with her fleeing from the northern invaders in 1127 as the line of demarcation. In the earlier stage, she concentrated on depicting nature and life in the boudoir. Her works describing natural scenes were refreshing and full of life, revealing her very deep love of nature. In the latter stage, she suffered the misfortunes of a broken home, a conquered country, and the death of her husband. She led a vagrant life; as a result, her poems are permeated with a deep feeling of rootlessness.

Apart from her poems, Li is also famous for her *tz'u* (another form of poem) and essays. She was a fairly prolific writer. Her realistic approach and singular style have given her an important place in the development of Sung tz'u. A hall in her memory was built in the Pao Tu Ch'un Yuan in Chinan, Shantung, to remind people that one of the many outstanding women in Chinese history was the writer Li Ch'ing-chao.

In that same generation another famous woman, Liang Hung-yu, was highly praised by historians. Distinctly different from Li's high social status and expertise in literature, Liang was a former prostitute who later became a concubine of General Han Shin-chung. Instead of being called Mme. Han, Liang was glorified by the imperial court as Mme. Liang. General Han, a heroic figure in the middle of the Sung Dynasty, had, with Mme. Liang's help, confronted attacking invaders several times to maintain the security of the Emperor.

Liang's first bold mission was carried out after she and her son were held hostage by an insurgent group in Linan where Emperor Kao Tsung was stopping. An emperor's counselor convinced the rebellious party to send Liang Hung-yu to her husband, General Han, who was stationed in another town waiting for reinforcements. They wanted her to persuade her husband to respond to the overthrow of the Emperor from outside the city. After galloping for 24 hours without a stop, she reached the destination. Based on her intelligence report, General Han decided to assail Linan immediately. The rebels, with little military power in hand, made a rapid escape from Lin-Ah, where Emperor Kao Tsung greeted General Han at the city's entrance.

Later, when General Han was commanding a crucial confrontation with the Kings at Huang Tien T'ang, Liang Hung-yu participated on the battlefield by drumming to encourage and coordinate the combat. The victory in this battle resulted in a period of peace between the Southern Sung Dynasty and its invaders, the Kings. The throne of Emperor Kao Tsung was then secure.

Liang Hung-yu's contribution to her nation continued even after her direct contact with the Kings. The countryside where her husband was assigned had been destroyed several times during the wars and she helped to rebuild it. They not only reconstructed the external appearance of the region but also formulated a district government. In addition, Liang Hung-yu mobilized local women to build camps for soldiers, take care of war refugees, and assist the returning refugees in rebuilding their demolished homes. The joint efforts of General Han and Mme. Liang fortified the country as a garrison to insure peace in the Southern Sung Dynasty.

During this vulnerable and tumultuous period in Chinese history, many famous generals and scholars were influenced primarily by their widowed mothers. Widows customarily preserved very close relationships with their adult sons. Ou-Yang Hsiu, a scholar and statesman, frequently cited his mother's comments about his late father. His mother transmitted his father's beliefs to him, and these in turn became an essential part of his life and philosophy.

Another widow who deserves mention was Yueh Fei's mother who admonished her son to be loyal to his country by tattooing the verse on his back. Yueh Fei, who was a prominent military leader during the King's invasion, was a newborn baby when the Yellow River flooded in Honan. His mother carried him in a large floating barrel until they were rescued by nearby villagers. She not only worked to earn a living, but taught him reading and writing as well. Because he could not afford paper and pencils, he practiced writing in the sand with twigs.

There are quite a few other remarkable mothers reported by historians (Hsu, 1913; Ch'en, 1977; Liu, 1978; Li,
1978a; and, Gross and Bingham, 1980). Their recognition
relied largely on the achievements of their sons in literature,
politics, and/or manuevers on the battleground. The most
common characteristics shared by these respectable mothers
are: (1) perpetuation of their value systems to their children;
(2) close mother-son relationships; (3) high expectations of
their sons; and (4) perseverance in the face of misfortune.
Historical records confirm the material influence on sons.
For example, the impact of an empress was critical to the
escalation or downfall of a dynasty.[41] In ancient times the
Chinese regarded the emperor as the father of the nation and
the empress as the mother of the people. The empress was
supposed to be a model for social conduct and for the education of women. A kind and intelligent empress, undoubtedly, was an asset. to her husband. Because of her unique
personal background, Empress Ma of the Ming Dynasty was
chosen to exemplify the important role played by empresses
in Chinese history.

Empress Ma was the queen of Chen Tsu, the first
Emperor of the Ming Dynasty. She was an orphan who was
raised by her late father's close friend, Kuo Tzu-hsin. When
Chu Yuan-chang (Chen Tsu) first joined in the uprising headed by Kuo Tzu-hsin against the Yuan Dynasty, his unusual
facial bone structure caught Kuo's attention. Very soon Kuo
married Ma to Chu Yang-chang. After Kuo's death Chu succeeded to the leadership and eventually defeated the Yuans,
inaugerating a new era.

Ma's benevolence and compassion for the people were
not terminated when she was crowned empress. Her innate
sensitivity to people frequently enabled her to differentiate
false accusations from real ones for Chen Tsu whose firey
temper often interferred with his ability to render fair judgments in his court. When people were afflicted with natural
disasters like drought and famine, she would fast with palace
personnel and pray for the catastrophe to end. Empress Ma
was also concerned about the meals served to court counselors and the food supply for the families of the students who
studied at the National Academy (which was like our institutions of higher education today). She proposed to im-

prove the menu for court counselors and initiated a program to distribute food to the Academy students' dependents. Her philosophy was to treat others better than oneself—especially the intellectual elite. She was very generous to the needy and often dressed in simple outfits while giving away nice clothing to elderly widows. She declined Chen Tsu's offer to search for her relatives in order to elevate their status. Being the first Empress of a new dynasty, she contributed tremendously to the political stability in the beginning of the Ming Dynasty. Constant self-improvement through the study of classical literature made her a model for court women in the succeeding generations.

Women from other social spectrums often had more diverse experiences than women in court. Historical evidence indicates that quite a few women disguised themselves as men to join the army in place of their elderly fathers (Hsu, 1913; and, Liu, 1978). Most of them were married after being discharged. Their bravery could not compete, however, with a well-known female commander who devoted her lifetime to military maneuvers during the end of the Ming Dynasty.

Ch'in Liang-yu was a woman who led a small army into battle against rebels in several southwestern provinces. During this time mobs were dispersed all over the nation; people were under constant attack and had to escape from town to town. Since the Emperor was incapable of coping with the spreading rebellion, the security of the local state depended on regional troops. Unfortunately corrupt district officers often accepted bribes to throw a battle. Many towns and cities were therefore trampled and destroyed by mobs.

Born in Ch'ungching, Szechwan, Ch'in used to fight alongside her husband, a governor of the province. After the death of her husband and her two brothers, she continued fighting to protect the southwestern areas. Her vigorous counteractions against rebel uprisings were recognized and honored by the Emperor who was grieved that no single man had the courage to crack down on the savage multitudes for the safety of the people as Ch'in had done. Sadly her endeavor was not endorsed by other male commanders who were in too much dispair to raid rebel camps. Yet her army of three thousand soldiers, called White Sticks, was so powerful that the surrounding areas of her home town were the only regions free from the revolts headed by Chang Hsien-chung and Li Tzu-ch'eng when they swept through Szechwan.

Although she was very strict with her soldiers, Ch'in was an elegant and refined lady. Warriors under her command were lionhearted and well disciplined, which explains why her small armed forces were able to defend a large area against the revolts of Chang and Li. Ch'in's talents, however, were not strictly confined to the military. She was also adept at writing quality poetry in which she reflected on her life and times.

Conclusion

The portraits of these women mentioned above influenced Chinese women who radiated strength and endurance in diverse areas eventhough they were treated unfairly by society in both psychological and physical domains. It seemed that the "brain washing" for female chastity during this period was not considered to adequately promote male egotism at the expense of women's total submission and loyalty to their husbands. Moreover, the male-dominated society demanded women to surrender their right to life and freedom to move due to self-destruction, infanticide, and footbinding. Nevertheless, the worst part of women's fate comes next in the Ch'ing Dynasty which opens a chapter of dramatic change in Chinese women's history.

NOTES

[1] Ch'en Tung-yuan, *History of the life of Chinese women* (Taipei, Taiwan: Commerce Publishing Co., 1977), pp. 129, 135.

[2] *Ibid.*, pp. 134-135.

[3] *Ibid.*, p. 137.

[4] Nich Chung-ch'i, "The traditional change on women's remarriage," in Pao Chia-lin's *Readings in Chinese women's history* (Taipei, Taiwan: Mu T'ung Publishing Co., 1979), pp. 128-138.

[5] Tung Chia-tsun, "Research on widows from Han Dynasty to

Sung Dynasty," *Historical literature of Central University* III.1 (March, 1934), p. 212.

[6]Tung Chia-tsun, "The statistics of sacrificed women," *Contemporary history* III.2 (1937), p. 5.

[7]*Ibid.*, p. 4.

[8]Ch'en, *op. cit.*, pp. 178-180.

[9]*Ibid.*, pp. 145-148.

[10]*Ibid.*, p. 207; see also Li Ch'ia-fu, *Lives of ancient Chinese women* (Taipei, Taiwan: Li Min Publishing Co., 1978), p. 84.

[11]Li Ch'ia-fu, *Chinese ancient women* (Taipei, Taiwan: Li Min Publishing Co., 1978), pp. 85-86.

[12]Li, *Chinese ancient women*, pp. 77-80.

[13]Mai Kuo, "Historical review of Chinese prostitution," in Pao Chia-lin's *Readings in Chinese women's history* (Taipei, Taiwan: Mu T'ung Publishing Co., 1979), p. 119.

[14]*Ibid.*, p. 120.

[15]Ch'en, *op. cit.*, pp. 96-102.

[16]Ch'uan Han-sheng, "Women wage earners in Sung Dynasty," *Journal of Shih Huo* I.9 (1935), pp. 8-9.

[17]Kao, *op. cit.*, p. 8.

[18]*Ibid.*, p. 119.

[19]Ch'uan, *op. cit.*, p. 8.

[20]Kao, *op. cit.*, pp. 122-123.

[21]Ch'uan, *op. cit.*, p. 10.

[22]Ch'en, *op. cit.*, pp. 187-188.

[23]*Ibid.*, p. 188.

[24]*Ibid.*, p. 198.

[25]Ch'uan, *op. cit.*, pp. 5-10.

[26]*Ibid.*.

[27]Li Ch'ang-nien, "Female infanticide and inequality of two sexes in China," *Eastern Magazine* (June 1935), pp. 99-100.

[28]*Ibid.*.

[29]Li, *Chinese ancient women*, pp. 178-179.

[30]*Ibid.*, p. 178.

[31]*Ibid.*; see also Li Ch'ang-nien, *op. cit.*, p. 100.

[32]Li, *Chinese ancient women*, pp. 179-180.

[33]*Ibid.*, pp. 180-181.

[34]*Ibid*, p. 153; see also Chia Shen, "Examination of women's footbinding in China," *Geographical and historical report* III.3 (1924), p. 69.

[35]*Ibid.*.

[36]*Ibid.*, p. 70.

[37]*Ibid.*, pp. 70-71; see also Li, *Chinese ancient women*, pp. 157-158.

[38]Chia, *loc. cit.*.

[39]*Ibid.*, p. 71.

[40]*Ibid.*, p. 67.

[41]Susan Hill Cross and Marjorie Wall Bingham, *Women in traditional China* (Minneapolis, Minnesota: Gary E. McCuen Publication, Inc., 1980), p. 24; see also, Liu Tzu-ch'ing, *Critical biographies of famous women in Chinese history* (Taipei, Taiwan: Li Min Publishing Co., 1978), pp. 108-114, 162-164, 178-181, 200-208, and 232-240.

Yunnan woman

CHAPTER FIVE

The Modern Period (1643-1949)

During this period of more than 300 years, the changing status of Chinese women can most easily be outlined in four stages. The first stage, 1643-1894, when Chinese women suffered greatly overall, precipitated the drastic changes of the second stage. The second stage, 1894-1915, began during the reformation period at the end of the Ching Dynasty. With the influence of political reformation, women's roles in the family and society were recognized, and their physical and educational needs reevaluated. In the third stage,1915-1926, women, especially educated women, were influenced greatly by the May 4th Movement. Their legal rights and liberal role in the family reached a peak during this stage. During the last stage, 1926-1949, the women's movement failed to reach a new plateau. Due to civil wars in the early years of the Republic, and the political conflict between the Nationalist and Communist Parties in later years, women, like the population in general, were divided and scattered. Therefore, thoughout this modern period, Chinese women's motives for liberation from their traditional roles were immensely influenced by their political ideology. They no longer shared the simple common goals as before; their struggle was geared to the ideology of revolution and the dream of a new nation.

A. *The Peak of Suffering (1643-1894)*

Prior to the political reformation in 1894, Chinese women were excessively suppressed with no sign of any possible improvement in their lives. They were considered sexual objects, personal possessions, commodities for trade, and were even evaluated as pieces of art. The standards of beauty required a soft, white complexion; long, narrow eyes; soft hands with pointed fingernails; and very small, bound feet. Their time-consuming make-up application, artificial mannerisms, and sophisticated gestures were geared to please men and win from them their physical admiration. When the Manchus first conquered China in 1656, the Emperor K'ang

Hsi abolished footbinding because Manchu women did not have such a practice.[1] K'ang Hsi tried to enforce the law for seven years, but to no avail. Ironically, Manchu women then imitated the Han women's footbinding in the course of their assimilation into Chinese society. Eighteen styles of footbinding were derived from five basic patterns: namely, lotus petal, new moon, harmonious bow, bamboo sprout, and water nuts.[2] Scent lotus was a nickname for bound feet and was evaluated according to a scale of nine different levels of beauty. Bound feet were not only for the sake of beauty by forcing women to walk wiggly, but also served the purpose of physically restricting them, especially young girls, from walking freely outside their rooms. Based on his study on footbinding in Chinese history, Chia Shen concluded that women's peak of suffering in footbinding was in the Ch'ing Dynasty eventhough it was not practiced nationwide.[3]

Besides footbinding, chastity and total submission were also emphasized during this period. For women, chastity was more valuable than life itself; they would sacrifice their lives for it. The definition of chastity became ridiculously broad—to the extent that a girl was considered unclean if she happened to see a man's sex organ when he urinated in a public place (Chen, 1926; and, Li, 1979a).[4] Unless she married him she had to commit suicide to protect her reputation. Married women were expected to be submissive to husbands and in-laws alike, and to serve them diligently. The husband retianed a high position at home regardless of any immoral behavior on his part, including polygamy and going to prostitutes. Prostitution became prevalent in the 1780s toward the end of the reign of Emperor Ch'ien Lung.[5] The city of Nanking was the capital of prostitutes prior to the Taiping Rebellion in 1849. When Hung Hsiu-chuan occupied Nanking and decided to make it the capital, all high-class prostitutes moved to Shanghai, which then became the central location for prostitution. After the port of Shanghai was opened to international trade, many prostitutes rushed to foreign concessions (Chuchieh) for better business opportunities. In Chuchieh, reserved exclusively for foreign residents, prostitutes were less restricted by Chinese law and enjoyed better living conditions.

Women's Advocates

Under such social climates, Chinese women began winning more sympathy than ever from educated men who subtly advocated women's rights through published novels and articles. Among these men the best known are Mao Ch'i-ling, Li Ju-chen, and Yu Cheng-k'uei. In 1710, Mao wrote about the chastity of engaged women whom he believed should not be required to remain single, or to commit suicide, or be buried alive upon the death of their fiancees. More than one hundred years later, Li Ju-chen spent more than ten years completing a book, *Ching Hua Yuan*, which portrayed Chinese women's humble status in the society and in the extended family. In his novel, Li presented his viewpoint on the following subjects: women's fashion, make-up, ear piercing, footbinding, concubinage, and marriage according to the zodiac (Eberhard, 1977). He stressed that men and women had equal intellectual capacities, and that women were as qualified as men for political activities. Li used projective techniques to make women conscious of their suffering. For example, when female readers felt pity for the fate of a poor princess who was forced to dress and be made up against her will and natural beauty to please the men around her, women undoubtedly compared themselves to the unfortunate princess. On the other hand, male readers gained a genuine picture of the painful processes of the old methods of ear piercing and footbinding. Li not only described in detail the bleeding steps for the binding of feet, but also pointed out the physical handicap that resulted to the ill-fated princess. Men did not realize the price women had to pay in order to please them. Furthermore, Li believed that a person's astrological sign should not be the dominating factor in choosing a marriage partner. Instead he thought that men and women should be matched based on socioeconomic class, age, appearance, and moral characteristics. Li's point of view definitely mirrored the social background of that time. His opposition to concubinage was based on the assumption of equality between men and women; a man should first ask himself if he would want his wife to have *Mien Shou* (male lovers, equivalent to concubines for the husband). If he wanted his wife to be faithful to him, then he should also be faithful to her. He focused primarily on the relationship between men and women as a result of their intellectual development.

Approximately ten years later another writer, Yu Cheng-k'uei, promoted women's status through his articles. First, he strongly opposed polygamy, which he believed to be the main cause of jealousy in women. Second, he felt women should not be criticized for remarrying since men were not criticized for doing the same. Third, he considered chastity to be valid only when both spouses were living. In order to promote the fame of a family, many parents in this period tended to exaggerate their daughter's chastity by asking them to commit suicide. Yu felt that parents should abandon such a fame-seeking demand. Fourth, he attacked footbinding for two traditional reasons: (1) women were weakened and handicapped by bound feet (according to an old Chinese saying, men would suffer when women were weak); and (2) shoes for bound feet were considered a type of cheap clothing in ancient times. When a woman dressed cheaply, her husband's status was lowered. Although Yu may have been influenced by Li's novel, Yu's views were not as broad as Li's whose cumulative experiences and observations contributed a great deal to his extensive analysis of women's problems.

Chinese women's suffering during this period of time was not only revealed by male literati but also expressed by their own literary works. In the beginning of the nineteenth century, a number of volumes of poetry were written by women. Among them, *Hsiang Ho Chi*, collected by Hsu K'uei-ch'en, contains over three hundred poems written by women. Many poetesses represented in this volume were students of Yuan Mei (1716-1797), who taught both males and females. Although some traditionalists accused Yuan Mei of being immoral and taking advantage of virtuous women, women were not convinced to forgo such an educational opportunity. Nevertheless the themes of these women's writings were still confined to romantic and sentimental expressions related to their daily personal interactions. There were at least ten volumes of women's poems released as a result of Yuan Mei's profound influence on women's learning. Among them, the collection of K'uei Hsiu published in 1908, was the largest volume; it contained

1591 poems written by 521 women. Meanwhile, some moralists opposed women's advancement in learning for fear of causing a declining moral standard among educated women. Thus, the statement, "ignorance is a virtue" believed to have originated by the end of the Ming Dynasty became a popular tool used by these moralists to counter-attack the increasing demands of women's education.[6]

On the contrary, the Taiping Rebellion (1850-1864) gave some women in southern China a booster to reevaluate their role and abilities. The Taiping Rebellion was launched with the influence of the Christian doctrine. Its leader, Hung Hsui-chuan, proclaimed himself to be the second son of the Almighty God, the brother of Jesus Christ. He believed that everyone was a child of the Holy Father and entitled to equal rights, regardless of their sex. Women were encouraged to participate in decision making and were even given high-ranking positions in his movement. Men and women were both eligible to qualify for civil service in Hung's "Heaven Government."[7] It is estimated that there were 100,000 female soldiers, commanders and generals in his army. Women served side by side with men on the battlefield and held a winning record against the Ching Army. Cultic brothers and sisters were required to abstain from sexual activities to assure their single-minded devotion to warfare. He also declared equal land allotments to men and women and abolished commercial marriage, one-sided chastity, prostitution, and footbinding.[8]

Although Hung's initial intentions for women's liberation did not last long, his impact on the women's movement cannot be ignored. When the Heaven Government became corrupt toward the end of the revolution, women lost their value on the battlefield and became cheap labor. They were once again treated as second-class citizens and their basic human rights were denied. They had no right to protect even their own lives; sexual and physical abuse were common.[9] However, as a result of the influence of the Taiping Rebellion people began changing their attitudes toward women.[10] First, the ideas of freedom and equality had seeded in the minds of the people in the southern part of China which consisted of more than sixteen provinces where Hung's government once prevailed. Second, traditional value systems were being challenged and women's roles in society and in the family underwent drastic changes during this 15 year rebellion. Third, women gained self-confidence through participation in various military and civil activities. Fourth, women not only proved to themselves that they were not inferior to men, but also made it clear to the privileged men who had considered themselves superior to women for thousands of years. Later, when the Chinese were defeated by Japan in the Sino-Japanese War of 1894, the Chinese people realized that a political reformation was needed to build a strong new China. And they were convinced, for the first time, that the reason Japan had won the war was due to its westernization, including its education of women.

B. Issues on the Women's Movement

In reality, the influence of foreign culture on the status of Chinese women began prior to the Sino-Japanese War in 1894. When groups of western missionaries arrived in China in the middle of the 18th century, they found Chinese women existing under miserable conditions. Following China's acceptance of the Open Door policy demanded by the west, and the subsequent Opium War in 1842, western traders also viewed the harsh realities of women's lives in China. Even though they might have laughed at the bound feet of ignorant Chinese women, westerners were hesitant to take action until 1878 when an American missionary, Young J. Allen, began advocating that women's feet grow naturally.[11] He simply could not comprehend why people would bind a pair of healthy and useful feet. His periodical, *The International Journal*, continued to oppose footbinding for over a quarter of a century (Li and Chang, 1975). Mr. Allen's opposition to footbinding was based on the conviction that all human beings are equal. He argued that both men and women had strengths and weaknesses, but that women were in no way inferior to men. He discussed the disadvantages of footbinding from the viewpoints of Confucianism and Christianity and tried to persuade people to abandon footbinding on the basis of the philosophy of Confucius, rather than by ridiculing their traditional attitude toward such practice. Allen also used cultural comparisons between

China and western nations as a basis for decrying footbinding. Regarding his stay in China he concluded that Chinese women had suffered most in four major areas: (1) they were deprived of an education; (2) they were physically confined; (3) they were handicapped; and, (4) they had no status whatsoever. He spent his later years in China promoting women's education hoping to eliminate such inhumane practices.

In response to Allen's advocacy for women's rights, many western educated scholars and journalists began campaigning for women's equality, addressing such issues as women's education and freedom in marriage. Publications recommended that in order to ensure family harmony, and well-brought-up and well-educated children, women should have freedom of choice in both marriage and education. They also urged men to abandon their feudalistic thinking, to promote the status of their daughters, and to support the movement for natural, unbound, feet. Later, between 1903 and 1904, the conflict with Russia in the northeastern states further spurred newspapers and journal articles to focus on women's issues. Men were advised to use womanpower against Russian aggression while women were urged to liberate themselves from their traditional familial role and become involved in saving the nation from foreign suppression.

According to the documents collected by Li and Chang (1975), the contents of women-related articles authored by both sexes and published by newspapers and magazines basically addressed the following eight areas which laid the foundation for women's issues emphasized later by the women's movement.

The first area concerned the abolition of women's bad daily habits and feudalistic ideas. This was particularly addressed to middle- and upper-class women who devoted much of their leisure time to personal grooming, gossiping, and gambling. Their lifestyle was shallow and their views were narrow. Most of the time they were content to place themselves in a pyschologically passive position in the family setting and to confine themselves physically within the courtyard of their homes.

Thus, encouraging women's participating in volunteer work outside the sphere of family life was the second area addressed. During a series of national crises, women slowly realized that caring only for one's family could not ensure the survival of China. In the process of resisting foreign military and political invasions, they were urged to contribute part of their time and energy to the survival of the nation. Examples of the actions of several foreign women were cited to demonstrate the type of work in which Chinese women could engage, including working for the Red Cross, reporting, spying, informing, assassination, fund raising, and even fighting on the battlefield.

Since women often had doubted their potential, their physical strength and capabilities were the third area discussed in many articles. It was argued that, in the beginning of human history, men and women had equal physical power. However, because of the length of the childbearing years, women lost some of their physical strength and were not as able as men to hunt or fish. Women had to look after their children while men used their strength to secure food and shelter. In order to renew their physical vigor, women had to discontinue the crippling habit of footbinding.

In addition to the physical aspect, women were advised to seek mental independence. At this time the issue of financial independence for women was not addressed, due to the limited employment opportunities available to them, such as tutoring, babysitting, nursing, and midwifery. However, mentally, they could be independent individuals entitled to certain freedoms and also be expected to equip themselves with broader knowledge in order to contribute what they learned to society. Since in the past, they had been accused of not being aware of their own human dignity and of lacking self-respect, they failed to demonstrate their unique abilities and characteristics in society. For example, the minimal education received by a few fortunate women in history was often inconsequential because they continued to restrict themselves to the family setting and household chores.

Of course, one should not deny the important role played by women in child-rearing which was the fifth issue of concern to women. The histories of both western and eastern countries verified the belief that mothers had a greater influence on child-rearing than did fathers. Therefore, women required and deserved the same educational opportunities as men. Women were encouraged to provide both daughters and sons with equal education.

Equal education for women should not be limited to primary or secondary education but should also include higher learning. The sixth area addressed by many articles was to encourage young women to go abroad for further studies. In order to alleviate the military and political threats from foreign countries, women needed to understand their responsibilities to their country and their role in warfare. Nevertheless, women's demands in education and social status could not be quickly achieved without the support of men who still dominated the direction of society. Therefore, the vital role played by men in the emancipation of women was recognized and promoted by many women advocates. Men were encouraged to first liberate their wives and daughters from traditional thinking and old social customs.

The eighth and most popular area presented by articles on feminism was the examination and comparison of women's education and physical freedom in other nations. Many authors who advocated women's rights in education and in the family tried to cite the experiences of women in such places as Japan, Europe, and the United States, to stimulate the women's movement in China. Quite a few comparative studies were conducted to illustrate that China was the weakest among these nations and liberating her female population was the answer to alter the fate of China (Li and Chang, 1975).

During this blooming advocacy by the news media there were several leading books and periodicals that played an influential role in promoting women's rights (see Table 4). Geographically speaking, Shanghai seemed to the be the center for most of the publications addressing women's issues. This hinted at the foreign influences on the Chinese women's movement since Shanghai was becoming an international city with quite a few foreign concessions.

Most importantly, the support of the news media was beginning to serve as a solid backbone for the following three major campaigns towards the end of the 19th century: the return of the natural foot, equal education for all, and women's participation in the revolution.

Table 4*

Publications by Women in the Early 1900s

Books

1900 *Story of Joan of Arc* (Yokohama, Japan)
1902 *Famous Women in Eastern Europe* (Yokahama, Japan)
1903 *Women's Voice* (Shanghai, China)
1903 *Elimination of Shame* (Shanghai, China)
1904 *Women's Captive Lifestyle* (Shanghai, China)
1904 *Stories of Women* (Shanghai, China)
1905 *Freedom of Choice for Marriage* (Tokyo, Japan)
1905 *Unsung Party Heroines* (Shanghai, China)
1907 *Story of Chiu Chin* (Shanghai, China)
1907 *Deeds of Chiu Chin* (Shanghai, China)

Periodicals

1903 *Nu Szu Pao* (Shanghai, China)
1903 *Nu Hsueh Pao* (Shanghai, China)
1903 *Women's World* (Shanghia, China)
1904 *Soul of Women* (Tokyo, Japan)
1906 *Chinese Women's News* (Shanghai, China)
1906 *Chinese New Women* (Tokyo, Japan)
1907 *Shen Chou Nu Pao* (Shanghai, China)

---

1. The Natural Foot Movement

As mentioned earlier, Mr. Allen's *International Journal* played a vital role in the movement to promote the acceptance of the natural foot for more than twenty years (approximately 1878 to 1900). Since the substantial influence of this periodical reached the decision makers at all government levels, many state governors took their first step toward supporting the women's natural foot movement (Li and Chang, 1975). In order to solicit more feedback from the general public, the *International Journal* launched an essay writing contest on this issue. Among the 230 papers submitted, 15 were chosen for their outstanding reasoning and analysis. The best article appeared in the October 1898 issue of the *Journal.*

*Source: P'i Yi-shu, *Chinese women's movement* (Taipei, Taiwan: United Women Publishers, 1973), p. 32.

Along with Mr. Allen's writings, the other articles collected by Li and Chang (1975) against footbinding basically presented the following arguments:

    a. It was against nature; all parts of the human body should be protected from any form of damage.

    b. It ignored the old teaching because ancient women did not have such a practice. According to Confucius the entire body is a gift from parents and should be free from harm.

    c. It invited illness; many illnesses found among youngsters were caused by infection during the process of footbinding. Infertility among women was found to be associated with footbinding.

    d. It endangered life; a woman with bound feet often found it impossible to escape during a fire, robbery, and other emergencies.

    e. It fostered unemployment; women with bound feet were not efficient in child care or in factories, and were effectively prevented from seeking employment.

    f. It handicapped women; physical care and help were often required by bound-footed women.

    g. It was a form of child abuse; how could a mother witness her daughter's screaming without thinking about another alternative?

Nevertheless, the formation of an organization to counteract against this deep rooted social practice was much more difficult than addressing it. Although people became more aware of the drawbacks caused by the handicap, to actually remedy the problem was a challenge to people of all social strata and required their collaboration. Mr. Kang Yu-wei (1858-1927), one of the six men involved in the political reformation of China from 1894 to 1898, was the first to establish a society for natural feet in Canton as early as 1881.[12] Unfortunately, he failed to achieve its goal to persuade women to abandon their suffering. Later, in 1887, the other reformation leaders, including Liang Ch'i-ch'ao (1873-1929), succeeded in forming a natural foot club in Shanghai.[13] The constitution and by-laws of the club are summarized below (evidently the following rules were designed to eliminate any marital problems for those girls with natural feet; by intragroup marriage, natural-footed girls had the same chance to marry as bound-footed girls):

  a. The feet of all members' daughters should not be bound.

  b. The sons of the members should not marry a woman with bound feet.

  c. Those members who had boundfooted daughters under age eight were to unbind them.

  d. All children of the members were to be registered for up-to-date information, such as the birth of baby girls, their age and progress of unbinding feet. This information will be important for matchmakers.

Mr. Allen and other western missionaries had not found any club to implement their philosophy until 1895 when the Chinese public were more ready for such social change. After all, their first priority was spreading the gospel of Christianity above any other controversial issue.

2. Equal Education for Women

Chinese women's desperate need for education was first recognized by missionaries from the West as a result of their outreach to Chinese women. Since oppressed women were more susceptible to religious preaching which was to soothe their depressed lives, they became the target population for western missionaries' work. Simultaneously, missionaries were enthusiastic to reorient Chinese women's traditional beliefs through the educational process as well as to introduce Christianity to them. Following the opening of trade relations with western countries in 1821, certain informal learning sessions for girls were sponsored by western missionaries. The first formal school for girls is believed to be the one established by the Methodist Church in Chenkiang in 1884.[14] Yet, missionaries had no desire to alienate the general public; therefore, the guidelines for the girls' schools were regulated by Chinese social norms. All females, regardless of age, were accepted. Later, in 1891, Miss Laura Heywood founded another well-known girls' school, Chunghsi, in Shanghai.[15]

Meanwhile some Chinese became increasingly aware of the importance of women's education and began promoting equal educational opportunities for all. During the reform movement, Liang Ch'i-ch'ao postulated educating women for the following reasons: first, education was the prerequisite for women's independence from husband and family. Without an education women could neither think independently nor survive in the job market. Second, a husband would benefit from having an intelligent wife. Education would promote a wife's intellectual capabilities and stimulate her reasoning abilities. Third, the proverb, "the hand that rocks the cradle rules the world," succinctly pointed out the importance of education for mothers. Better-educated mothers would, theoretically, raise better generations. Liang was convinced that women played a vital role in raising offspring who would be capable of building a strong China. Many journals and newspapers also advocated education for women. The pressing need for both a healthy family unit and a strong nation was the incentive for promoting women's education. The general public had gradually come to accept the fact that some educated women did not share with men the responsibility of restoring the strength of China by contributing what they learned to their country.

The collapse of the reformation was a setback for the women's movement, especially with regard to educational opportunities. However, when the Boxer Rebellion ended in 1902, revolutionary thinking once again became popular, with women's rights focusing on education.

In 1905, the government set up a new division in the administration to direct educational affairs. The issue of women's formal education was first introduced to the legislature as part of family education. One year later, women's formal education was integrated into the Division of Educational Affairs. However, women were restricted to teacher education, which was considered the best field for women whose only choices were to be either a teacher or a mother. The curriculum and textbooks leaned toward traditional values; students were required to read all classics for women and to learn domestic skills. The proposed guidelines for normal education can be summarized as follows (Li and Chang, 1975):

a. The purpose of normal education for young girls was to gain knowledge in child care and family life. The curriculum should consist of moral education for women, classical literature for women, Chinese history, geography, mathematics, science, painting, homemaking, sewing, handicrafts, music and physical education. The entire curriculum should be a period of four years, 45 weeks annually, 34 hours per week. A sample of the schedule of all required courses can be found in the book of Li and Chang (1975).

b. Each county must set up a normal school supported by local funds and participants should not pay tuition fees. Private girls' schools were allowed but were subject to evaluation by the local government and concerned citizens.

c. A student must be recommended by a prominent member of the community. Those girls entering the fourth year must be under 15 years old. Students had to live in dormitories except for special events, and wear a standard blue uniform and no make-up.

d. Each school should have no more than 200 students, with a class limit of 40 students. All school facilities had to meet the standard and requirements of the government.

e. Personnel and staff were recruited and placed according to qualifications specified by the government.

f. All graduates were obligated to teach in local educational institutions for three years, or else they had to repay the cost of their education.

The educational opportunities provided by western missionaries, on the other hand, offered different perspectives to Chinese girls. The curriculum and texts adopted by missionary-run girls' schools were different from those of the normal girls's schools designed by the government. The former emphasized foreign language, science, mathematics, social science, and Bible studies, and put aside Chinese classical literature. As an example, the guidelines for the missionary girls' school, Chunghsi, were summarized as follows: [16]

a. The arrangement of the classroom was in accordance with the traditional setting, including an altar to Confucius.

b. There was one teacher for every 20 students, with westerners comprising half of the teaching faculty. The school board consisted of 24 members, with half in charge of external business.

c. All employees were female; males were not even allowed in the school. When males attended a board meeting, it had to be held in a separate courtyard.

d. The age range for students was from 8 to 15 years old. Girls with bound feet were accepted in the beginning, but not in later years.

e. Students first learned both English and Chinese, with history, art, and science secondary. A student could choose one of four specializations: mathematics, medicine, law, or education.

f. Tuition was one silver dollar per month, excluding room and board.

g. Donations such as books, money, and equipment from individuals and business groups were accepted.

h. All graduates were given a diploma in their specialization to qualify them for employment in later years.

According to Young J. Allen's survey in 1902, the number of female students in various missionary schools was 4373, over 43% of the total student population in missionary schools.[17] The following table (Table 5), illustrates the distribution of students in different types of missionary schools. Obviously, college education was not as common as secondary education among female students.

Table 5*

Student Distribution in Missionary Schools

Type of School	Number of Schools	Total Number of Students	Number of Female Students
College	12	1813	96
Junior College	66	1315	543
High school	166	6393	3509
Craft school	7	191	96
Medical school	30	251	32
Nursery	6	194	97

During this period, education for girls under the age of 15 had two tracks: one was supported by the government with an emphasis on traditional Chinese education; the other was established by western missionaries and/or local Chinese elders and included English studies. Consequently, graduates of these two different educational tracks manifested different cognitive abilities, value systems, life orientations and social functions in Chinese society. As far as the students were concerned, one track offered a free education with three years of teaching obligation, while the other was more expensive without any commitment. Girls from the lower socioeconomic classes tended to enroll in the former, while girls from wealthy families were attracted to the missionary schools.

Although the founding of the Republic in 1911 introduced many reforms in education, educational systems for boys and girls remained separate. For instance, normal girls' schools went up only to junior high in 1917. The first

*Source: Ch'en Tung-Yuan, *History of the life of Chinese women* (Taipei, Taiwan: Commerce Publishing Company, 1977), p. 347.

statistics released by the Ministry of Education in 1916 (Table 6) reflected the enormous increase in the number of young female students during the first five years of the Republic. The sharp decline in these students in 1916 revealed the impact of Yuan Shih-ka'i's attempt in 1915 to reestablish the monarchy upon the drive towards education for women. That Yuan almost succeeded in reviving monarchism deflected the people's attention and energy from the education movement. Nevertheless, the figures indicate that public education provided by the government had a greater and faster influence on women's education than missionary schools.

Table 6*
School Enrollment by Sex

Sex	1912	1913	1914	1915	1916
Boys	2,792,257	3,476,242	3,898.065	4,113,302	3,801,730
Girls	141,130	166,964	177,273	180,949	172,724

In addition to basic education for women, the importance of advanced studies overseas was recognized by women as well as by men. The threat from foreign super powers to China's security encouraged many young people to go abroad and absorb new knowledge for use in restoring the strength of their mother country. Women were no exception to these social trends. Prior to 1907, some Chinese girls sponsored by American missionaries, crossed the ocean to study in the U.S. It is believed that Kang Ai-tei and Shih Mei-yu, assisted by American missionaries, were the first women to complete their western studies in the U.S. in 1880.[18] In 1907, the first examination for those students who intended to study abroad with government support was held in Kiangsu. In this examination, girls competed with boys on an equal basis, and from a total of 13 students three girls were accepted.[19] Besides those going to the U.S. and other European countries for advanced learning, some other students chose Japan as the place for their higher education. Due to the geographical

---

*Source: Ch'en Tung-yuan, *History of the life of Chinese women* (Taipei, Taiwan: Commerce Publishing Co., 1977), p. 362.

proximity, similar cultural background and the lowest cost of living compared to other nations, Japan became a popular nation for progressive learners including quite a few well known revolutionary women.

3. Revolutionary Women

Because of the recognition of women's role in saving China from foreign imperialists' suppression as described earlier, some educated women, especially those who once went abroad were encouraged to participate in the uprising against the Ch'ing Dynasty. They assumed an active role in raising funds, smuggling ammunition, hiding wanted revolutionaries, delivering messages, working on the Red Cross team and even fighting in the field. When the revolution was dramatically ignited in Wuch'ang on October 10, 1910, it spread quickly around the country. A number of women with unbound feet formed various militia, such as the Women's Military Brigade, the Women's Exercise Team, the Women's Civil League, the Women's Assassination Corps, the Women's National Army, and the Women's Dare to Die Squad (P'i, 1973; and, Young, 1973). Following the birth of the Republic, all the female militia groups were dissolved by the Provisional Government. But Yuan Shih-kai's conspiracy for imperial restoration during 1913 evoked a momentary revival of women's military action.

Women's suffrage organizations, however, continued to pursue their goals. The names of these organizations reflect the seriousness of their role: the Shanghai Society of Comrades for Women's Suffrage, the Women's Suffrage Rearguard Society, the Women's Militant Society, the Women's Alliance, the Women's Peace Society, the Society for the Support of Equal Rights for Men and Women, and the Women's Citizen's Society (Young, 1973). However, when the Provisional Constitution was introduced in Nanking on March 11, 1912, no equality between men and women was mentioned. When a discussion with male representatives failed to reach any agreement on this issue, a skirmish ensued the next day between the Women's Suffrage Alliance headed by Tang Ch'ung-yin and the guards around the Provisional Parliament. The incident proved that women could and would take action against men as necessary.

Yet not all women were in favor of such violent action. Other moderate women, led by Mme. Wu T'ing-fang and Mme. Chang Ching-chiang, believed that women's rights should be promoted through a better communication, and that the education of women should be a gradual process. Thus, Chinese women concerned about women's rights began to split into two groups: one was radical, actively attempting to upgrade women's legal status through a socialist revolution, and the other was moderate, composed of women who felt that the education of women was the first step in elevating their status and uniting the nation.

As a result of the above-mentioned developments in physical liberation, educational opportunities and participation in the political process, women were gradually able to enter the job market and become financially independent. In Shanghai, the most westernized city, women were recruited by a farm laboratory to grow vegetables and raise poultry; by a factory to manufacture women's hats; and by other business establishments.[20] At the government level, the Railroad Administration in Canton initiated the first extensive female recruitment in the history of the female labor force.[21] Such employment trends for women could be contributed to by both the changing public attitude toward women's strength and abilities, and by women's advancement in physical freedom and the educational ladder.

At the conclusion of this period an increasing number of Chinese women had begun to realize their potential and exercise their inherited rights. They no longer believed that they were inferior to or should be enslaved by men. They were unfettered from the bondage of traditional norms which society had prescribed for them for thousands of years. With the commencement of the Republic, equality was guaranteed to everyone, including women, who then had the freedom to organize their own groups and solve their own problems. Nevertheless, the women's movement at this point involved only a few well-educated, upper-middle-class women, whose insufficient understanding of the problems of the majority of Chinese women resulted in a failure to attack women's problems and to define long-term goals. They lacked the support of and response from the mass female population as a foundation for the large scale change in their social status and legal rights. Furthermore, these educated women who were impressed by the technology of imperialist countries but against their suppression failed to recognize the force of traditional culture on Chinese women's new role under a new political system. Progressive thinking on women's emancipation should be balanced by cultural heritage. After all, changing the system without altering the minds of the "system designers" only scratched the surface of the issue without making sustained impact.

C. The May Fourth Movement

The founding of the Republic did not guarantee women's total emanicipation even though some educated women were actively involved in the revolution because the majority of women had no knowledge of women's emancipation until the May Fourth Movement paved the way for it. The May Fourth Movement, an intellectual, cultural, social, and political crusade was so named because on May 4, 1919, students of the National Peking University led a demonstration against the unstable government and its pro-Japanese adherents. Put simply, the May Fourth Movement was a reaction to Yuan Shih-kai's attempt at an imperial renaissance and the aggression of foreign powers, particularly Japan and Great Britain (P'i, 1973). The unsuccessful formation of a republican government immediately following the revolution in 1911 created an opportunity for ambitious warlords who wielded military power in the provinces. Yuan's plot at imperial restoration reflected concern over other warlords' eagerness for local control. They were anxious to extend their territory by any means, including warfare among themselves and seeking the support of foreign imperial countries. To gain personal power and wealth, the warlords disregarded the interests of the nation and the well-being of their countrymen. Because of his craving to be an emperor in Peking, Yuan Shih-kai signed a secret treaty with Japan. He acceded to a number of Japanese demands in 1915, known as the "Twenty-One Demands". This treaty virtually made China a colony of Japan. This selfish attitude shared by other warlords was attributed to traditional feudalism. As a result, feudalistic ideas which were blamed for the unstable political situation, were attacked by a group of young intellectuals: Hu Shih, Ch'en Tu-hsiu, Tsai Yuan-pei, and Wu Chih-hui. They realized that the political revolution had failed to change the dominant feudalistic thinking of the general public. They tried to convince people that an ideological alteration was essential to save and unite the nation. In 1915, Ch'en Tu-hsiu published a periodical, *Hsin Ching Nien* (*New Youth*), aimed at starting a cultural movement to eliminate feudalism and to reevaluate history through critical thinking and self-criticism. This movement demanded the abolition of Confucianism, and changes in the traditional value system, family structure, and ethics. "Down with Confucius and Sons" was the slogan and egalitarianism was the goal during this period.

Following the downfall of Yuan's short lived monarchy, the vulnerable government in Peking was helpless to defend the rights and lands of her people. Foreign powers continued to assert their rights in China. For example, at the Paris Peace Conference after World War I in 1919, China was denied the right to protest against colonial transferability when the decision was made to transfer Shangtung to Japan in the Treaty of Versailles. Such a resolution stimulated Chinese nationalism; demonstrations, labor strikes, student boycotts, and public speeches heightened people's sensitivity to the survival of China. In Peking a demonstration broke out on May 4, 1919, in which 34 college students were arrested. Subsequently, more and more people were jailed after several violent demonstrations. On June 3rd, fellow students from Peking Girls' Normal School rallied students from other schools to sign and deliver a petition for release of the prisoners (P'i, 1973). Later, this movement spread rapidly to the south. People throughout the country responded enthusiastically to various activities, including the boycott of Japanese products, and general strikes in Shanghai.

During this historical moment, women were given another chance to be liberated from their traditional roles. Although the legal status of women had been enhanced a great deal since the Republic, the women's movement was neither widespread nor well accepted due to both political instability and the involvement of only a small number of women. Until now, as a result of literature on women brought out by the May Fourth Movement, the social expectations of women had been swiftly transformed from such traditional thinking as "ignorance is a virtue," "three obediences and four virtures," to the modern idea, "faithful wife and good mother."

In providing for the intellectual backdrop for the May Fourth Movement in 1919, the magazine *Hsin Ching Nien* also advocated a modern role for women in China. Publisher Ch'en Tu-hsiu launched the magazine with a stirring commentary in praise of democracy and science. He denouced the old political system, traditional ethics and moral standards, religion, classical literature and paintings. His first article on women appeared in the magazine in January, 1916, in which he advised women not to be thwarted by traditional norms, and not to consider themselves as men's possessions. Later in the year in response to a legislative proposal to designate Confucianism as the national religion, Ch'en attacked the philosophy for not giving women equal rights, and attributed all women's suffering to the enthrallment of Confucian orthodoxy. Everything he advocated, such as participation of women in politics, remarriage for widows, open social activities for girls, opportunities for financial independence for women, and nuclear families, was contrary to Confucianism.

Another writer during the same time, Liu Pan-nung, was the first person to outline an utopia for suppressed Chinese women in his article which appeared in *Hsin Ching Nien* in August, 1918.[22] He believed that women at all socioeconomic levels shared the same fate—living for the family, not for one's self. Individualism could only become a reality when circumstances allowed. Without favorable circumstances, individualism for women was merely a fantasy. He put forward his concept of a cooperative neighborhood which was similar to the commune system in Communist China in later years. In order for women to contribute to society, they needed to be organized and mobilized for various tasks in the local community. He believed that many services could be achieved by a group effort, including childcare centers for children under four, pre-school programs for older children, creches for the entire neighborhood, laundry and tailor shops for the community, and street sweepers who would also take care of errands and delivery services. Through collaborative labor, women were given the choice of being employed outside the home and contributing to the nation, while their children were cared for by others. According to his calculations, at least half of the female population in a community could be employed in this manner.

Although the women's movement had been frustrated since Yuan's imperial restoration in 1915, it was boosted by the cultural breakthrough during the May Fourth Movement and Chinese women once again took another important step toward emancipation. In addition to Ch'en's discussion on women's inferior status, several other writers for *Hsin Ching Nien* also examined the controversial issues of chastity, contracted marriages, and the attitudes, education, and employment of western women.[23]

The May Fourth Movement not only influenced people's attitude toward other women but also provided women with an opportunity to work with the opposite sex and demonstrate their equal abilities for the same social cause. Since group effort and propaganda were stressed by the May Fourth Movement, women were involved in numerous collective tasks such as publication, drama production, and fund raising. The propaganda literature on ideological revolution, open social contacts, women's liberation, freedom to love, and equal educational opportunities, was published and disseminated by young people. Through these team events, young women had more social contacts with men and won the respect of men as individuals.

Furthermore, women obtained some substantial privileges during this period. For example, in 1920, girls were permitted to attend colleges in Peking, assuring equal opportunity for women in higher education.[24] At the same time, quite a few women's organizations were formed in Shanghai, focusing on various interests, such as religion, social gatherings, family, and career. In other provinces, like Szechwan, Chekiang, and Hunan, women took advantage of the receptive social climate and urged the local governments to grant legal rights with respect to political activities, educational opportunities, marital freedom, property and monogamy to women. Between 1922 and 1923, two major women's organizations for the suffrage movement were created by female college students in Peking. These were the League of Women's Rights, and the Women's Suffrage Association, headed respectively by Chou Min and by Wong Hsiao-Yin. They had different objectives as stated below.[25] The seven issues emphasized by the League of Women's Rights were:

a. All jobs in the field of education should be open to women.

b. Guidelines for equality between men and women should be legally established, since all people are equal under the Constitution.

c. Family codes dealing with family relationships, property, and inheritance should be ratified to ensure equal rights for women.

d. New marriage laws guaranteeing sexual egalitarianism should be introduced.

e. The criminal law should declare concubinage a form of bigamy.

f. Public prostitution, commerce in women, and footbinding should be prohibited.

g. Based on the principle of "equal pay for equal work," laws should be drafted to protect the rights of female laborers.

The platform presented by the Women's Suffrage Association included the following goals:

a. Reexamination of all legal codes to ensure equal rights for men and women.

b. Abolishment of the traditional male inheritance system, and inclusion of women for such rights.

c. Revision of the educational system, allowing women a choice of curriculum other than homemaking.

These two groups extended their organizations in an attempt

to reach women throughout China. Active members of these groups traveled around the country to advocate their views. Simultaneously, several other women's groups were formed in Canton and Shanghai with similar goals.

In 1924, women advocates found that all their individual local efforts to promote women's legal status had been in vain, since voting rights were granted only to educated men, as stated in the "Guidelines for Presidential Delegates" enacted by the Provisional Government. As a result, female leaders from different parts of the nation met in Shanghai and agreed to establish a national organization which was named Association of Chinese Women to fight for this common goal. The branches of this organization penetrated into many towns and cities where local chapters were formed. This group of concerned women played a vital role in 1925, following the May 30th Tragedy in Shanghai, the Hankou Tragedy on June 11th, the Shachi Tragedy on June 24th, and the Lungmen Tragedy on July 2nd. The tragic massacres of Chinese labor leaders and laborers by Japanese and British factory owners reflected the semi-colonial oppression from foreign nations and provided the Chinese public a realistic picture of imperialism. Female groups joined the vast population in calling for strikes and patriotic demonstrations. Now, the women's movement had become a movement not only for educated women, but also for female laborers.

In conclusion, as a result of the May Fourth Movement, Chinese women were given the opportunity to be liberated from the traditional value system. They assumed an active role in the suffrage movement and in activities against imperialism. Although their accomplishments were limited by the unstable political environment, and often their efforts and intentions were ignored by the powerless Peking government, women struggled to convey their message across the nation and reached out to recruit women from the labor force.

This period was the turning point for the forthcoming two-track women's movement in China. The women's movement encountered a politically turbulent period in China as people sought to resist imperialism and traditionalism and embrased western science and belief of individualism. Thus, its development paralleled the challenge of cultural and ideological conflicts which eventually induced the birth of two major parties in China: the Nationalist and the Communist parties. Since the women's movement had close ties with the political structure, it was inevitable that women were divided according to their ideological beliefs.

D. Post Second Revolution (1926-1949)

The 1911 revolution created the Republic of China. However, the Provisional Government formed in Nanking and presided over by Dr. Sun Yet-Sen, was unable to unite the nation immediately following the overthrow of the Ch'ing Dynasty.

Several cultural and situational factors complicated the tasks of forming a democratic society that encompassed a diverse ethnic population in a vast land. Democracy which, to Chinese progressives at the turn of the century meant having no emperor to enslave laborers or to control the thinking of the elite, was an enormous challenge—even a threat—to the Chinese people who had been influenced greatly by the political hierarchy emphasized by Confucianism. Because the immense populace lacked an understanding of the essence and implication of democracy, they were not eager to pursue it. Meanwhile, the military strongmen who dominated various parts of the country continued to exploit their power for economic and political gains. These so-called "feudalistic" warlords paid no respect to the Provisional Government. In addition to these internal problems, Russia and Japan continued to penetrate, using both diplomacy and military might to occupy more and more of China. After the founding of the Republic, most of the western powers such as Great Britain, Germany and France, had rescinded the unjust treaties imposed on the Ch'ing Dynasty and recognized China as an independent nation. However, the ambitions of Russia and Japan to control Chinese resources, including territorial acquisitions and manufacturing rights, grew unchecked. Their interests intensified when the warlords competed for their military support—Yuan Shih-kai being one of them.

Before his death, Dr. Sun Yet-Sen was convinced that a second revolution was inevitable in order to unite the nation against the ambitious foreign powers. In January, 1926, Chiang Kai-Shek, his successor, launched the Northern Expedition from Canton. During the Northern Expedition, Chiang exercised both military strength and political muscle to consolidate the hold of the Kuomintang (KMT) over the nation. By the end of 1928, China was finally under the nominal control of one government with one party—the Nationalist Party (Kuomintang).

Actually, the counterpart of the KMT, the Chinese Communist Party (CCP), first created under the guidance of the Communist International in 1921, continued to survive after the KMT claimed its victory of the second revolution which lasted from 1923 to 1927. To struggle against warlords and resist foreign imperialists, the CCP joined the KMT to form a united front from 1923 to 1927. During the Northern Expedition in the spring of 1927, differences between the two parties over goals and means led to an assault by the KMT on the Communists in Shanghai. Surviving Communist forces were reorganized by Mao Tse-Tung and Chu Teh as the Red Army. They preyed on scattered rural areas in south-central China. Later, pressed by the Nationalist military power, the Red Army was forced to undertake the "long march" during 1934-1945 to relocate in the northwestern province of Shensi, with headquarters at Yenan. During the War of Resistance against Japan (1937-1945), the CCP cooperated with minimal enthusiasm with the KMT on the battlefield against Japanese imperialism on one hand, and began its own guerilla warfare, supported by the Soviets, and extended its territory through mobilizing the rural population in the northwestern region of the nation on the other. The Communist party introduced new social and economic policies which liberated the peasants from the control of the landlords.

Simultaneously, the women's movement in the rural areas, which had received little attention from the public since the May Fourth Movement in 1919, started to gain momentum. In the liberated rural areas women were encouraged to participate actively in guerilla warfare in such areas as intelligence, communications, medical care, message delivery, food preparation, and other sex-oriented tasks. In 1922, the creation of a special bureau to incorporate women into the CCP resulted in their being better organized in the labor force as well as prepared for political gain and military advancement (Ch'en, 1960). Through participation in these revolutionary activities, women's consciousness was raised and their knowledge broadened. Furthermore, the Marriage Law, implemented in the liberated areas, had enhanced the prospects of wives and daughters-in-laws' rights at home. However, such egalitarian family relationships were not welcome by husbands and mothers-in-law. When "purchase marriages" became less popular, divorce was acceptable under the new law. In order to save their marriages, some peasants had to modify their male dominant attitudes toward their wives as an alternative to an unhappy marriage. The CCP not only played a major role in the improvement of women's family status but also ensured that instances of family discord could be resolved through the consulting efforts of cadres. Along with the new Marriage Law, agrarian reform in the liberated areas provided Chinese women with the possibility of becoming financially independent; rural husbands and wives obtained an equal share of the property when fields were allocated (Document, 1949).

Nevertheless, the legal actions and ideological propaganda designed to liberate women in rural areas generated fewer achievements than expected, due to the following reasons (Yang, 1945; Document, 1949; Crook, 1959; and, Davin, 1976): Unable to shed the deeply-rooted ideas of sexism and conservativism, peasant women suspected and feared strangers who advocated "unheard of" ideas, and disapproved of "liberated" women who had short hair and big feet. The traditional belief in the woman's role in the family was particularly strong in older women who had gone through the bitter period of being daughters-in-law, and had just come into their own period of authority over their daughters-in-law. Such conflicts of interest between older and younger women in rural families was one of the obstacles to the women's movement. Unlike urban female laborers who were single and not dependent on their families, peasant women were family oriented. Marriage, children, and relationships with in-laws meant more to them than their urban sisters. Thus, for peasant women, the price of emancipation was much higher. In addition to the social factors the political decisions of the CCP also contributed to the slow progress of the women's movement. During the 1920s, female cadres working in rural areas received only moral support from the Party and lacked money to recruit more cadres to help the needy peasant women. Furthermore, women tended to be segregated from men in the early stages of the revolution. Female cadres were assigned mainly to work with peasant women and to deal with those problems related merely to family affairs, thus being denied an opportunity to be involved in important decisions which often mingled both revolutionary struggle and women's liberation.

In urban areas where light industries were established by foreigners, women were employed as cheap labor and exploited by imperialistic capitalists. Due to the job opportunities for uneducated women, many young girls left their country homes, voluntarily or involuntarily, to seek financial independence in urban living. Very often they were recruited by questionable means and ended up being housed in crowded dorms, cut off from any contact with their parents in the remote countryside. The less fortunate had to work for many years to pay off their passage to the middlemen who recruited them into the factories.

Since women represented the majority of the labor foce involved in light industries during the 1920s (Chesneaux, 1968; and Fang, 1931), their major means for liberation was through the labor movement. Oppressed and underpaid female workers caught Hsiang Ching-yu's attention during the labor strikes of 1922, which were in response to foreign exactions, particularly from Japan. Hsiang traveled among the major cities to agitate for and organize strikes in silk and cotton factories. She demanded better working conditions and higher wages for female laborers. Her essential goal was to form a women's force which could generate some sort of impact upon the productivity of the country, and thus be used as a political tool. She recruited uneducated female workers into her movement. Although she had once headed a girl's school and had been educated in Paris, Hsiang condemned suffrage groups of educated middle-class women and mistrusted women who had a college education. Hsiang firmly believed that the women's labor movement should be incorporated into the CCP's labor movement and not be treated as a separate bureau. On May 31, 1927, the Party formed the Shanghai General Labor Union headed by Li

Li-shan (Chesneaux, 1968; and, Klein and Clark, 1971) as a result of the advantageous climate generated by the labor movement since May 30, 1925. Yet, women remained segregated. When the Northern Expedition led by Chiang Kai-shek was accomplished two years later, the Communists abandoned their urban strategy which had focused on the labor movement, and turned their attention to rural villages and peasants.

Although employment opportunities were gradually opening up for women in both urban and rural areas, their status in the family usually remained unchanged. As discussed previously, legal protection of women was partially implemented in the 1920s. After nearly 20 years of advocacy and propaganda, women finally mustered enough courage to demand the right to get a divorce. In the liberated northern states, between January and June of 1948, 64% of all civil cases were petitions for divorce filed by women (Hsin, 1949).

In terms of political advancement, women were given the chance to participate but were neither well accepted nor recommended for high-ranking positions. The female and rural population which the CCP aimed to mobilize for the revolution was less educated and more culturally and economically suppressed by country gentry or landlords. Therefore, the Party had less confidence in the women than the men, and tended to confine the women to certain female-related jobs in the Party (Young, 1973). In many liberated areas, political control was in the hands of students or peasants (Brandt, 1959), with very few women assuming positions of leadership (Wilburn, 1970). In 1947, only 30% of the elected village representatives, 20% of the cadres at the district level, and 10% at the county level were women (Tang, 1973). For some reason, women simply could not win Communist leaders' confidence even though they had demonstrated both their enthusiasm for the Party and their abilities in public affairs during the late 1920s and early 1930s (Young, 1973).

Like other female leaders in the early 1900s, several women's action groups, such as the Women's Army, Women Guard, and Women's Aid Corps, were formed under the CCP toward the end of the 1920s. During the Anti-Japanese War, female-related work was directed by the Women's Committee of the Central Committee. In 1945, the Preparatory Committee of the Women's Association of all liberated areas was set up in Yenan with 13 members (Documents, 1949). In the villages this organization was known as the Women's National Salvation Association until the Japanese surrender in 1945; from then on it was referred to as the Women's Association, or the Peasant Women's Association. The Peasant Women's Association once played an active part in land reform, but later merged with the local Peasant's Association, which often reflected local cadres' negative feelings toward women (Document, 1949). When the CCP occupied the entire nation in 1949, the All China Democratic Women's Federation was established to be in charge of women's advancement in social status.

The problem of women's emancipation was also recognized by the Kuomintang (KMT) as early as the beginning of the revolution led by Dr. Sun Yet-Sen. Documents on women's issues and problems are found in the 1905 proclamation of T'ung Meng Hui, the former body of KMT (Li and Chang, 1975). Upon the founding of the Republic in 1911, the KMT stressed the importance of women's educational opportunities. In 1923, the proclamation of equality between men and women signified the government's intent to protect women in China. At the first KMT Congress the following year, women's equality was interpreted more specifically in the legal, economic, educational, and social areas. The implementation of the proclamation of equality consisted of two dimensions—legal and administrative—and was outlined at the Second KMT Congress in 1926. Among the legal steps to be taken were: (a.) legislation to ensure equal rights for women; (b.) regulation of women's rights to inherit and own property; (c.) abolition of human purchase; (d.) passage of a marriage law based on freedom of marriage and divorce; (e.) protection of oppressed run-away women; and, (f.) enactment of a labor law in accordance with the principle of equal pay for equal work, and with guidelines for women and child laborers. The administrative steps included: (a.) encouraging the education of women; (b.) examining the education of peasant women; (c.) creating job opportunities for women in government and other occupations; and, (d.) organizing child care facilities.

Since women also participated in the Second Revolution (known as the Northern Expedition), most of the public speeches delivered by the KMT touched upon women's role and status to a certain extent (P'i, 1973). A speech addressed to the entire nation on National Day (Double Tenth) in 1928 declared that the educational goals for women were to develop and facilitate motherhood. When the Third Congress was held the following year, women's education was guaranteed as part of the legislation on educational goals and implementation. Once again, the traits and virtues of motherhood and good housekeeping were stressed. (This philosophy directed the KMT policy on women's issues until the present day, and is discussed in Chapter 7.) In November, 1929, the Central Executive Committee declared that forced or purchased marriages, infanticide, concubinage, prostitution, footbinding, and ear piercing should be gradually abolished.

During the Northern Expedition, masses of the population—laborers, farmers, youth, and women—were mobilized to eliminate the feudalistic warlords. Women participated in the attack on warlords by sabotage in various parts of the nation for the preparation of the arrival of the KMT troops. Their cooperation with the KMT accelerated the military maneuver and the restoration of the cities controlled by the warlords. When the KMT troops arrived in Wu Han, more than 500,000 workers in Shanghai joined a strike to demonstrate their support of this operation. It was estimated that over 40% of the strikers were women.[26] When the nation was nominally united after the Second Revolution, many female leaders felt that the women's movement had achieved its goals and no longer needed to fight for any additional rights. They believed that women were protected by legal codes, and that women's problems could be solved through legal channels. Thus women's organizations gradually became devitalized and passive immediately after the Northern Expedition.[27]

Later, in May 1930, a development among the women in Nanking, the capital, revived demoralized women's groups in other parts of the nation. A meeting was called by three women's groups in Nanking: the Nanking City Women's Association, Nanking Young Women, and the Voice of Women, to determine the number of female representatives in Congress. Female delegates from every part of the country were invited to participate in the selection process. Negotiations with the KMT Party resulted in designating ten regular seats and seventeen observer seats for women, which constituted one percent of the total seats in Congress. The Congress passed the Provisional Constitution on May 12. In the spring of 1933, as a result of the efforts of a group of women led by Wong Hsiao-ying, the committee for the revision of civil and criminal laws adopted a resolution that extramarital relations be penalized, with one year in prison for the parties involved; this is considered one of the major victories for Chinese women in their legal battles.

Without any effective agency to enforce the law codes alone generated very little impact on the improvement of Chinese women's lives. Realizing this, the KMT renamed the women's committee the Ministry of Women, which paralleled the peasant, labor, and business ministries. However, all four ministries were later merged to form a new Public Training Committee. In 1938, the National Provisional Congress decided to place women's affairs under the newly established Ministry of Social Affairs. Later, the women's bureau was directly responsible to the Central Organization of the KMT.

Anti-Japanese War

The Anti-Japanese War, which was officially declared on July 7, 1937, was China's resistance to the years of Japanese aggression toward China. Japan was an isolated nation prior to the Meiji Restoration which began in 1867. The Restoration transformed it into a leading industrial and military power. New found national strength in turn fueled its expansion and territorial ambitions with China as the main target. Before the Sino-Japanese War of 1894, Japan correctly diagnosed the inferior military strength of the Chinese government. After its victory, Japanese military power gradually penetrated throughout the northeastern part of China. The success of the Northern Expedition in 1928 resulted not only in national unity, but disturbed the Japanese government a great deal, for such unity interferred with their attempt to detach the northeastern provinces from China's central government and put them under local "self-rule" puppet governments. As a result, the Japanese instigated several military confrontations with Chinese forces after 1930. With well-planned military maneuvers and careful use of Chinese resources, the Japanese were able to penetrate the eastern portion of China rapidly and thought that they would be able to claim victory within three months.

The declaration of the Anti-Japanese War fired Chinese nationalism and promoted internal unity, regardless of differences in sex, age, occupation, ethnicity, and geographical location. Everyone, both men and women, was eager and anxious to make a contribution to the country during this national crisis. Women were reminded of their traditional virtues by Mme. Chiang Kai-Shek in her Mother's Day address in 1938 (Women's Department, 1979). By presenting examples of several famous mothers in Chinese history, she concluded that Chinese women: (1) had an unique philosophy toward lifetime goals; (2) were able to tolerate crises with peace of mind; (3) could utilize available meager resources during difficult times; (4) preseverd in the face of obstacles; (5) possessed unusual courage and determination; and, (6) had unbelievable potential. During the eight-year Anti-Japanese War, Mme. Chiang organized women to carry out various different tasks; basically, there were four organizations through which women contributed to the war effort:

> a. The Chinese Women's Resistance Federation was set up in Nanking on August 1, 1937, immediately after the declaration of war. The goal of this organization was to mobilize women to accept responsibilities in the rear while men were fighting in the front lines. Women in China and overseas responded by forming 42 branches of the Federation around the world to support the anti-Japanese effort. Their major tasks were to sew uniforms for soldiers, to rescue and assist refugees from Japanese occupied territories and/or bombed areas, to raise funds for military spending, to visit troops on the battlefield, to care for the wounded and to wash and mend clothes for soldiers. Women from different age groups, socioeconomic classes, and educational backgrounds joined in these significant activities. Many former bar girls

and dancing girls worked hard in the hospitals to help care for the wounded.[28] Women who had lost their families volunteered to work with the poor and to prepare clothes, bandages, and sheets for the soldiers. Over one hundred women were engaged in the sale of one million dollars worth of bonds to help the nation. Some young girls were in charge of dangerous ammunition transportation. Numerous students, both boys and girls, helped to make stretchers and crutches. In order to assist bereaved families the Women's Resistance Federation set up home visits, job training programs, and established schools for war orphans. Women in remote areas organized collective shops and prepared lands in CheKiang and Shansi for cultivation (Women's Department, 1979). In the Japanese-occupied regions, women were wary of strangers in their villages. One day, as a group of women were washing clothes by the river, three strangers approached them for directions to Japanese occupied areas. One woman gave them confusing instructions, while another said, "Please follow me because it is not easy to find. My house is in that direction, too." While she prolonged the journey, the other women were able to notify local authorities, who then arrested the three spies (Women's Department, 1979). Using only their hands, women contributed their labor to build roads in the provinces of Hopei, Kwangsi, Ch'inghai, and Kansu.

b. The War-Time Child Care Association was founded by Mme. Chiang in Wuhan in March of 1938. The major task of this unit was to locate orphans from war districts and then transport them to safe locations for care. Over forty orphanages, aiding over 20,000 war orphans, were set up in various cities.[29] These orphanages were forced to close or evacuate to Szechwan when the Japanese overtook the city.

c. The Women's Committee for the New Life Movement was organized by Mme. Chiang in July, 1938, as an effort to serve the nation through a fundamental change in daily living (P'i, 1973; and, Women's Department, 1979) Five goals were identified: *to promote women's cultural standards; to provide vocational training; to enhance women's employment opportunities; to improve the living conditions of female laborers;* and, *to alter female-related social customs.* The process of mobilization involved training to meet the needs of women from various backgrounds. Nine task forces were organized under the committee to look after specific areas: coordination, training, service on the battlefield, service in villages, guidance and counseling, child care, production, visitation to the soldiers, and publication and cultural activities. Their job assignments were similar to those carried out by the Chinese Women's Resistance Federation. Later in 1939, this organization established several light industries in Szechwan to support the War.

d. The Young Women's Army was formed in 1944, when Chairman Chiang called for "one hundred thousand young people to be one hundred thousand soldiers." Many college students, both men and women, discontinued their studies and joined the army. A separate women's division led by Ch'en Yi-yun consisted of eight units with 100 women in each. Each unit was divided into four teams to deal with either cultural, first aid, fund raising, or communication and publication needs.[30]

Social changes are often accompanied by problems; such was the case with the Chinese women's mass involvement during World War II. Women's contributions to the nation and their demonstrated qualifications—both mental capacity and physical strength—were recognized by society. However, the basic concept of serving the people was inadequately shared by many influential women. Mme. Chiang tended to organize women's groups by inviting prominent women, including the wives of state governors and military leaders, to head the branches or sit in on the governing committees. Very often these women, who were accustomed to being waited on in their own homes, lacked the commitment to devote themselves to the basic task of serving the nation through work. They were able to outline very impressive but unrealistic plans, often bragging about imaginary achievements. Therefore, Mme. Chiang urged these female leaders to help the nation by action, not by lip service (Women's Department, 1979). Furthermore, since these women played a coordinating role in their local areas, their active participation was essential; otherwise, the propsed programs would have difficulty being implemented (Women's Department, 1979).

Women's contributions to the war effort greatly improved their social status.[31] Consequently, they were given greater opportunities to participate in the process of political decision making. Upon winning the Anti-Japanese War, the Nationalist government decided to hold a general assembly on November 15, 1948, for the purpose of writing a permanent new Constitution. Once more, the issue of reserved legislative seats for women was raised. There were some people who disapproved of such an idea because women's equal rights had been guaranteed as early as 1931 by the Provisional Constitution that indicated all people were equal in all respects regardless of sex and ethnicity. However, the rationale behind the provision of "reserved seats" was that Chinese women had been suppressed by society and were deprived of education and cultural exposure for so long that much time was needed to compensate. Legal equality was not adequate for women to better themselves from an inferior starting point. Equity, rather than equality should be considered to enhance women's opportunities in politics. The eighty female representatives to the Assembly tried vigorously to win support for their resolution of reserved seats for women. Finally, it was accepted as follows: 10% of the Assembly seats, 10% of the legislative seats, and 20% of the Examinational seats were reserved for women.[32] Since then the number of female Representatives at all levels has followed similar proportion.

In general, the Anti-Japanese War generated two different kinds of impact upon the women's movement in the regions controlled by the Nationalist government. Women's self-concept was improved because they had been given the chance to challenge and develop their potential. Meanwhile, the image of Chinese women as perceived by Chinese society had changed. After 1945, however, the women's movement seemed to have lost its drive. Again, women found their place at home and had no incentive to work after the eight harsh years of resistance to Japan. Accrording to P'i's analysis (1973), limited educational opportunities for women contributed to the regression of the women's movement in the postwar period. She believed that the success of the women's movement hinged on universal education; women could not be emancipated without basic education.

E. Famous Women

The experiences of Chinese women varied enormously from the beginning to the close of this period. Under the Ming Dynasty the social status of women declined rapidly. Women were required to submit to the most inhuman social norms, with no other choice than to continue accepting their suffering in an effort to win social recognition. When their affliction reached its apogee in the Ch'ing Dynasty, without other alternatives, they were forced to finally fight back and the women's movement was launched. The potential power of women was recognized through the revolutionary process which freed Chinese poeple from foreign colonialism and Manchu misrule. Many talented and intelligent women took advantage of this revolutionary opportunity and demonstrated their leadership in the women's movement which grew rapidly in the late 19th century.

The following stories of five women represent a very small part of the literature on outstanding Chinese women. However, this selection is intended to portray women's lives, value systems, achievements, and participation in the women's movement in an era in which women's role and social status underwent enormous changes.

The story of Maiden Ts'ao reflects the vicious demands chastity put on women during the Ch'ing Dynasty.[33] Maiden Ts'ao was a native of Anhwei, a province nestled on the banks of the Youngtze River. Near her house was a temple. Although in general the monks residing in temples were honest and dutiful in performing religious ceremonies and social services for the villagers, one who lived in the temple near Ts'ao's home was not. This lustful monk did not refrain from sexual activities. He lured women with good reputations to the temple to satisfy his own sexual desires. Because of the fear that social pressure would force these women to commit suicide after such an adulterous relationship, all of the victims chose to endure in silence. One day, a neighborhood boy stumbled unwittingly upon the monk having sex with a woman. To conceal his lewd behavior, the monk killed the boy and buried him behind the temple. When the boy's father discovered the truth and accused the cruel monk of murdering his son the monk realized that, with all the evidence against him, he would be given the death penalty. To postpone his death, the monk implicated more than thirty innocent women with whom he claimed to have had sexual relations. Because of the proximity of her house to the temple, Maiden Ts'ao was one of those mentioned. The inept magistrate took the monk's word and decided to bring these women to trial for verification. On the witness stand the monk declared that he had a longer and more initimate relationship with Maiden Ts'ao than with any of the others. Ts'ao replied, "If your statement is true, you should be able to name an identifying mark on my body." The monk made no response. Then Maiden Ts'ao submitted to an examination by a court official who saw a peculiar mole near her sex organs, a mole which would have been noted by anyone having an affair with her. Because he had no knowledge of this obvious mark, the monk was found guilty and the rest of the women were set free. Without Ts'ao's fearless decision, these women would have had no way to exonerate themselves and would have been forced to take their own lives because of social pressure.

Maiden Ts'ao saved the lives of these innocent women by sacrificing her own life. After being dismissed from the court Maiden Ts'ao took her life as the socially acceptable means to relieve her personal shame and preserve her reputation. It was considered shameful for a woman, especially an unmarried one, to expose her body to a stranger and reveal such a personal characteristic to the public. Her courageous story was then recorded in the volume of virtuous women of the Ch'ing Dynasty.

Maiden Ts'ao had little control over her fate and was the victim of tyrannical social norms prescribed for women. In contrast, the Empress Tz'u Hsi (1835-1908) was not. She was one of the strongest personalities found in modern Chinese history. Tz'u Hsi of the Manchu tribe of the Yehe Nara played an active role in Chinese politics and had a great influence on the destiny of Chinese people in the last decades of the Ch'ing Dynasty.

Yehonala (Tz'u Hsi), the daughter of a minor Manchu official from the province of Anhwei, possessed extraordinary intelligence, ambition, and a beautiful melodious charm. These talents, and the birth of a son, enabled her to be raised to the rank of Empress Consort. Prior to the death of her husband, Emperor Hsien-feign (reigned 1851-1861), she was one of the most influential persons in court, advising the Emperor on both public and domestic affairs. Emperor Hsien-feng's attempt to transfer power smoothly to his son was frustrated by Tz'u Hsi, who was determined to become the regent for her five-year-old son, T'ung-chih (reigned 1862-1874). On assuming the Joint-Regency with another Empress Dowager, Satoka, who had not given birth to a son for the late Emperor, she took the title of Tz'u Hsi ("Kindly, Motherly, and Auspicious"), while Sakota assumed the title Tz'u An ("Kindly and Serene"). Having established her authority over her co-Regent and all her entourage, Tz'u Hsi soon dominated her chief minister, Prince Kung, through a plot set by her most trusted eunuch, An Te-hai.

In 1873, Tz'u Hsi's regency officially came to an end when her son T'ung-chih reached the age of 16. The mysterious deaths of T'ung-chih in 1874 (some historians suggested that he died of smallpox or venereal disease; see Hibbert, 1970; and, also, Li, 1978), the death of Empress Dowager Tz'u An, and the suicide of her daughter-in-law, was believed to be associated with Tz'u Hsi's thirst for power. Knowing how to manipulate people and exploit human emotional weaknesses, she suppressed all opposition from the imperial princes, including Prince Kung, and installed her sister's son Kuang-hsu as the emperor (Chesneaux, *et al.*, 1976). She was then restored to the regency in January 1875, over the three-year-old emperor Kuang-hsu. She climbed to power as absolute ruler while China became more and more vulnerable to foreign encroachments. Later, when Tz'u Hsi learned of Emperor Kuang-hsu's active involvement in reform and his sincere efforts to save the nation from being divided by western powers, she was furious and reassumed her regency on his behalf by making the Emperor a prisoner in Ocean Terrace until his death in 1908. Later she also arrested and had executed the leaders of reform.

While historians, as well as the Chinese people, have denounced Tz'u Hsi, her influential role in Chinese politics cannot be denied. In her early years, soon after the death of her husband, she contributed greatly to the restoration of social order after suppressing the Taiping rebels (1850-1864).[34] In addition, Tz'u Hsi had a positive impact on the movement against child bethrothals and girls' footbinding. Western missionaries who had previously been wary of interfering with native customs had stiffened their opposition to these two practices during the Tz'u Hsi regency.

Tz'u Hsi's original vitality and eagerness disappeared, however, as she continued to assert her supremacy over young emperors, including her son and nephew. She was criticized by many for her obscurantism and her extra conservativism. Among her most widely known political errors and misconceptions were her belief that the European powers were as barbarian as her neighboring tribes, and her blind trust in I Ho Chuan ("Righteous Harmonious Boxing") who, she was convinced, would be able to chase the foreign aggressors out of China without using a single bullet. Such ignorance led to the Boxer Riots which provoked the foreign powers to send an invading force. Her opposition to reform resulted in her inability to understand the realities of world politics and her misconceptions about modernization, which she believed would destroy the domination and prerogatives of the Manchus and the gentry. The flight of the royal party to Joho during the Boxer Riots finally awakened the Empress Dowager to the need for reform. In 1904 she decreed the reforms, which were very modest, and were never fully carried out. Such political changes were too late to win the people's confidence. Furthermore, her inordinate extravagance and, in particular, her lavish expenditures on a summer palace, known as the Hill of a Myriad Longevities, invited more criticism and dissatisfaction because it drained the Imperial Treasury of funds which were supposed to be reserved for the establishment of naval forces. Consequently, many reformers became underground revolutionaries and actively plotted to overthrow the Manchu Dynasty.

In 1908, at the age of 75, the Empress Dowager fell ill. When she felt that her end was near it was said that she had the captive Emperor Kuang-hsu assassinated. He died at 5:00 p.m., on November 14, for unknown reasons; Tz'u Hsi, herself, died the next afternoon. Evidently she was determined that this man whom she had ill-treated and oppressed all of his life should never regain his independence. Since Emperor Kuang-hsu had no children, she picked two-year-old Prince P'u Yi, her sister's son, as Emperor Hsuan-t'ung (1909-1911) on the day of her death.

There are many stories about the Empress Dowager's personal life and her relationships with two well-known eunuchs: An Tei-hai and Li Lien-ying. An Tei-hai was rapidly promoted and gained the Empress' confidence after Tz'u Hsi successfully seized power following the death of the Emperor Hsien-feng. He acted as Tz'u Hsi's messenger during the intrigues involving the power struggle between Tz'u Hsi and the Joint-Regents appointed by the late Emperor on his death bed. He was not only the Empress' most trusted servant and her constant companion, but also played the leading role opposite her in court entertainments and masques, even going on trips with her to the palace lake wearing the Dragon Robe which was reserved for the Emperor. In 1869, An Tei-hai's arrogance went too far during a journey down the Grand Canal. He traveled wearing the splendid clothes, attended by numerous servants and other eunuchs, acting as if they were the royal party. On learning from the governor of Shangtung that An Tei-hai had flagrantly broken the rules, Prince Kung seized his opportunity and had him executed. Furious at Prince Kung's actions, the Empress later found a suitable replacement for her former Chief Eunuch in another eunuch: Li Lien-ying, an ugly former cobbler who, it was said, castrated himself in order to qualify for a life of enjoyment and power in the Imperial Palace. He was known as a cruel, vindictive, and avaricious man—but was devoted and loyal to his mistress. He was excellent company, a brilliant raconteur, and a generous, amusing host, capable of exercising a strangely persuasive charm over his guests (Hibbert, 1970). His superciliousness and political influence lasted until the death of Tz'u Hsi. Because of Li Lien-ying's dominance, imperial decision-making reflected his egoism, ambition, narrow-mindedness, and short-sightedness, and the Court became more bungling and corrupt than ever. Even the loyal, courageous, out-spoken and highly regarded chief minister, Prince Kung, was dismissed with impunity for taking offense at Li Lien-ying's extravagance and corruption at the Imperial Court, which finally helped lead to revolution.

Tz'u Hsi's nearly one-half century of rule was marked by mishandled diplomacy with western nations and continuous internal turmoil and revolutionary agitation. Her unique life and historical importance have attracted the attention of many Chinese. Numerous books have been written on her childhood, sex life in widowhood, eating habits, clothing, leisure activities, and use of cosmetics (Hibbert, 1970; Li, 1978b; and, Liu, 1978). Frequently her story is dramatized and distorted to arouse readers' interest.

Before Tz'u Hsi died in 1908, many Chinese women had become involved in establishing schools for women and even in revolutionary activity. The following three renowned women were, in fact, born during Tz'u Hsi's last years.

Chiu Chin, a martyr of the revolutionary period, was a native of Chekiang and nicknamed Chien Hu Nu Hsia ("The Knight of Chien Hu") (Hsu, 1913; Li and Chang, 1975; Ch'en, 1977; Liu, 1978; and, Pao, 1979). Because of her father's political appointments her family moved to several different provinces during her childhood. With her wide experience and unusual intelligence, she learned reading and writing very quickly. At the age of 18, she was married to a wealthy man named Wong Ting-chun, to whose family she had been betrothed in her childhood. She gave birth to one boy and one girl. Her marital life lasted less than ten years and ended in separation. She objected to the political ambition of her husband, Wong Ting-chun, and denounced the corruption and misgovernment of a few ambitious, selfish and greedy politicians in Peking. Political incompatability finally led to the end of the marriage. A friend stole the assets from her separation settlement, so she had to sell all of her personal jewelry in order to travel to Japan for advanced studies. Leaving her two young children behind with her mother, she arrived in Tokyo in March, 1904. She not only learned Japanese, but also dressed in a kimono—the Japanese costume. She formed the Kung Ai Hui (Common Love Society) to advocate revolutionary thought and joined the Tung Meng Hui in 1905, to assume an active role against the Manchu Empire.

Chiu Chin's concern for women's rights was displayed even before the end of her marriage. Once she helped to free two concubines from the dominance of their husbands; and, she helped an educated young girl protest her betrothal to a wealthy merchant as a concubine. She believed that women should be respected as individuals instead of being treated as property of their husbands. She felt women should become more independent by fighting for their rights, including the right to take part in serving their country, freeing China from foreign powers and the merciless rule of local warlords.

Since she realized that women's education was the key to their building a strong China, upon her return to China in 1906, she established the Min Tao Girls' School and published the first women's newspaper, *Nu Hsueh Pao*, in Shanghai, to promote sexual equality. Chiu Chin firmly believed that China could not be strong without educated women and that China would continue to be weak while women were not educated and were restricted physically. Therefore, she formed a natural foot club to protest footbinding. Chiu Chin not only advocated women's rights through her writings and her dedication to women's education, but also actively participated in the revolution, hoping that the political, social, and economic conditions in China could be changed to the benefit of all people. She secretly engaged in manufacturing ammunition to support underground revolutionary activities. When she substituted for her cousin, Hsu Hsi-lin, as the headmaster of the Ta Tao High School, she often dressed like a man in military clothing and rode a horse in and out of town. The local gentry was not pleased with her style, which increased her difficulties in recruiting young girls for her school. She taught her students, both boys and girls, military tactics to prepare them to overthrow the Manchu government by military force. In 1907, after an attempt to assassinate the governor failed, she was arrested and executed at the age of 31. She and her cousin Hsu Hsi-lin had planned to lead the schools in an armed insurrection after the assassination. Unlike Chiu Chin's aggressive attitude and actions, Chang Chu-chun's deeds represent another type of revolutionary women (Hsu, 1913; Li and Chang, 1975; and, Ch'en, 1977).

Chang Chu-chun came from a well-to-do family in Canton, and studied four years at a medical school established by American Presbyterians. During the late 19th century, western medicine was not well accepted by the Chinese. Most Chinese still believed in traditional Chinese methods of curing illness. However, because of her outstanding medical practice and out-going personality, she won immense respect, popularity, and friendship from local people regardless of age or sex. Her practice, which aimed to help the poor as well as the rich, kept her clinic crowded with patients night and day. In a short while, with financial assistance from her friends, she founded several western-style hospitals and schools in different provinces.

Chang Chu-chun usually dressed in western clothing and rode a specially designed sedan chair held by four men. To escape the summer heat she stayed in a boat along the river. Because of her personality and achievements as reported by newspapers, many prominent young men admired and pursued her. Yet, her close social ties with several famous men in the news-media, politics, and business did not result in marriage.

Being a devout Christian, Chang Chu-chun conducted regular Bible study groups outside her clinic on Saturdays and Sundays for friends and even non-believers. In addition to preaching the gospel and practicing medicine, through her speeches and newspaper writings she also advocated equality between men and women in accordance with Christian doctrines.

In 1904 Chang Chu-chun moved her practice to Shanghai. Again, she was warmly accepted by the local people and continued to play an active role in social circles. On the eve of the Wuhan Uprising in 1911, which led to the revolution, she was asked by Hsu Chung-han, a very close friend who once financed her hospital construction, to protect some revolutionaries crossing the Youngtze River in order to reach Hankou and prepare the uprising. To do so, she united several local hospitals and organized the first Red Cross, consisting of 69 men and 54 women. Claiming that the wounded in Hankou needed help, they formed two teams leaving Shanghai spearately for Hankou on September 3rd, and September 29th. The leaders of the Wuhan Uprising, disguised as members of the Red Cross, were able to arrive at their destination safely. Chang Chu-chun's efforts contributed considerably to the success of the Wuhan insurrection. After the revolution, she gradually disappeared from social and political life. She remained single and devoted herself to healing people.

Hsiang Ching-yu was born at a time when Chinese people were suffering from domestic feudal rule and foreign imperialist intervention. The collaboration of imperialist powers and local warlords for personal economic and military gain at the expense of many Chinese peasants and laborers made revolutionaries out of many Chinese, especially the young. Hsiang Ching-yu was one of the most active (Young, 1973; and, Liu, 1980).

Hsiang Ching-yu was convinced that women must first gain access to education before they could free themselves from feudal bondage and share with men the responsibilities of national salvation. After graduation from Chounan School for Girls in Changsha, Hsiang Ching-yu returned to her native county of Chupa and set up a school of girls to teach them democracy, patriotism, and promote sexual equality. At the age of 21, she went to France on a work-study program and there joined other progressive Chinese students who were eagerly searching for a way to save China. In France she studied Marxist theory—including that concerning women—and came into direct contact with the French working class. In "A Thesis on the Emancipation and Transformation of Women," written in France, she emphasized that the women's movement should be integrated with the political movement of the proletariat. She argued that the women's movement for emancipation ought to aim at freeing them from the burden of housework so as to involve them not so much in women's suffrage, but rather in building a social system similar to that of Soviet Russia.

Upon her return to Shanghai in 1922, she was selected by the Communist Party's Second National Congress to be a member of the Central Committee and the first Director of its Women's Department. She convinced the Party of the enormous potential of women for the revolutionary cause and argued that it should not neglect the mass of working-class women who were not educated, but could be. Her sympathy with the mercilessly exploited working women drove her to devote herself to support and guide women in labor movements. She frequently visited female workers in textile factories and taught them Marxist theory. Through her close ties with female workers, she was able to organize several large-scale female labor strikes in Shanghai and Wuhan. Her message was that the evil social system (local warlords) and external forces (foreign imperialist powers) denied women's rights. To rally and organize female factory workers, peasant women, and revolutionary women intellectuals, the Party entrusted Hsiang Ching-yu with the task of setting up the "Women's Emancipation Association". The association quickly took shape in many locales. From that time on, the women's movement, previously limited to a few intellectuals, became an important force against imperialism and feudalism and expanded to become a mass movement under the guidance of the Communist Party—with females and peasants as its mainstay.

In 1927, as a result of serious conflict between the Kuomintang (KMT) and the Chinese Communist Party (CCP) the Communists were forced to go underground. The Party advised publicly known Communist figures to withdraw from cities to the rural areas and prepare for future armed uprisings. Hsiang, however, insisted on remaining in Wuhan to continue the underground operation. In the spring of 1928, she was arrested by the KMT and was executed on May 1st. Eventhough she died at 33 years of age, she had a profound impact on the emancipation of Chinese women and laboring people.

152

Conclusion

The women's movement launched at the end of the 19th century was the result of the climax of societal suppression of women and the influence of western powers. When women were no longer able to tolerate such inhumane treatment as female infanticide, footbinding, and unilateral chastity, they had to seek a solution to free themselves from further suffering. Complimented with the cultural, educational, economic and military influences of the industrialized nations, women and women sympathizers began to recognize women's problems and advocate their rights.

After the Republic was founded in 1911, as a result of the Chinese people's dissatisfaction with the Manchu rulers and the oppression of foreign nations, the process for women's emancipation gradually became related to political ideology. Under the two different political parties—the KMT and the CCP—women had different experiences in terms of changes in value systems, lifestyle, political, social, and family status. The gap between these two tracks of women's movement had been widened as these two parties have had the defined territory since 1949. Women in Mainland China and in Taiwan will be the theme of the next two chapters.

NOTES

[1] Li Ch'ia-fu, *Chinese ancient women* (Taipei, Taiwan: Li Min Publishing Co., 1978), p. 159.

[2] Ch'en Tung-yuan, *History of the life of Chinese women* (Taipei, Taiwan: Commerce Publishing Co., 1977), pp. 232-240.

[3] Chia Shen, "Examination of women's footbinding in China," *Geographical and historical report* III.3 (1924), p. 70.

[4] Ch'en, *op. cit.*, p. 246.

[5] *Ibid.*, p. 292.

[6] *Ibid.*, p. 282.

[7] Li Yu-ning and Chang Yu-fa, eds., *Documents on the Feminist Movement in modern China* (Taipei, Taiwan: Biographical Literature

Publishing Co., 1975), p. 9; see also, Vincent Y.C. Shih, *The Taiping ideology* (Seattle: University of Washington Press, 1967), p. 62.

[8]Li Yu-ning and Chang Yu-fa, *op. cit.*, pp. 722-725.

[9]*Ibid.*, pp. 726-731.

[10]*Ibid.*, pp. 724-725; see also, Pi, *loc. cit.*, p. 9.

[11]Ch'en, *op. cit.*, p. 321.

[12]*Ibid.*, pp. 316-317.

[13]*Ibid.*, p. 317; see also, Liang Ch'i Ch'ao, *Essay of Ying Ping Chi*, pp. 220-223.

[14]*Ibid.*, p. 319.

[15]*Ibid.*, p. 321.

[16]Li Yu-ning and Chang Yu-fa, *op. cit.*, pp. 995-1003.

[17]Ch'en, *op. cit.*, p. 347.

[18]*Ibid.*, p. 350.

[19]*History of contemporary Chinese students overseas*, pp. 129-132.

[20]Pi, *op. cit.*, p. 36.

[21]*Ibid.*.

[22]Ch'en, *op. cit.*, pp. 378-380.

[23]*Ibid.*, pp. 372-374.

[24]Pi, *op. cit.*, p. 47.

[25]*Ibid.*, pp. 49-50.

[26]*Ibid.*, p. 60.

[27]*Ibid.*, p. 61; see also, T'an Shei-ying, *Forty years of the Women's Movement*, pp. 31-34.

[28]Pi, *op. cit.*, p. 75.

[29]*Ibid.*, p. 76.

154

[30]*Ibid.*, pp. 80-81.

[31]Olga Lang, *Chinese family and society* (New Haven: Archon Books, 1968), p. 345.

[32]P'i, *op. cit.*, pp. 82-84.

[33]Liu Tzu-ch'ing, *Critical biographies of famous women in Chinese history* (Taipei, Taiwan: Lin Min Publishing Co., 1978), pp. 267-268.

[34]*Ibid.*, pp. 252-255.

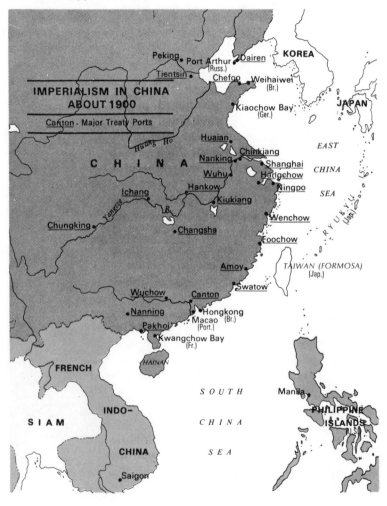

CHAPTER SIX

Revolutionary Women of Mainland China

Since the beginning of their revolution, the Chinese Communists have considered women's liberation part of the revolutionary process. Revolution aimed at changing tradition and liberating the victims of the traditional society, mainly women and peasants. Traditional Chinese society was formed by the thousands of years old value system under which scholars were highly respected and society was controlled by a rigid hierarchy of authority, including families. The family system, by demanding blind obedience from women of any age, gave rise to countless family and personal tragedies. Women were suppressed by the authority of clan, parents, husband, and grown sons. In addition to this, the prevailing Confucian idea that men who worked with their brain were superior to those who worked with their hands led to the revolution. The dominance of educated people reinforced the inferior status of uneducated peasants and women. As a result a great majority of people, both men and women, were downtrodden and exploited. Their ignorance kept them in constant poverty. In many cases they had to sell their children and even their wives to avoid starvation. Their educationally and economically deprived offspring faced the same fate and went through the same experience. This vicious cycle continued for over a thousand years, and the gap between the rich and the poor naturally grew wider as time went by. Often in desperation farmers were forced to sell their land to the rich on extremely unfair terms. Consequently lands were controlled by fewer and fewer rich people while the number of tenant farmers enslaved by these wealthy landlords increased. Such practices victimized the great majority of the rural Chinese and eventaully paved the way for the Communist movement in which the liberation of women and peasants became a major issue. Even though these two groups of people were the majority they had no power to control their destiny. Husbands and masters had absolute authority over the labor force, daily activities, use of resources, and even life and death. These authority figures stripped from women and peasants all opportunities for education and economic betterment in order to relegate them at the bottom of society. Due to their similar oppressive experience, peasant liberation and women's emancipation joined together to fight against their common abusers. In the emerging Communist Party of the early 1920s, women's emancipation was an integral part of the Party goal: social reconstruction and economic reformation.

A. *Changing Political Role of Women in China*

Women were not only a target of liberation, they were also an instrument for achieving such a goal. Moreover, they were recognized as a powerful contributing force to social reconstruction. In order to improve their self-concept and raise their political consciousness they were encouraged, as a first step, to speak out against those who mistreated them and to attend local classes which taught politics. In the early stages of the revolution, when guerrilla warfare was used, women fought alongside men. Because of their family responsibilities, however, they were less mobile than men and more likely to be given assignments such as laying mines, digging tunnels, and acting as nurses, messengers, and food collectors. For these tasks they did not have to move around as much as soldiers (Davin, 1976).

The Communist Party has played a very important role in promoting women's political consciousness and status in the government. Since the success of the Communist revolution in 1949, women have been organized for social reconstruction and encouraged to take on new responsibilities. First, they were constantly reminded of their bitter past, then they were urged to continue to speak out in public meetings against it as they had done in the early stages of the revolution. The government believed that if it promoted women's political knowledge and ideological sensitivity through self-study and political classes, women could better serve the country and would be more willing to devote time and energy to their countrymen rather than to their individual families. Women were required to put their political ideology into practical day-to-day living. They collectively attacked problems such as childcare, family discord, and changing values. The following case demonstrates the factors which have changed traditional ideas and practices more drastically than ever:[1]

> One night in the winter of 1967, when Kuo Ai Lien was at a meeting in the commune, her baby at home cried for a long time and her husband was in a dither. The mother-in-law also was displeased. Ai Lien came home late to a fuming husband and a row ensued. When the Party branch heard of this, it immediately sent Chen Yung Kuei to talk with the husband. "If we men are away at work, the women hold down the fort and never complain when we come home late," he said. "So why can't we look after children for a change when they go to meetings? Women are the other half of the brigade, you know. Just imagine half the brigade chained at home—how can production and revolution go ahead then?"

The Communists believed the family to have a causal effect on society. The interest of the community and society was considered the interest of the family as well. Not uncommonly the local party brigade or officers interfered or interceded in family affairs for the welfare of the country. Women were often given advice and assistance in solving the problems of marriage, childcare, housekeeping, and inheritance.

A more recent case reported in the March 1980 issue of *Women of China* reflects the enforcement of the Marriage Law by a local court judge and police to protect women's rights to inherit property from their parents. Chiu-ti was the only son of a retired worker, Ch'en Chuan-gan, who was living in a people's commune in Chuansha County, Shanghai. He allowed his oldest son, Chi-ti, to use the two east rooms when Chi-ti got married some twenty years previous. Chuangan and his wife continued living with their youngest daughter Yun-pao in the two west rooms. Yun-pao was married in 1974 and agreed to take care of the old couple. As he and his wife were both approaching 70, Ch'en Chuangan decided to divide his house during his lifetime between his only son and his youngest daughter. Ch'en Chuan-gan's intention was vigorously opposed by his son Chi-ti, who used all means to block this division of property. Chi-ti's reason was that it had been common practice since ancient times to hand down family property to one's son and he considered himself the sole heir of the entire property. Relatives and close friends failed to mediate the family dispute. Finally, the case was solved in the county court and the house was divided as the elderly couple wished. Because of Chi-ti's defiance of the court's decision, the court sent a court judge and police to Ch'en's house to construct a wall, dividing the house and carrying out the court's verdict. From then on, Yun-pao and her parents enjoyed a peaceful life on her own property.[2]

Women in Communist China not only are protected by legal codes, but also have played different roles during each stage of political development of the Communist Party. It is increasingly clear that women's liberation is closely related to the development of the socialist revolution as implemented by the Party. The pre-1949 history of Chinese Communism shows that top Party leaders highly valued the potential women held for the revolution. Most Chinese, however, held the opposite attitude toward women's liberation. As a result, competent women were often caught between the contradictory expectations of the Party and of society. Married female cadres were chastised by the conservative segment of society for not fulfilling the woman's role at home and became the target of rumors concerning romantic relationships due to their association with men in the Party. Politically uninvolved women were not free from attack either. They were often condemned by the Party for staying at home. To show their devotion to the revolution and to gain greater personal satisfaction in serving the country, some women postponed marriage. The most active and talented female cadres were between 20 and 25 years of age. Those who decided to remain in the political arena after marriage were usually assigned by the Party to the positions related to women's issues and problems.

Although Communist women's voluntary labor to neighborhood associations for community service have given them status and recognition from the Party, their long-term leadership goal remained undeveloped. The female cadres were considered by their parents as nothing more than manual laborers who earned little or no money and made even less an economic contribution to the family or to the country.

Geographical location and working experience were often the factors influencing a Communist woman's advancement in a political career. Urban women had a better chance of entering politics than their counterparts in rural areas. Working rural women were more likely than rural housewives to be given the opportunity to assume political responsibilities.

The Marriage Law which, along with Land Reform, was considered part of the political movement, was adopted by the Central People's Government Council at its 7th meeting on April 13, 1950, and promulgated on May 1, 1950, by the order of the Central People's Government.[3] While the Marriage Law provided women an opportunity to reassess their marital relationship, the ownership of land as a result of the Land Reform law assured them financial independence from their husbands. Granting women land was only a by-product of the three major goals of Land Reform in 1950. First, the Party intended to improve the economic conditions of millions of peasants. Second, they hoped that land distribution would give peasants more incentive to produce crops. Third, they aimed to destroy the wealthy, rural land-owing gentry. With the land allotment from the government and the legal protection of marriage, women were not only self-supporting but also began having equal status in the family. The incompatible victims, both male and female, of arranged marriages were given the option of divorce. Thus, people frequently refer to the Marriage Law as the divorce law. As a result, even women who kept their marriage felt that the government supported their liberation from traditional family roles and encouraged them to enter male-dominated fields such as politics. Following the proclamation of the Marriage Law, a movement was launched during the period 1950-1953 to radically reexamine women's relationships with their spouse and parents-in-law. They were encouraged by the Party to form small groups, attend grievance meetings, use the mass action of the women's organization, and participate in special interest groups from different age brackets to attack the issues of arranged marriages, mistreated wives, inheritance of property, and the right of divorced mothers to child custody. To eliminate remnants of traditional values which regarded chastity or widowhood as a virtue, the Communists in some cases encouraged widows and nuns to marry. Land Reform and its accompanying liquidation struggles against the landlords, however, created difficulties for women from landowning families. They often suffered at the hands of their persecutors and cases of suicide were known to exist.

The Communists were forced to moderate their radical implementation of the Marriage Law in late 1952 because the institution of the family was threatened with possible collapse. After that, the Party took less drastic steps and assumed the role of mediator in coping with women's family problems. During this period, women started testing their political talents with the encouragement of the Party. Unfortunately, a politically favorable atmosphere to women did not last long. The active implementation of the Marriage Law diminished in 1953 with the onset of the First Five Year Plan, which was intended to improve the productivity of the nation. Urban-centered economic development failed to provide women with adequate employment opportunities. Once again, women found that traditional housewife and mother roles dominated their choice. In 1956 only ten percent of the party members were women,[4] although the percentage of women in the total group of cadres increased in the fifties.[5] In 1951, 8% of all cadres were women; by 1955, 14.6% were women.[6] At the same time, their proportional representation declined at the highest level of senior county and provincial administrative positions.[7]

The political situation once again favored women during the Great Leap Forward (1958-1960) which required mass labor participation of men and women in communes, street industry, and industrial management. Women's political activities were enhanced. Stimulated by political learning, many educated urban women were motivated to go to rural areas (hsia-hsiang) to transmit their liberal ideas to peasant women and bring new knowledge to the countryside. The neighborhood factory boom which was promoted by the Party to stimulate economic growth gave numerous women employment in light industry. The government encouraged families to establish small shops in the neighborhood or even in their own homes. Some women did open their own business in their homes or neighborhoods. This work experience helped women make great gains in occupational knowledge and self-confidence. Work and training gradually cured their inferiority complex. Women slowly developed leadership in politics as they advanced in political studies and activities. Some aggressive women started their political career during this period and became recognized later (Croll, 1978).

Fluctuating political and economic policies disturbed men as well as women in China. Self-study of Marxist theories did not always guarantee a rise in women's political status; instead their chances for political advancement often depended on Party decisions on social change. On the eve of the Socialist Education Campaign (1962-1966), because of economic retrenchment and the scarcity of job opportunities, Chinese women again lost political ground and were discouraged from participating in the labor force. The Party emphasized women's role in reproduction and household economy (Young, 1973). It preached respect for the aged and re-strengthening of kinship ties (Chin, 1970). Once again, most female cadres (70%) were young, below 25 years of age, and tended to drop out from politics after they married.[7] Fewer women were active in politics, even at the bottom of the political hierarchy. It was estimated that 5-10% of the lower jobs in communes were held by women during the early 1960s.[9] In Kwangtung Province, 25% of the cadres on the production team (the basic rural unit) were women.[10] Cadres in urban areas had a better chance of being involved in political affairs. In Peking over 30% of the cadres were women in 1963.[11] Because of their greater experience, urban women usually enjoyed advantages over rural women in politics. The behavior and social activity of women in cities were more acceptable to their peers and in-laws than those of women in the country where old traditions were still observed. Urban women also had help with their housekeeping. They had the advantage of some social services, such as childcare, and canteen and mending shops, and the assistance of their husbands around the house. Apartment type housing and various residents' committees provided women with the chance to work and compete with men on a more equal basis. Full-time housewives had the opportunity to be active on fire prevention and street sanitation committees, and in political study groups, literacy classes, and day-care. Nevertheless, political leadership in industrial cities remained sexually imbalanced.

In China, all the managerial positions in industry are filled by political appointees. Only 8 to 15% of the middle and top level positions in light industry were held by women.[12] Women's slow political advance during this period can also be attributed to several reasons related to traditional thinking. First, heavy housework and traditional family responsibilities have prevented women from going to political meetings or classes, and usually the husband automatically represented the family at political gatherings (Myrdal and Kessel, 1970). Moreover, in-laws and parents still tend to discourage their girls from having contact with men other than family members in order to avoid rumors about their moral and sexual conduct. Finally, high-ranking Party members were still skeptical about women's abilities and hesitated to recruit and train young women.[13] The conservative years were followed by a radical period. The Cultural Revolution (1966-1969) aimed to invigoriate the socialist consciousness of all citizens regardless of sex, age, or occupation. Women, once again considered a deprived group, were encouraged to be vocal, active in politics, and in criticizing family members for their "wrong-doings." Depending on the area, 10 to 16.4% of the revolutionary committees were composed of women.[14] These could be called "token appointments," since many women were still burdened with household chores. They had to adjust their family life to the realization of political ambition, by reducing family size and childcare arrangements among others.

Overall, Chinese women have been given less substantial political power than men. The former have acquired more power at the local level through hard work while the latter exerted more influence at central or higher levels of the political hierarchy (Mandel, 1975). Fortunately, things have been changing for the better in the 1970s. Since then active female cadres have often been seen holding a leading post at the communes, brigades and in the militia organizations, the Communist Party and Communist Youth League branches. Volunteer cadres became paid personnel in the early 1970s. The New China News Agency reported that in one district in Peking, 95% of the leaders of the residents' committee were women.[15] At higher levels of political hierarchy more female figures are also found today. Of the Congressional representatives, 21% are women.[16]

The Ministry of Trade, newly formed by combining four former ministries, is headed by Ch'en Mu-hua, who was the former vice premier responsible for family planning.[17] The vice chairman of the Standing Committee of the National People's Congress of China, Teng Ying-ch'ao, is a woman.[18] The former Minister of Water Conservancy, Ch'ien Tseng-ying, was recently appointed as the new Minister of Water Conservancy and Electricity (or Electric Power).[19] Female deputy ministers in clothing and textile education and other governmental branches also appeared in the past decade.

However, discrepancy still exists between theory and practice, ideology and reality; women are still facing a great deal of challenges and struggling for total equality. One of the major obstacles is in the training of leadership. Female cadres well-trained enough to assume the responsibilities in the Party and the Communist Youth League have been in great demand. In 1973, a case study demonstrated that female cadres could be trained by fighting against more precise hardships and obstacles, by being called to speak first in meetings, by studying Marxism-Leninism seriously, and by raising their understanding of Marxism-Leninism through practical work (Croll, 1978). After many years of struggle, delegates to the Tientsin's Sixth Congress of Women held June 27 to July 1, 1973, were not satisfied with their accomplishments in the political process. In her report Comrade Wang Man-tien, Secretary of the Community Party of Chinese Tientsin Municipal Committee stressed:[20]

> Party organizations at all levels should strengthen their leadership over work regarding women, be concerned about the vital problems of women and solve them, and oppose exploiting-class ideas of esteeming and respecting men while considering women inferior and discriminating against them.

A resolution adopted by the Congress points out:[21]

> Women should regard love, marriage, family, and the education of children from the proletarian point of view; late marriage and family planning should be encouraged, husbands and wives

> should be encouraged to share household chores,
> and work to protect the health of mothers and
> children should be strengthened so that women
> can take a better part in political activities, in
> production, and other work, and in study....

This resolution, which addresses the issue of female labor, women's education, women's welfare, and women's role in the family, reflects the fundamental ideology behind the women's movement in China.

Organizing women to form a mass force for liberation tied in closely with Party policy. The women's movement in Communist China was encouraged and strengthened by the late Chairman Mao's adage that women support half the sky. After the Communist Party took over Mainland China, the women's movement continued to retain its own independent organization. The All-Chinese Democratic Women's Federation (ACDWF) was founded in Peking on April 3, 1949. It was later renamed National Women's Federation (NWF) and has further developed its goals and interests throughout the post-revolutionary period. It aims to unite all women of different classes and occupations, raise their levels of socialist understanding and vocational skills and protect the newly-won rights of women in all respects. "In general, it strives to bring about the complete emancipation of women and to rally all peace-loving women the world over in defense of peace."[22] The NWF is composed of a number of affiliated groups at different administrative levels, paralleling the Communist Party's village, county, city, municipality, province, and national organization. In the course of the development of the women's movement, Party committees have worked closely with NWF at various corresponding levels. Now the name of NWF is All-China Women's Federation.

The setback in the training of female leaders during the Cultural Revolution led to a shortage of qualified young female leaders, a loss of direction for women's emancipation, and the inadequate planning for goal-oriented activities by the Party. During this period the women's federation, like youth league branches and trade unions, stopped functioning while most factories, communes and government agencies remained semi-paralyzed.[23] In an interview, Teng Ying-ch'ao, Vice Chairman of the Standing Committee of the National

People's Congress of China and Honorary President of the All-China Women's Federation, pointed out:[24]

> The women's liberation movement in China has always been part of the revolutionary movement of the Chinese people. Since the founding of New China, the women's movement has been closely linked with the socialist construction of the country. The government regards women, who make up half of the population, as an important force in revolution and construction.

The present goal of this organization was indicated by Teng Ying-ch'ao in the same interview:

> The central task of the women's movement today is to mobilize and organize women throughout the country in China's socialist modernization drive, and at the same time, in further developing their own capabilities and for equal rights in this great cause.

She concurred with the comments which Mme. Soong Ching Lin made more than a decade earlier.[25] They both agreed that Chinese women's liberation from traditional thinking and practice had a long way to go. Mme. Soong was the widow of Dr. Sun Yet-Sen, founding father of the Republic of China. She devoted her life to Chinese women's emancipation and was highly respected by the Party, once serving as Vice Chairman of the Communist Party. After her death in 1981, she was named Honorary President of the People's Republic of China.

B. Women in the Labor Force

One of the major objectives of the Communist Revolution was to mobilize the entire population, both men and women, in the economic reconstruction of the nation. In addition, women's direct participation in the labor force was believed to be the only road to equality (Mao, 1964). They would develop a positive self-image through learning vocational skills, and they would establish financial security as wage earners. These two elements would enable them to function independently, unconfined by traditional roles.

However, since 1949, Chinese women's employment opportunities have fluctuated with the Party's changing economic policies (Sidel, 1972). The role played by women in the work force was closely linked to the economic conditions. When the economy was slow, jobs held by women were the first to be eliminated. Between 1949 and 1957, female workers in the total labor force rose from 7.5% to an average of 15%, or between 13% and 18%, depending upon the region. In nonagricultural labor, the percentage of working women increased from 14% to 20%.[26]

Prior to the mid-1950s, and following the Land Reform and Marriage Law, the Party insured equality between men and women (Johnson, 1976). The land redistribution on a collective basis granted women the right to own property and to cultivate the land they received. The implementation of collective economic policy in rural areas enabled women to work outside the home as wage earners. Working at collective production and providing of social services, women earned extra income by doing the same tasks which they had performed for years at home. Their status in the family was raised as they contributed to family finance. Actually, it was not a novel idea for women to work in a commune for wages. As early as the 1920s during the May Fourth Movement, a renowned writer, Liu Pan-nung, advocated this type of society to free women from domestic chores for outside employment.[27] In a collective community, as promoted by the government, daily household chores, such as laundry, mending, cooking, and childcare, were accomplished by a collective force which was organized by a small group of community residents, both men and women. Consequently, other women in the community were freed from these chores and were able to work in factories for extra income. Meanwhile, the people, mostly women, working for the collective organization or shop(s) were also paid for their contribution. Yet, the family unit was threatened by losing its basic function as a place for meals, childcare, and personal interaction.

During the mid-1950s, women were discouraged from employment because of economic and organizational problems government policy encountered in both urban and rural areas. The government concentrated on the development of intensive heavy industry by using the available capital. One result was the flow of male migrants from rural areas to the cities. Since women could not compete with men in physical strength they made little employment gains during this period. In fact, it was found that non-agricultural employment did not increase at all for both male and female during 1953-1957.[28] Owing to strong job competition between men and women during this period of industrial collectivation, women were found holding unskilled, low-paying jobs and were at times even driven completely out of the job market.

The growing unemployment rate among women during the 1957 and early 1958 meant many women were compelled to return home and be a good "socialist family woman." Party policy adapted to the change. A full-time housewife was considered "productive social labor" at home. Women's role in the family once again was confined to submission to in-laws and obedience to husbands. The *wu-hao*, or "five good" program, became a national campaign. Women were told to (1) arrange their homes in a proper way; (2) help and unite with neighbors; (3) encourage their husbands to work hard and study diligently; (4) educate their children in the proper way; and, (5) study hard themselves (Chi, 1967). Especially in the rural areas, women were heavily burdened by domestic work, which included producing goods for consumption by the family. Thus they were inhibited from participating in the rural economy as wage earners.

When street industry was developed in response to the Great Leap Forward (GLF) in 1958-1959, neighborhoods consisting of several families were encouraged to start small factories, producing such things as bicycle parts, in their homes. Its location greatly facilitated women's involvement in this type of work. As a result of this experience, there was a 14% increase in female laborers in industry between 1958 and 1959.[29] However the percentage of non-agricultural labor force women remained the same: approximately 18%.[30] In rurual areas, several hundred million women were involved in commune-run industries, water conservancy, afforestation and construction projects (Diamond, 1975). Collectivized household tasks, which were carried out by paid female workers in both urbal and rural areas, alleviated many working women's household chores. Commune nurseries, dining halls, sewing and laundry stations, processed food centers and other social services hired 12 million female workers, turning them from unpaid household workers into wage earners in collective communes. The advantageous employment climate that had existed in the early 1950s returned.

The ambitious GLF, relying on mass mobilization, communes and indigenous methods, eventually failed, largely due to poor administration and policy implementation, aggravated by bad weather. Declining industrial investment in small neighborhood factories and bad harvests in the country returned the job market back to male workers. When many nurseries, mess halls, and other services were scaled down or abolished, large numbers of women lost their jobs (Johnson, 1976). Even some male workers were forced to return to agriculture and handicrafts. The setback after GLF not only affected the employment of female workers, it also meant the return of an old direction in women's lives. Many articles published by women's magazines and leading newspapers emphasized that women's place was again to be found at home. Women again resumed the full-time household duties they held before the GLF. When the government failed to reconcile the discrepancy between the ideology of sexual equality and the reality of the traditional family role played by socialist women, economic circumstance was not blamed by the government as the factor contributing to the insignificant improvement of women's employment (Johnson, 1976).

During the Cultural Revolution of the mid-1960s, which emphasized a return to the fundamental Communist ideas of mobilizing the general population, women were better trained and often became semi-skilled, non-agricultural employees. Barefoot doctors, veteranarians, and agro-technicians were the most popular occupations among working women. Because of holding these relatively "high status" positions, women were less discriminated against. While communes, production teams, brigades, and factories visited by foreigners or overseas Chinese had a much higher percentage of female workers (between 50% and 75%), most Chinese women did not do so well. Nevertheless, in many areas, more than one quarter of the agro-technical positions on production teams, the basic rural unit, were young women.[31]

With the new economic policy and the four modernizations launched by the government after the downfall of the radical "gang of four," women's employment continued to be supported by the government. The reopening and expansion of nurseries and kindergartens in the late 1970s enabled women to devote time and energy to their jobs instead of being worried about childcare problems. In some places women count for 46% to 80% of the commune's total labor force.[32] Based on Kessen's visits in China, there were 90% of the women under the age of 45 in the labor force.[33] At the same time, the female worker's committee in factories assumed an active role in attacking the problems encountered by employed women.[34] It demanded fee reduction at nurseries and regular gynecologic check-ups, took care of sick family members, mediated family quarrels or disputes between colleagues, tackled housing problems, and solved individual emotional problems. With the counseling provided by local party officers, family problems involving employed mothers were often resolved.

Theoretically speaking, women in Mainland China were given the opportunity to perform any type of task that suited them. In practice, since the government assigned jobs primarily according to training and background, women were frequently restricted to light industry, such as textile factories, while men were placed in heavy industry, such as steel mills. Today, a request for a job change will be granted for what the authorities consider legitimate reasons. Certain types of jobs are still sexually specified. For instance, workers in nurseries and teachers in kindergarten are strictly female while petrochemical workers in remote areas are predominantly male.

"Equal pay for equal work" has been a cry since the mass participation of Chinese women began. Wage disparities do exist, especially in communes (Weitz, 1977), where the system of basing pay on working points was introduced in the early 1950s. Women earned less than men because they accumulated fewer working points. These work points were based on the individual's strength, skill, training, and experience, and they affected women unfairly. The semi-skilled or skilled jobs accomplished by women did not accrue as many work points or units as the jobs done by men. Because of their physical strength and/or better education, men were able to hold jobs requiring hard manual labor or professional abilities and earn more work points for higher wages. Once such inequality was gradually eliminated by the Commune Movement in the late 1950s, female laborers had greater representation in communes and were given more opportunities to be wage earners. However, the policy of equal pay for women has never been truly implemented with fair evaluation by local commune officers. It was pointed out in *Front Line* in 1964, that the contributing factor of unequal pay for equal work was the cadre's thinking which revealed his feudal thought about women.[35] In her visit to China, Sidel (1972) found that women generally earned less than men, because equal pay for equal work alone does not insure equal income for both men and women.[36] The type of job also determines the wage. Unless both sexes are entitled to the same job choice and employment opportunities which require education and training, equal pay for equal work is merely one of the steps toward the ultimate goal of job equality in wage and promotion. During the author's visit to China in 1982, she found that "equal pay for equal work" is well implemented in large cities and the interviewed women were proud of being able to earn a higher salary than their spouse.

Following the Cultural Revolution, formal education for women has broadened. Chinese women have been found trained as doctors, engineers, masons, airplane pilots, policewomen, welders, oil-well operators, vegetable growers, and fruit pickers—all of which were traditionally filled by men (Sidel, 1972). After all, these jobs occupy only a small fraction of the female population. Most women are still segregated in sex-stereotyped jobs.[37] Workers in childcare centers and primary-level teachers are predominately women. Medicine, pediatrics, obstetrics/gynecology, and psychiatry, attract more women than other specialties (Weitz, 1977).

Despite the government's constantly changing economic policies, however, the number of working women has grown rapidly since 1949. Nevertheless, men still dominate the top levels of all occupations. Several factors contribute to this discriminatory hiring practice (Johnson, 1978). First, society holds that women should stay at home, except for the few occupations which are considered appropriate for them to engage in outside the home. The notion shared by factory managers that women are less efficient workers mirrors the general public's attitude toward women's abilities and prevents women from obtaining jobs. Furthermore, it costs more to hire female workers who need to take maternity leaves, requires childcare facilities, and presents more sex-related physical problems. Finally, surplus unemployed male laborers constantly compete with women for scarce jobs.

Undoubtedly family responsibilities, particularly childcare, are the most obvious obstacles to women's employment.[38] During the Great Leap Forward, the people's communes were found to be an excellent form of organization leading to the complete emancipation of women.[39] As a result of the Communist Party's general line for building socialism and political and economic reconstruction, communes demanded women's total participation in collective production. Nevertheless, despite women's widening involvement in social, economic, and political activities outside of the home, they were still confronted by the challenge of bearing traditional family responsibilities, housekeeping, and child-rearing. Only about 30% of women worked in neighborhood factories and to them childcare was not a problem.[40] A working mother could send her child to local creches or a kindergarten run either by the local collective-owned factories or by the state 56 days after the birth of the child until the child was ready for primary school. However, the qualifications of child caretakers were questionable. Of the 20 nation-wide schools for training kindergarten teachers, 19 were closed during the Cultural Revolution in 1966 and had not been reopened by 1971, severely damaging China's childcare system.[41] During the early 1970s, untrained childcare staffs were usually accepted as long as they were patient, warm, concerned, and had a minimal knowledge of hygine.[42]

Recently, because the goal of four modernizations requires more womanpower, the problem of childcare has attracted attention from both the government and community groups. To restore the childcare system after the destruction of the Cultural Revolution, all 19 kindergarten teacher-training schools that had been closed were reopened during 1978-1980, and eight new ones have been established to meet the increasing need.[43] A national conference on childcare work was convened in August 1979, under the joint sponsorship of the Ministry of Education, the Ministry of Public Health, the State Bureau of Labor, and the All-China Women's Federation. Following the conference, an agency with special responsibility for childcare was established under the State Council with the former Vice-Premier Ch'en Mu-hua in charge. Branches with similar structure have been set up in almost every province, municipality, and autonomous region. Quite a number of provinces and municipalities have made plans to restore the old nurseries and kindergartens and open new ones.

Neighborhood committees and female worker's committees in factories have also embarked on an effort to establish more well-equipped regular nurseries and kindergartens for employed women and more busy-season childcare programs in the countryside. An article in the March 1980 issue of *Women of China* revealed that childcare facilities used to serve only a limited number of "privileged" people.[44] With their expansion after 1978, they have become more accessible to the general population—and were even free to parents who commit themselves to having only one child.[45] School holidays, however, remain a perennial problem for working couples. Some plants run a supervised activities center for youngsters during the summer which organizes sports and provides books and the use of recreational equipment.[46] Owing to the distance between work and home, many working parents are unable to return home for lunch and do not arrive home until well after their children get out of school. As a result, their children run on the streets and cause destruction in the neighborhood. A program, organized by local community people in the Haining neighborhood, Hongkou District, Shanghai, proved very successful in keeping latch-key kids off the streets.[47] In many districts, well managed childcare systems could be found to alleviate women's anxiety over their children's safety and welfare when they are on a business trip. With trust and confidence in childtakers and kindergarten teachers, employed mothers are able to concentrate on their job.[48]

In order to live up to society's expectation of playing various kinds of roles, women's biological limitations and physical strengths have been taken into consideration by the government. Beginning in the early 1960s, the circumstances of female workers during the "four periods" drew the attention of both male and female team leaders. During these "four periods"—menstruation, pregnancy, childbirth, and breastfeeding—a rational work arrangement was needed to protect women's health. As Croll writes:[49]

> In order to give successful protection during the menstrual period, the chief thing to do is to exempt women from heavy work and from work carried out in icy water or deep water. . . . It is stipulated that during the period of menstruation, pregnancy or breastfeeding, the female commune members can be assigned only "to a place nearby but not far away, to the dry field . . . and to lighter work. . . ."
> When a woman gives birth to a child, the chief form of protection that can be given is to give her the necessary rest and proper nourishment. The lying-in women in the countryside can generally rest from 30 to 56 days. In accordance with the production and economic conditions of the different production brigades, they are given a commensurate number of work points as subsidy, so that they can feel at ease when taking rest.

Women on maternity leave are allowed 70% of their salary for one year. Full pay was extended recently from 56 days to 3 months, then to 100 days. A child is usually weaned at about one year. During the breastfeeding period, the working mother is allowed to nurse the baby twice every eight hour shift. A full-time nursery is also available to mothers who want to leave their children for Saturday or Sunday night, but considered expensive by most women (Croll, 1976).

From observations or interviews it is found that most Chinese women share the daily housework with their husbands. But household chores are not always divided equally in every family. Many working mothers work hard to live up to the dual role of employment and housekeeping. Nevertheless, working women are no longer criticized by society for leaving their children and husbands in their home town and working in a separate city or even a separate province. As long as they can contribute to the nation, working women as men are praised for their personal sacrifice for the Party.

C. Educational Opportunities

A lack of education and leadership training for career advancement seems the major handicap in promoting women's status in China. Even today, proportionately more boys than girls attend school (Mandell, 1975; and, Townsend, 1979). The discriminatory attitude about training women is attributed to the common opinion shared by people that education for girls is a waste as they will merely become wives and mothers. In 1934, only 15% of the students in institutions of higher education were women. The most popular field for women was education, followed by liberal arts, science, and health. By 1946, 28% were studying to enter the health professions.[50] Among nine counties in Szechwan Province during 1942 and 1943, 52% of the men and 81% of the women were illiterate.[51] In addition to being denied an education, women were discouraged from developing any skills outside the home. After the promulgation of the Marriage Law in 1950, the Communist government placed special emphasis on the literacy of the vast female population. Literacy classes were organized in rural as well as urban areas (Sidel, 1972). It is difficult to say, however, how successful the campaign was. Available statistics do not allow an accurate estimation.

Basically there are three different models of formal educational systems identified with each political period: Pre-Cultural Revolution, Post Cultural Revolution, and Post-Mao Period. All models consisted of three levels of education: primary, secondary, and higher.

The Pre-Cultural Revolution model is very similar to the education system in the U.S.: with six, six, and four years for each respective level. This model emerged gradually during the years between 1949 and 1965. Because it emphasized training of technical specialists, with middle school and college enrollment growing at a faster rate than primary school students, it was attacked vigorously during the Cultural Revolution for not adequately addressing the needs of Chinese society. By 1960, roughly 10% of the primary students went on to the middle school, and one out of ten middle school graduates went to college (Townsend, 1979). The number of college students declined thereafter and all schools were shut down during the Cultural Revolution.

The Post-Cultural Revolution model reduced the length of formal education. In general, primary schools were re-opened first after the Cultural Revolution and universities were last. The rapid expansion of primary and secondary education alongside a reduced number of university slots made college entrance difficult (Townsend, 1979) and led to some unreasonable entrance requirement, one of which was the political background of the applicant's family going back three generations[52] and only about one percent of secondary enrollments. Consequently, the quality of those accepted college students was poor. Another characteristic of the educational system in Mainland China during this period was that education became more or less localized which permitted the years of school to vary upon local conditions, such as the demand in the job market and the availability of school facilities. Primary school had four to six years, secondary had four to five years, and college education lasted two to three years. No single pattern of schooling was adopted nationwide. Academic standards, research, and examinations were downgraded while an emphasis was placed on political criteria and practical study. Two to three years of participation in the physical labor force was required for admission to college.

The Post-Mao model began after the death of Mao in 1976. With the purge of the "gang of four" in October, 1976, the educational system has improved and an academic orientation, examinations, and scholastic criteria have been restored.[53] However, the length of formal education remains five-five-two (or three) years for each level. Today, the government has shown its desire to strengthen both the enrollments and quality of higher education, with particular emphasis on training scientists and technicians and encouraging research. Higher education concentrating on training engineers, teachers, and medical personnel, provides a distinct contrast with the years between 1928 and 1932 when there was much more interest in political science, law, literature, and the arts.[54] Since most universities were shut down during the Cultural Revolution, many young college-age people missed the opportunity for higher education. Thus, very few people now between the ages of thirty and forty have a college education and are qualified for advanced learning. To remedy such a shortage of human resources, the government has extended the age for college entrance from 25 to 30 years of age. The college entrance examination is held at 200 locations in July each year. Besides good test scores, the criteria for college admission also includes the applicants' previous schooling, good health, and all-around standards consisting of political, intellectual, and physical appraisal by their superiors.

Regardless of the changes in the educational model, Chinese women still have less educational opportunity than men do. Legally speaking, girls have the same chances as boys for an education—but in actuality, fewer women than men are educated. Orleans (1972) estimated that in 1970, 41% of the population completing six years of primary education were girls, 27% of the high school graduates were girls, and 29% of those who completed at least two years of college were women.[55] When Nanking University reopened after the Cultural Revolution in 1972, only 27% of the enrolled freshmen were women.[56]

In addition to the above-mentioned regular education, there are three other less formal types of education. First, local groups in various parts of the nation often run preschool programs. Second, a large scale vocational program allows students to study half-time and work half-time to gain technical or compensatory experience. Third, participation in study groups, political classes, and other on-the-job training teaches students about work, society, and politics. Besides these opportunities, women often learn from team leaders how to improve their work skills and how to raise their socialist consciousness through meetings and activities. Informal education and working experiences are most important and practical for female cadres who seek political advancement.

In the area of sports, girls, like boys, are encouraged to participate in all kinds of sports. The Chinese Women's Volleyball Team won the Asian zone Preliminaries of the World Cup Volleyball Championships held in Hong Kong in 1981. The Women's Table-Tennis Team was also the winner

Above: Tong Ling, winner of the women's singles at the 36th World Table Tennis Championships.

of the 36th World Table-Tennis Championships held at Novisad, Yugoslavia, in April, 1981. The mass media often portrays individual winners in chess, gymnastics, swimming and riflery. For example, the victory of Shih Mei-chin over both the Soviet and the U.S. champions at the Martini International Diving Competition held in London in November, 1980, was widely publicized.

D. *Women's Family Life*

As the political scene changes, Chinese family life en-
counters the same revolutionary challenge. The Marriage
Law promulgated in May, 1950, prescribes new intra-family
relations. It distributes family responsibilities and privileges
evenly. Women's status in the family has been promoted as
a result of their rights being insured by this law. "Overall
the aim is not to abolish the family, but to change its structure and reduce its central position in society by removing
certain of the family's former social and economic functions."[57] Since the implementation of this law thirty years
ago, Chinese women have also been gradually shaking off the
fetters of the feudal marital and family system and encount-
ering a new morality as a result of today's recent political
changes. Therefore, a revised "Marriage Law of the People's
Republic of China" was introduced to the Third Session of
China's Fifth National People's Congress in September, 1980,
and came into force on January 1, 1981. For example, the
revised law changes the minimum marriage age from 20 to 22
for men, and from 18 to 20 for women, and encourages
marriage and child-bearing to actually exceed these age
requirements. Another interesting revision is that the husband can become a member of the wife's family which was
peviously prohibited by law. Now this law stipulates that
with the agreement of both parties, either the husband or
the wife could become a member of either spouse's family
and both parties should undertake an equal obligation to
support their elders and share equal rights to inherit
property.[58]

The extended family no longer exists. The birth control policy imposed by the government is the first, although
not necessarily the most important reason for the elimination
of the extended family. The size of the family has been
shrinking during the past two decades. Second, family relationships based on the six kinship relations have been diluted
by the relocation of family members and the ideological
requirement that each individual serve the nation. The six
kinship relations are between (1) husband and wife; (2) hus-
bnd and children; (3) brothers; (4) the children of brothers;
(5) the brothers' grandchildren; and, (6) the brothers' great

great grandchildren. The first four of these kinship relations determined the size of the extended family; the last two enlarged it to a clan. Villages named after certain families disappeared because of the reorganization of the residential composition and implementation of new social structure. The central government introduced a political hierarchy at all levels from lane to province and administered it closely through the Communist Party. Social, economic, and political construction were to be the top priority in every individual's life. To reconstruct the nation, the Party required numerous people to leave towns where they had long resided near relatives and friends, for remote areas. Family members were scattered according to the government assignment. Only the nuclear family had much of a chance of remaining intact.

Because of the increasing number of smaller families and government's enforcement of the Marriage Law, relationships among family members have changed greatly since the revolution. Nowadays, the average family size is about five and consists of married couples, their offspring, and their parents or in-laws.[59] With the drastically diminishing authority of mothers-in-law, a young wife has more power in decision making, particularly if, as is very common, she works. The historical resentment and bitterness between the daughter-in-law and the mother-in-law are vanishing. The daughter-in-law is no longer the target of the mother-in-law's anger against traditional suppression. A woman's role in the family is no more specifically to serve and please her in-laws. Instead it is geared to her husband and her children. As a result, the marital relationship between husband and wife in a small family becomes more intimate than in the large family headed by the oldest family member, either grandfather or grandmother. Parents and chldren are also closer than in an extended family, where more siblings and other cousins lived under one roof.

Urbanization has discouraged some older peasants from living with their married children in the cities, because, most likely, they prefer to stay in the more familiar environment where they were born and raised. Hence many urban families do not have the company of the older generation. However, the government requires that the older generation, especially if they have no retirement benefits, be taken care of by their grown married children. If a married child refuses to support his or her parents, he or she will face court charges. The case of Chu Ai-feng reflects how this law protects old people.[60] Chu Ai-feng had lived in Shanghai with her foster son, Chu Chiang-yuan, and his family for many years. One day in 1975, the young couple and their two children moved to the home of the wife's parents in Nanhsi in another part of the city, leaving the old lady alone and destitute. This move was the result of long drawn-out conflicts between the old woman and the young couple. After the family dispute was amicably settled by the court, Chu Ai-feng regained her foster son's care and support.

Grandparents have played a vital role in the labor force since the Great Leap Forward. When childcare facilities are not available to working parents, aged parents or in-laws often take care of the preschool grandchildren. In many instances, senior citizens were found tending young children while working in the field (Kessen, 1975). By taking care of children, the elderly do not have to live separately or to rely on social welfare, which is minimal.

Due to the mandatory birth control policy, the sex of a child no longer concerns grandparents and parents, who, after their retirement, can be taken care of by either sons or daughters. That parents are less reluctant to live with married daughters and sons-in-law and the fact that husbands are willing to move in with their wive's families further facilitates the diminuation of traditional tension between mother and daughter-in-law.[61]

The shrinking size of households is the result of not only the relocation of clan members and the redistribution of population, but also the government's population control policy. The Communist Party has recognized since the 1940s that the rapid growth of population in China is a social, political, and economic problem. In order to reduce the birth rate, several official measures have been taken since that time. First, late marriage has been encouraged in both rural and urban areas. When Kessen was visiting China (1975), the average marriagable age for females was about 23, for the males it was 25. In the cities the minimum ages for marriage were about 25 for females and 28 for males. Recently, due to young people's increasing knowledge of contraceptives and willingness to use them, the regulation for late marriage has been relaxed. Second, the government has tried to restrict the number of children. Prior to the mid-1970s, two children several years apart was considered most ideal. But, during the past few years, in order to achieve zero-population growth by the end of this century, a new government policy encouraged one child per family.[62] A preview of the zero-population-growth plan was contained in an article published August 11, 1979, in the *Official People's Daily* written by former Vice Premier Ch'en Mu-hua, Director of the States Council Birth Planning Leading Group. She spelled out three reasons for launching this project. A growing population (1) is detrimental to the acceleration of capital accumulation, (2) hinders efforts to raise quickly the scientific and cultural level of the nation, and (3) is necessary to improve the people's standard of living. Nevertheless, the number of children per family and the implementation of the plan vary according to geographical location. To effectively enforce Party policy, the government has used food coupons and cash rewards to crack the traditional value system which stresses the multiplication of offspring and sons' inheritance of the family name. Since having no son has been considered one of the three kinds of unfilial behavior, many people have had difficulty complying with governmental policy. Food rationing is the most effective way to destroy such thinking. The second child, regardless of sex, does not receive food coupons. Illegitimate births are usually avoided by either marriage or abortion. In addition, the salary of both parents will be proportionately reduced if more than two children are born. Cash rewards to families that agree to have only one child and extra pension payments for those retired couples who raise only one child of either sex also motivate people's cooperation in this effort.[63]

The government makes various birth control measures available but only after marriage. The most popular contraceptive is the condom. Next is oral contraceptive. Tubal ligation is more prevalent than vasectomy, which implies that women play a more important role in sterilization than men (Mandel, 1975; and, Croll, 1978). The government first launched the movement for family planning in the late 1950s and emphasized it in the 1960s. The Chinese government stated in its National Program for Agricultural Development (1956-1967) that, other than in areas inhabited by minority peoples, birth control should be publicized and popularized and family planning advocated in all densely populated areas.[64] Public health workers and female cadres penetrated all regions to advocate the importance of population control and the methods available for contraception. In the meantime, people were taught about the human reproduction system to clear up a great deal of misconception about sexual organs and their behavior. The following table (Table 7) by Sidel (1972) shows the results of family planning in Hangchow:

Table 7*
Family Planning Chart
Silvery Lane Health Station, Hangchow

Methods Used	Number	Percent
Total number of married women	369	100%
Permanently sterilized	99	27%
Vasectomies	10	3%
Tubal ligations	89	24%
Total using contraceptives	172	46%
Oral contraceptives	65	17%
Condom	69	19%
IUCD	22	6%
Rhythm	7	2%
Other	9	2%
Not using contraceptives	88	24%
Husband outside the city	21	6%
"Has not been pregnant"	6	2%
Breast feeding	16	4%
Newly married	7	2%
Chronically ill	13	3%
Other	25	7%
Abortions	0	0%
Pregnant	10	3%

During the last few years, the population growth in

*Source: Ruth Sidel, *Women and child care in China: a firsthand report* (Baltimore: Penguin, 1972), p. 53.

many places slowed. In Peking, Shanghai, Tientsin, Szechwan, Hupeh, Chekiang, Shansi, Shensi, Shantung, Kansu, and Hopei, the growth rate figure has fallen to less than ten births per thousand population. In Szechwan, China's most populous province, it dropped from 29 per thousand in 1971 to 6.1 per thousand in 1978, and in Shanghai, from 7 per thousand to 5.1 per thousand. The national population growth rate is expected to come down to about 5 per thousand by 1985.[65]

In a sense, women benefit from the Party effort for population control. In his report on the work of the government delivered in 1978 at the First Plenary Session of the Fifth National People's Congress, one of the reasons the former Premier Hua Kuo-feng gave for population control was the health of the mother and child.[66] It was not unsual for a woman to have seven or eight girls followed by a son or sons who pass on the family name and use it to entitle them to numerous prerogatives which daughters could not claim. Under tremendous social and family pressure, many women would have one pregnancy after another until giving birth to a baby boy. Such an attitude contributed to a rapid population growth and stripped women of freedom of choice in childbirth. Constant pregnancy often damaged her health or even endangered her life. Forced birth control procedures imposed by the government have given women a free choice in childbirth. The policy that termination of an unwanted pregnancy could be decided by the woman has shown women's changing status in the Chinese family. With the facilities provided by the government, women can easily have an abortion performed without any charge in a local public health clinic. Indeed, all contraceptives and related services are free to women.

The above-mentioned drastic measures for population control parallel another change in the format of dating and marriage. As discussed in earlier chapters, marriage in China used to be considered a lifetime agreement and commitment between two families rather than two individuals. Courtship was a novel idea to many young couples when it was first introduced and practiced in the early 1900s. Following the May Fourth Movement during the late 1920s, young people loudly demanded an end to the traditional matched marriage and called for the freedom of choice for love and marriage. Happy marriages, however, were not guaranteed to these vocal young lovers, and some matched marriages do survive.

Presently, in a society where young men and women feel free to express their affection for each other, matched marriages coexist with freedom of choice of marital partners. In the public places of large cities, display of affection is common among dating couples who no longer feel uneasy holding hands in public. The rigid moral codes for young lovers imposed by the Party have also been relaxed. Communists are not prohibited from dating non-Communists. The Tientsin *Daily News* published pamphlets of tips on dating in addition to its regular classified columns where readers could advertise for a prospective spouse. The government has made some effort to serve as an "official matchmaker," setting up matchmaking centers in large cities. The application includes a $1.35 fee, a 2"x2" photograph, and a written discription of the mate of the applicant's dream. However, the centers found out that both male and female applicants were very picky.[67] Only a small percentage of applicants have been successfully matched.

Fathers or male heads of some families, however, still hold traditional ideas about marriage.[80] Daughters are considered a commodity requiring a large sum of money for betrothal gifts from the bridegroom's family. The centuries-old tradition which gives the senior member of the family a great voice in matrimonial affairs continues to exert itself in many ways despite the unremitting legislative and public efforts over the last three decades to eliminate patriarchal intervention in marriage. The following case is not an isolated instance.[69] Tao Mei-chi's experience shows that in China, older ideas affecting women's freedom of choice in marriage die hard. Tao Mei-chi, a member of Tong Feng Hung People's Commune in Chekiang Province, overcame many obstacles to her second marriage to the man of her choice. Her first husband died shortly after she became pregnant. Because of her condition, a member of her production brigade started coming over to help her. Soon they fell in love with each other. Unfortunately, her older brother was so eager to obtain some betrothal gifts from a man in a neighboring county that he arranged her second marriage behind her back. She resisted the arrangement, but her brother and the suitor overrode her objections. When help from her co-workers in the production brigade failed, she appealed to the local government and the women's federation. With powerful backing from the social forces organized by the two groups, she was finally able to marry the man of her choice.

After the Communist Party's accession in 1949, marital rites were kept very simple. Official registration and approval were required prior to the announcement of the husband-wife relationship because local party officers first had to conduct an investigation of both parties. On the wedding day, both bride and groom donned their best attire, most likely brand new jacket and trousers for the male, and tunic and trousers for the female. No big feast was given by the newlyweds or their parents. Instead, sweets or pastries were passed around to relatives, close friends, and co-workers.[70]

Things have changed a great deal since the normalization of relations with the United States, including the wedding protocal and expense.[71] The complicated old traditional ceremony, designed to ensure good fortune to those involved, cost both the bride's and groom's families a good deal of capital. Amid the confusion which began in 1966, the old wedding customs began to return and extravagant wedding ceremonies welcomed. Many marriages again began to resemble business deals.[72] Dowries commonly contained wardrobe, desk, clock, and bedding—often provided by the bride's parents. In return, the bride's family requested betrothal presents. Items, such as television sets, sewing machines, cameras, and furniture are the most popular dowry items after the fall of the "gang of four". Because people nowadays like material possessions and festive elegance, weddings have become extravagant.[73] The expenses of the matchmaker, an introductory meal for the bride-to-be, cash gifts to the bride's parents, and setting up a nest with the above-mentioned furniture—all these add to the rising cost of weddings. On the wedding day, a groom in the city, unlike his counterpart in the country who could ride his bicycle to fetch his fiance from her parents' home, is expected to obtain a car, either borrowed or rented, to escort the bride to his family. The banquet for relatives and friends could have up to several hundred invited guests. As a result, many families either deplete all their savings or fall deeply into debt which easily exceeds their annual income.

Such a trend creates some social and family problems. When wedding festivities became excessive, people had the tendency to compete with each other. Consequently, a man's financial condition has become a major consideration for the girl's family. In order to have a lavish wedding and material advantages, many parents are often open to "bids" before making the marital choice for their daughter.[74] Frequently, their choice does not correspond to their daughter's wishes. Women seem, again, to be caught in another form of purchased marriage. Although women have they legal right to choose their spouse, parents still control their children's marital decisions. Due to their parent's growing cupidity, many young girls have difficulty taking advantage of the legal codes and maintaining filial piety to their parents. The amount of debt varies and affects the family life of the newlyweds. Repayment may take several years of hard work by the young couple. The burden of this debt often makes their marital adjustment even more arduous than it might otherwise be.

Lavish spending on weddings during the past three years has been publically criticized—but no official measures have effectively stopped them. One alternative, group weddings, was tried in Peking; these joint weddings were jointly sponsored by six organizations: the Peking Municipal Trade Union, the Peking Women's Federation, the Communist Youth League of Peking, the Peking People's Broadcasting Station, the Peking Television Station, and the Peking *Evening News*.[75] It was held at the Worker's Cultural Palace on April 26, 1980. Fifty couples were seated at tables with their relatives and friends. They were greeted and congratulated by Party leaders and entertained by professional singers and famous comedians. Each couple paid a fee of 20 yuan (which is less than one-half of one's monthly salary). The magazine *Women of China* commented that this form of wedding—simple, dignified, and in good taste—was unanimously appreciated by the newlyweds, their families, and their guests.

The marital life after the wedding ceremony, whether simple or lavish, is different from the traditional one. While the traditional tie between family members has loosened, the tie between husband and wife has become stronger. The Party encourages joint dedication to its goals as a cement for a stronger marriage. Families are expected to be responsible to the nation, not to individuals. Especially before the 1970s couples geographically separated due to their work assignments or military service were not uncommon in China and created no problem in their marital life since they both shared the same goals for the welfare of the nation (Sidel, 1973; and, Kessen, 1975). For example, because of participation in agricultural development or military service in a remote territory, a husband might have to leave his family behind with his parents. Normally the children continue to live with the mother, while the grandparents might help with childcare if the mother works outside the home during the separation. If both parents left the home village, then the grandparents might assume total responsibility for raising their grandchildren. Since the Marriage Law gives no advantage to husbands, they are not as much in favor of divorce due to physical separation as their predecessors were. Consequently, the marital bond of separated couples has remained cohesive and the relationship between spouses involves more personal effort for mutual adjustment.

The shrinking family size has also fostered an intimate relationship among husband, wife, and children. Some retired parents prefer to stay in their home towns when their grown-up children leave rural areas for cities. Without the presence of the older generation, the young married couple are free to express their affection to each other. Meanwhile, each needs the other's support for survival in a new environment. Problems, such as employment, life adjustment, domestic chores, and possible sickness and accidents, all require mutual dependence. They are forced to become more independent of elderly parents. Some widowed parents may later join this nuclear family and offer their services to help care for their grandchildren. But even this trend is declining, which further isolates the nuclear family. Since widowed women, old or young, are encouraged by the government to remarry, the number of older widows is declining. It is actually becoming popular for older widows to remarry.

While everyone works in a socialist society (Russell,

1971), men and women do not yet divide domestic responsibilities equally. Older women still feel obligated to perform the domestic chores which younger couples, particularly in large cities, divide more evenly.[76] Women are usually expected to carry out more of the household chores than husbands, even though husbands do share such tasks as cooking and washing. They still assume more responsibility than their husbands for child rearing. They breast feed, take care of sick children, and communicate with teachers (Croll, 1978; and, Kessen, 1975).[77] Sometimes, they can ease their domestic responsibilities by giving top priority to ideological studies. Then the team leader or cadre can communicate with the husband or in-laws concerning a woman's unfair responsibilities at home (Croll, 1978). Married female cadres are not encouraged by the Party to "indulge" in domestic activities. On the contrary, they are supposed to continue their revolutionary work and to make political progess after marriage (Croll, 1978). Recently, young men in large cities have easily accepted those traditionally female-associated tasks such as cooking, washing dishes, changing diapers, and grocery shopping when their wives are also employed and making a financial contribution to the family.

The new policy on birth control and the reality of employed mothers has changed the parent-child relationship. The single child family receives various benefits from the government, and often the only child is over indulged and becomes a problem for many young couples. With two incomes parents are able to spoil their only child with excessive toys and sweets. The fear of losing the child might cause the parents to be overly protective of the child. The relationship has become more like companionship; children have a louder voice at home than ever before. In addition, employed parents, as in the other parts of the world, have less time to spend with their children who sometimes have no adult supervision at all after school. Fortunately the educational philosophy of the family and of the school coincide, minimizing many potential juvenile problems. Concern for the education of the only child and family education has been recognized by the Women's Federation.[78]

E. Minority Women in Mainland China

Because of the vast size of the nation, China is made up of people of numerous racial and subcultural groups with different languages, religions, and social customs. There are 56 major ethnic minority groups scattered over Mainland China. Unusual marriage customs of some of these groups which have been diminishing, are introduced briefly in this section (Ch'en, 1975; Chen, 1977; and, Li, 1978a).

1. Marriage Customs Among Ethnic Minorities

Peasants or serfs in the northern part of the nation customarily married their young teenage sons, who were usually around 12 to 13 years old, to young women in their early twenties. The bride then played a maternal role in taking care of her young husband. Several incompatibilities and differences in maturity often created serious marital problems and caused many family tragedies.

Ning Ku Ta is the ancestral home of the Manchus and is located in the northeastern part of China. Polygamy was practiced in this area; men could have as many wives as they wished. Women were the bread winners. They supported their husbands and were responsible for the household chores. When a man died, the concubine of his choice was buried with him. Formally dressed, the selected concubine would sit on the heated bed, shed no tears, and await her death. The wife of the dead man would lead the rest of the concubines to pay their final respects to her. Then she would be hung until dead. If she resisted, the other women would choke her to death. The only privilege women had was that widowed concubines could remarry.

Another type of polygamy was seen in Kansu, where men outnumbered women, and several brothers frequently shared a wife. To avoid any embarrassment they either took turns spending the night with the woman or hung a skirt on the door to signify an on-going intimate affair behind it. The first-born child was named after the oldest brother, the second child named after the second oldest brother, and so on. Not uncommonly, a bachelor leased a wife from someone for a two or three year term to bear a child. Yet, women had no right to make decisions on sexual relations, or on childbirth.

Due to the proximity, Chin Chuan, located in the northwest of Szechwan and Tibet, also had unique customs. Young men and women first made their own marital choice. Then the parents of the groom-to-be had to divinate a lucky date for the wedding. On the wedding day, guests would rush the bride to the groom's home where dancing, drinking, joking, eating, and sexual activities took place. After all well wishers became drunk and left, the bride disappeared. She would wander around without a permanent residence until she bore a child for her husband. Then she was allowed to reside with her husband and in-laws.

Young people in Haian Island enjoyed the same freedom of marital choice. Premarital sexual relations were allowed for both girls and boys and they lived together after building their own home. Married women, easily identified by a facial tattoo designed by their husbands, were expected to be faithful to their husbands forever. Widows were not permitted to remarry. The sexual role of these men and women was opposite that of most of the Chinese population: women worked outside in the field while men kept the house and took care of the children.

Minority groups in the southwest (such as Meo and Yao) were less serious about marriage. Usually young people met at social gatherings and chose their own partners for sexual activities. Parental approval and gifts came after the fact. The following cases reveal this custom.

2. Two Cases of Changing Marital Life

Like the majority in Mainland China, ethnic minority groups have also experienced a great deal of change in their marital life and "male/female" relationship. This section illustrates the change for two minority groups in southwest China.[79]

The Nachi people belong to an ethnic group called Mushuas. They cultivate the land along the mountains of Shihchi, Houniu, and Tayue, in Yangning. Before 1949, women headed the family in a hierarchical matrilineal society. It was actually a partnership between men and women. The partner was called Achu, referring either to man or woman, who had no legal tie to his or her partner. Women raised the children and inherited the property while men shared no financial responsibilities. The "husband" lived and worked with his mother's family and went to spend the night at his "wife's" home, returning to his mother's at daybreak. Thus, such relationships were not stable. When the size of the female-headed household expanded, the oldest woman gained more authority over the members of the "family," which was frequently headed by a grandmother or great-grandmother living with her offspring. Since children lived with the same grandmother or her sisters, they were not familiar with their father. In fact, no special name or title such as uncle or grandfather was even given to a male.

The Nachi believe this system originated in legends. For them, Shihchi Mountain is the reincarnation of the Goddess Kanmu. She not only decides the size of the tribal population, the number of animals, and the amount of crops produced, but also exercises a great power on women's beauty, marriage, and childbirth. The legends say that the goddess lives like an ordinary Nachi woman, practicing Achu. She has several achus, all of them mountain deities. Even nowadays, on the 25th day of the seventh month of every year, the Nachis dress up and go to the Shihchi Mountain to offer sacrifices. This is also a social occasion for men and women to select the Achus.

Prior to the revolution, Nachi people never heard of marital relations or illegitimate children. Under the system of patriarchal monogamy established since 1949, the relationships of men and women have changed to various degrees. Many grandmothers or great-grandmothers still retain their supreme status in the household, assigning jobs, allocating food, and making decisions. Some young wives are reluctant to go to their husband's family and prefer to stay with their mothers.

The Tai is another ethnic group located in Yunnan. Like the Nachis, they also possess an unique cultural heritage. Before they were liberated by the Communists in 1949, the marriage of young people from official and aristocratic families was arbitrarily arranged by social status. Among the toiling poor, people had their own choice of marital partner and the couple could choose to live with either the bride's or the groom's family, depending on the manpower needed.

The social and familial status of women was low. They had no right to voice opinions, had to walk behind men, and were not allowed to sit with male guests, and received no help from men in household chores. Men refused to help women dry clothes in the sun for fear that they would become poor hunters or fishermen haunted by witches and demons if they accidentally touched a woman's sarong. Nowadays, Tai women have become more assertive and participate in various sectors of the labor force and political activities. Yet, they still encounter resistance from native men who maintain strong feudalistic ideas and traditional thinking concerning women's role and women's "proper place".[80]

Conclusion

Overall women in Mainland China have had diverse experiences in the labor force, in political and social advancement, in educational opportunities, and in family life since the founding of the Communist Party in the late 1920s. Like their counterparts in the West, Chinese women have found employment opportunities to fluctuate with the economic and political climate, the needs of society, and the policy imposed by the Party. Even so, they have gradually improved their political, social, and educational status. Women in high ranking offices are much more acceptable in Mainland China than in many other countries. The Communist Party has intervened in domestic life, asserting its influence in child rearing, relationships of spouse and in-laws, and household management (Croll, 1978; Russell, 1971; and, Snow, 1968). The implementation of the Marriage Law in the 1950s resulted in a radical change in family life: criticism and self-criticism were supposed to apply to the relationship between husband and wife; women not only attended and contested divorce proceedings, but could also initiate divorce proceedings (Russell, 1971).

Following the turmoil of the Cultural Revolution and the new contacts with the U.S. in the late 1970s, the government announced new approaches to modernization. Many radical policies have been revised or relaxed since then. Interpersonal relationships, especially within the family, now involve less political consciousness and teaching in restoring this intimacy. Affection rather than Party pressure was behind equality within the family. Men are more willing to share household duties with their employed wives in order to have a higher standard of living—not in just meeting the demands of the Party.

The pursuit of material gain, which is strongly influenced by China's recent open foreign policy, has generated some concern for women's emancipation in Mainland China. Capitalism, imported from western countries, is nuturing the revival of lingering feudalistic ideas about women and their traditional role. As Vice Chairman Teng Ying-chao recently pointed out, Chinese women have a long struggle ahead of them to reach the goal of complete emancipation.[81]

NOTES

[1] Elizabeth Croll, *The women's movement in China* (London: Anglo-Chinese Educational Institute, 2nd ed.; 1976), p. 84.

[2] Hsu Chu-ju, "Women's rights to inherit property protected," *Women of China* (March, 1980), pp. 39-40.

[3] The marriage law was revised and adopted in January, 1981.

[4] Teng Hsiao-p'ing, *Report on the Revision of the Constitution* (Peking: Foreign Language Press, 1956), p. 91.

[5] Hou Chi-ming, "Manpower, employment, and unemployment," in *Economic trends in Communist China*, ed. Alexander Eckstein, *et al.* (Chicago: Aldine, 1968), p. 371.

[6] Chang Ts'ai, "Actively train more and better women cadres," *New China Semi-Monthly* (November 6, 1956), p. 99.

[7] *Ibid.*.

[8] Janet Salaff, "Institutional motivation for fertility limitation in China," *Population Studies* XXVI.2 (July, 1972); reprinted in Marilyn Young's *Women in China*, p. 119.

[9] *Ibid.*.

194

[10]*Ibid.*.

[11]Barry Richman, *Industrial society in Communist China* (New York: Random House, 1969), pp. 304-305.

[12]"Pay attention to the development of the female party member," article in *People's Daily News* (September 13, 1971).

[13]*Ibid.*.

[14]Salaff, *op. cit.*, p. 120.

[15]"Sexual equality is the Order of the Day in China," article in *Houston Chronicle* (October 22, 1979).

[16]"My impression of the tour in the U.S.A.," article in *People's Daily* (August 8, 1979).

[17]"Four new Ministers are named," article in *World Journal* (March 9, 1982).

[18]"Vice-Chairman, Deng Ying-chao on U.N. Decade for Women," article in *Women of China* (August, 1980), pp. 6-7.

[19]"Four new Ministers are named," *loc. cit.*.

[20]Croll, *op. cit.*, p. 28.

[21]*Ibid.*, p. 29.

[22]*Ibid.*, p. 4.

[23]Nan Ling, "In the interest of women workers," article in *Women of China* (August, 1980), pp. 25-28.

[24]"Vice-Chairman," *op. cit.*, p. 6.

[25]William H. Mandel, *Soviet Women* (New York: Anchor Press, 1975), pp. 308-309.

[26]Hou, *op. cit.*, pp. 365-366.

[27]Ch'en Tung-yuan, *History of the life of Chinese women* (Taipei, Taiwan: Commerce Publishing Co., 1977), pp. 378-380.

[28]Hou, *loc. cit.*, calculated by the author.

[29]Tien, H. Y., *China's population struggle* (Columbus, Ohio: Ohio State University Press, 1973), p. 304.

[30]Hou, *loc. cit.*.

[31]Salaff, *op. cit.*, p. 123.

[32]Croll, *op. cit.*, p. 66.

[33]William Kessen, ed., *Childhood in China* (New Haven: Yale University Press, 1975), p. 23.

[34]This was discovered during the author's trip to China in the summer of 1982; see also, Nan Ling, "In the interest of women workers," *Women of China* (August, 1980), pp. 26-27.

[35]Croll, *op. cit.*, p. 71.

[36]Ruth Sidel, *Women and child care in China* (New York: Penguin, 1972), p. 31.

[37]Even women in those cities visited by the author could not avoid such a trend.

[38]Shih Wen-ju, "My daily life," *Women of China* (March, 1980), pp. 11-12.

[39]Croll, *op. cit.*, p. 62.

[40]*Ibid.*, p. 69.

[41]"China's child-care system today," *Women of China* (April, 1980), pp. 12-13.

[42]Mandel, *op. cit.*, p. 314.

[43]"China's child-care system today," *loc. cit.*.

[44]Nan Ling, *loc. cit.*.

[45]The author's observation in China in 1982.

[46]Nan Ling, *loc. cit.*.

[47]Hsia Chi, "Keeping Latch-key kids off the street," *Women of China* (November, 1980), pp. 20-21.

[48]"A talk between a reader from Denmark and four Chinese working women," *Women of China* (October, 1980), pp. 24-27.

[49]Croll, *op. cit.*, pp. 70-71.

[50]Leo A. Orleans, *Professional manpower and education in Communist China* (Washington, D.C.: G.P.O., 1961), p. 172.

[51]C. K. Yang, *Chinese Communist society: the family and the village* (Cambridge, Mass.: M.I.T. Press, 1965), p. 112.

[52]"University entrance examination, 1977" *China Reconstructs* XXVIII.4 (April, 1978), pp. 9-12.

[53]*Ibid.*.

[54]Orleans, *op. cit.*, p. 71; and also his article "Communist China's education," in the U.S. Congress, Joint Economic Committee, *An Economic Profile of Mainland China* (Washington, D.C.: G.P.O., 1967), p. 511.

[55]Leo A. Orleans, "China's science and technology," in the U.S. Congress, Joint Economic Committee, *People's Republic of China: An economic assessment* (Washington, D.C.: G.P.O., 1972), p. 215-219.

[56]Mandel, *op. cit.*, p. 314.

[57]Croll, *op. cit.*, p. 30.

[58]Yang Wen, "The Chinese people endorse revised Marriage Law," *Women of China* (November, 1980), pp. 8-9.

[59]Sidel, *op. cit.*, pp. 10, 52; see also Kessen, *op. cit.*, pp. 18, 22.

[60]"No longer a deserted mother," *Women of China* (March, 1980), pp. 40-41.

[61]"Letter says marriage in China like business deal," *Houston Chronicle* (February 10, 1980).

[62]"Sexual equality is the order of the day in China," *Houston Chronicle* (October 22, 1979).

[63]Interview with the street people in China by the author during travel/study in 1982.

[64]*China, a general survey* (Peking: Foreign Language Press, 1979), p. 199.

[65]*Ibid.*.

[66]*Ibid.*.

[67]"Comrade Lonelyhearts," *Newsweek* (December 29, 1980), p. 27.

[68]Wong K'ao, "Law upholds freedom of choice in marriage," *Women of China* (July, 1981), pp. 40-45.

[69]"Widow marries the man of her choice," *Women of China* (November, 1980), pp. 16-17.

[70]"A country wedding," *Women of China* (April, 1980), pp. 2-4.

[71]Pao Feng, "A welcome style of wedding," *Women of China* (April, 1980), pp. 2-4.

[72]"Letter says marriage in China like business deal," *loc. cit.*.

[73]"Hubby's family pays for Chinese wedding," *Houston Chronicle* (November 20, 1979).

[74]Pao, *loc. cit.*.

[75]*Ibid.*.

[76]"Women in China have way to go," *Houston Chronicle* (November 27, 1979); also the author's observation while in China.

[77]Such a trend continued during the author's 1982 visit to China.

[78]Hsia Chi, *loc. cit.*; see also, "A talk between a reader from Denmark and four Chinese working women," *loc. cit.*.

[79]Chung Hsiu, "Matriarchal families," *Women of China* (July, 1981), pp. 11-15; see also her article, "Dai—a free people," *Women of China* (November, 1980), pp. 2-5.

[80]*Ibid.*.

[81]"Vice-Chairman, Deng Yingchao on UIV Decade for Women," *loc. cit.*.

CHAPTER SEVEN

Contemporary Period
Women in the Republic of China in Taiwan

Japan capped its rise to power during the late 19th century with a military victory over China in 1895. At Shimon-
oseki, in April, 1895, Japan forced China to sign the most
humiliating treaty in her history. The treaty declared an end
to China's sovereignity over Korea, the payment of a huge
indemnity, the opening of Chungking and three other river-
side cities as treaty ports to the Japanese, and the cession to
Japan of the Liaotung Peninsula in southern Manchuria, the
Pescadores off the west coast of Formosa (Taiwan), and the
island of Formosa.

A. Post World War II:
Political Change and the Legal Status of Women

During Japan's fifty-year colonial rule, the Taiwanese
people on the island experienced many cultural and social
changes and assimilated a great deal of Japanese culture—including language, both verbal and nonverbal, social norms,
and community structures. The social status of Taiwanese
women was as suppressed as their counterparts in Japan.
Both were expected to be totally subservient to their husbands (Chang, 1966). But Japanese domination only intensified the already existent submissive nature of women's position. The growing women's movement in Mainland China at
this time had no effect on Taiwanese women under Japanese
rule. The experience of these two groups of Chinese women
in Taiwan and Mainland China, was reunited when China regained sovereignity over Taiwan after the defeat of Japan in
World War II. Restoration of Taiwan provided a constitutional change in legal status for Taiwanese women, entitling
them to the same rights as their sisters on the Mainland.
These two groups of women were again divided, however, when the Kuomintang (KMT) and its Nationalist
Government retreated to Taiwan in 1949. Since that time,
Taiwan has become the fortress of the KMT against the Com-

munist government on the Mainland. Assuming the guardian-
ship of Confucian tradition and cultural heritage, the Nationalist government has emphasized motherhood as the foundation for building a mighty base for anti-communism. The
government has encouraged all women on the island, whether
migrant Mainlanders or native Taiwanese, to share the same
goals for women's social and political advancement. The
Nationalist government has approached these issues differently than the Communists. Basically, the experience of contemporary Chinese women in Taiwan reflects a strong,
ancient tradition and value system which has been modified
by modern ideas about women and their role in the family
(Wei, 1975).

The Constitution of the Nationalist Government, formally adopted in 1947, and the Civil Laws, enacted in 1936,
are applicable to the people in Taiwan. The egalitarian
principle of the Constitution appears in Article 7: *"All citizens of the Republic of China are equal under the law
regardless of sex, religion, race...."* Under this constitution
women have the same rights as men to vote, be elected to
public office, inherit property, obtain an education, and
make contracts. With regard to marriage and divorce, women
have gained equality. For example, in past centuries conjugal
infidelity was a prerogative of husbands but brought punishment to wives. Now it is grounds for divorce for both men
and women (Article 1052 of the Civil Laws).

Yet the 1936 Civil Law still deals imperfectly with the
rights of women and certain parts of its need to be revised to
coincide with the current social changes. For nearly half a
centuy Chinese women have become increasingly aware of
their legal rights in family relations. In 1968 a group of
women's rights advocates formed a commission under the
Ministry of the Interior Committee on Promotion of
Women. They developed a ten-year proposal to promote the
social/legal/family status of women in Taiwan. They hoped
that all proposed goals would be realized by the end of 1978.
While progress toward these goals has yet to be evaluated, the
1979 Draft of Revision on Civil Laws has incorporated a few
of the proposals in an attempt to rectify the legal status of
women. The neutral terms "spouse" and "the marriage
parties" replace, for the most part, older terms such as

"father," "mother," "husband," "wife," "male," or "female." In general the revision eliminates automatic regulation by the husband and leaves decisions regarding such matters as place of residence after marriage, retention of the wife's surname, and determination of the child's surname to both partners. Table 8 illustrates some of the changes.[1]

Table 8*

Comparison of the Civil Laws and Its Revision of 1979

Present Civil Laws	Draft of the Revolution
Marriage cannot be forced and must be decided by both parties	No change
Wife must adopt husband's name	Decision is made by mutual agreement
Wife must live in husband's residence	Same as above
Children must carry father's name	Same as above
There are nine reasons for a divorce petition; some examples are given below:	
1. Desertion of three or more years	1. No change
2. Serious illness and/or handicap	2. No change
3. Jail sentence of 3 or more years	3. Jail sentence of 3 or more years, spouse can apply for divorce immediately
4. Physical or mental mistreatment of in-laws by wife or vice versa	4. Physical or mental mistreatment of in-laws by wife or husband and vice versa
Divorced women must wait 6 months before remarriage	If divorced woman is not pregnant, immediate remarriage is allowed
Joint property is awarded to whoever earned it	Wife's contribution to family receives property is divided equally
Alimony and monetary compensation should be given to the needy spouse	No change
Divorced woman legally resumes maiden name, even though employed Chinese woman is always addressed by maiden name.	No change
The sequence of inheritance is spouse, children, parents, sibling and grandparents unless specified	No change

*Source: Ministry of Justice, *Revision on Civil Laws on Family* (Taipei, Taiwan: Executive Yuan, 1979).

In addition to Civil Laws, women's legal status is also governed by the Labor Laws and Criminal Laws. Some relevant provisions in the Laws are:

>—Female criminals who are over four months pregnant or who have an infant less than two months old are not incarcerated but transferred to a detention or medical center.

>—Abortion is allowed only in the case of incest, rape, retarded fetus, or mental illness of the pregnant woman.

>—Female laborers receive equal pay for equal work.

>—Female workers are not allowed to work more than ten hours a day and at no time are they to work between 10:00 p.m. and 6:00 a.m.

>—Women employed for more than six months are entitled to eight weeks maternity leave at full pay, while those employed less than six months are entitled to eight weeks maternity leave at half pay.

Unavoidably, the discrepancy between the legal provisions and implementation of them has persisted during the past decades. The sexual eqalitarianism of the Constitution and Civil Laws has not overcome the enormous and profound impact of Chinese traditional thinking on women. Even today, many women, as well as men, remain conscious of the traditional roles imposed on them, especially those women who have been confined at home with limited social contacts or experiences with the outside world. They are not only unaware of women's changing role but also ignorant of their recently won legal rights. As a result, the legal codes designed to ensure them equality have not become fully effective, and men continue to thake advantage of these uniformed women. For example, the practice of dowry and matched marriages endures even though they have been outlawed. The marriages of socially isolated women have to be settled by a matchmaker. The only difference in such practices from previous generations is the presence of both matched parties—so that they both might have a say in the matter. The amount of the dowry still bothers some young brides whose parents have failed to present a sum commensurate with those of their sisters-in-law. Consequently, they often become the target for humiliation and subject for gossip (Wei, 1975).

Divorce is not common in Taiwan. Only 3.3 married people in a thousand take this option (Ministry of the Interior, 1980). Part of the reason may be the inconsistency between the legal rights of women and their actual treatment in a divorce case. Although the Constitution declares that men and women are equal, article 1051 of the Civil Laws deprives divorced women of the right of child custody. Fear of losing their children causes many women to endure physical and mental abuse rather than divorce their husbands. The proposed revision of the Civil Laws has left this article untouched. The draft of the revision, however, no longer requires that property gained from profits and interest from a wife's assets belong to the husband. In addition, it proposes that a family fortune acquired during the marriage be divided equally between husband and wife.

The continued influence of traditional values becomes particularly obvious when elderly parents prepare their will. By law, the parents' property should be divided equally among their children, regardless of sex. But the law of inheritance cannot override the parents' will, which most often designates the sons as heirs. An interesting recent case was reported by the *China Central Daily News* on April 19, 1982. Three daughters of a major stockholder of an enterprise went to court after their father's death. The charter of the real estate company required that the board vacancy created by the deceased should be filled by his eldest son, or an immediate male family member. Thus, according to company policy, these three daughters had no claim to their father's property, which consisted of 83 pieces of land. The daughters won in municipal court because of the provision of the Constitution which proclaims equality regardless of sex.

Although polygamy is against the law in Taiwan (Civil Laws, Article 1052), men suffer no social sanction for their extramarital affairs since unilateral fidelity was required of Chinese women for over two thousand years. Today women's faithlessness either generates inner guilt or invites public criticism, both of which easily leads to the dismissal of the woman by her husband. The double standard for sexual behavior also affects the young. Premarital sexual relationships cause more suffering and grief to girls than to boys (Wei, 1975). Lu Hsiu-lien (1977a), the pioneer of the feminist movement in Taiwan, conducted a survey of men's attitudes toward women in 1976. Her results indicate that those men who have a positive attitude toward women's abilities and potential tend to have a higher education. Very possibly better-educated men are more aware of the legal rights granted to women and women's changing social and political image in the male-dominated society. Even so, full implementation of the Civil Law remains a long way off, and more up-to-date revisions are required.

Despite the changes in legal codes, women themselves need to continue their collective efforts used for women's emancipation in the 1920s by the May Fourth Movement for their ultimate goals. The Communists adopted the same tactics when they sought to mobilize women, half the Chinese population, for social reconstruction. Some of the older women advocates who had fought for women's education and suffrage fled to Taiwan with the Nationalist Government in 1949. Yet, their enthusiastic attempts to promote women's legal rights further have been blocked for political reasons. Anti-Communist campaigns and social stabilization have been the top priorities for the government. Any organized movement, including the women's fight for equality which might disturb the existing order, is discouraged. Nevertheless, besides some private women's organizations dedicated to the social, cultural, and professional advancement of women, the Kuomingtang sponsors three major women's organizations, which are led by the wives of higher echelon party members. The activities of these organizations (the Taiwan Provincial Women's Association, the Anti-Communist Women's League, established by Mme. Chiang in 1950, and the Women's Department of the Central Committee of Kuomintang, founded in 1953) have been less for the advancement of women's rights than for the mobilization of women for the anti-Communist cause. Similar to the experience of women during the Anti-Japan War, women are once more encouraged to participate in organized activities for the sake of the country. However, at least a mass of women have been involved for the specific goals set up by the government and trained by party leaders. Through these experiences, some female leaders emerged in the Party.

The Taiwan Provincial Women's Association is the first women's club in Taiwan. Upon the termination of Japanese colonial power in 1945, many educated urban Taiwanese women, like their sisters on the Mainland, started working to improve the conditions of women in Taiwan. This evolved slowly, reaching out to all women from Taipei, the capital of Nationalist China. By 1976 it had 383 branches in different cities, counties, towns and villages.[2] Since the women it hoped to recruit as members had had little or no education during the fifty years of Japanese colonization, the goals of the Association focused on that, attempting (1) to guarantee a free, six-year education to women, especially those in rural areas, (2) to offer basic skills training in housekeeping and home improvement, (3) to educate women mainly through the use of printed materials, (4) to provide services and counseling in employment and family crises, and, (5) to contribute to the country by serving the military in several ways, such as sewing uniforms, entertaining soldiers, and visiting the wounded.[3]

The Anti-Communist Women's League (ACWL) was born in 1950 to unite all women in Taiwan toward the ultimate goal of recovering Mainland China. Unlike the Taiwan Provinicial Women's Association, all the officers of the ACWL are appointed by Mme. Chiang rather than elected by the members. As stated by P'i (1973), the major tasks of the ACWL are to: (1) provide training in basic homemaking and childcare, and mobilize woman power; (2) assist the servicemen and their dependents; (3) take care of the poor and needy to attain social stability; (4) unveil Communists' crimes to gain better understanding of the goal of, and steps for, restoration of the Mainland; (5) extend social education for proper moral conduct; (6) develop methods of psychological warfare against Communism; and, (7) establish diplomatic relations on a personal, one-to-one basis, with citizens in other anti-communist countries.[4] The ACWL was chaired until recently by Mme. Chiang, and is presently directed by Mrs. Y.C. Wong. In 1976, it had 422 branch units and 273 work teams.[5]

Similar to the ACWL, another women's group emerged in 1953 within the Kuomintang (KMT) and administratively parallel to other branches of the Party. Because women had played a vital role during the revolutionary period at the end of the nineteenth century, their power and problems were recognized by Dr. Sun Yet-sen and other Party members in the beginning of the Republic. However, no single independent branch of the KMT engaged in women's work until 1953, when a separate Women's Department was established under the Central Committee of the KMT. This department has mobilized nearly 300,000 women in Taiwan at different levels, from the local to the central government and from different occupations, from unskilled to professionals (Women's Department, 1976). Unlike previous women's organizations, which had focused on breaking down traditional customs and improving the status of women, the Women's Department organizes women to fight for the benefit of their country. Training women for leadership is geared to the welfare of the country rather than specifically to women's rights. The aims of the Department are (1) improving living conditions in rural areas, (2) teaching women to fulfill the family role as good housekeepers, and (3) understanding and serving the needs of countrymen.

In addition to the above-mentioned major women's groups, a number of other organizations exist, including 19 professional groups and 308 Women's Working Units in government and private enterprises. The most popular and well-known women's organizations in Taiwan are the International Women's Association in Taiwan, the Association of Professional Women, Chinese Girls Scouts, the Association of Women Writers, the Family Planning Organization, the Association of Women Physicans, and the YWCA.

B. Universal Education for Women

Since Confucianism highly values intellectuals, the Chinese have emphasized education a great deal. Before this century, self-instruction and private tutoring furnished the two major ways for youngsters to obtain an education. Because of the highly respected status of intellectuals, many youngsters studied diligently in hoping to reach their goals someday. Normally, their educational attainment would lead to a successful career in government. The government sponsored an annual Imperial Examination for civil service, beginning in the Han Dynasty, to recruit qualified men, but not women, to serve the nation. Prominent appointments were awarded to those who made the highest scores, and youngsters even from very poor families were encouraged to work and study hard to achieve this goal.

When the Republic was founded in 1911, public education was soon introduced. Since then, the Nationalist Government has continued to develop an universal education for all Chinese people, including those in Taiwan. The astonishing expansion of education since the relocation of the government to Taiwan can be found at all levels and in all areas, as reflected in the growing number of schools, teachers, and students, and the size of the budget (Ministry of Education, 1980). To further improve education, in 1968 the government extended free compulsory education from six years to nine years. All school-age children are entitled to this privilege. Basically, the school system in Taiwan resembles America's; the 6-3-3-4 pattern is the core supplemented by vocational schools, teachers colleges, junior colleges, and evening schools.

The educational opportunities for contemporary Chinese women in Taiwan are different from their predecessors. In the past, sons were often educated at the expense of daughters, particularly if the family was poor and could only afford to educate a limited number of children. Because sons could support the family and also bring success and glory to the family name while daughters married into another family, and, like a pail of spilled water, made no contribution to the fame or wealth of her family. Even in a wealthy family, daughters were only allowed to learn poetry, embroidery, and other domestic skills to prepare them to be good wives and mothers. Girls from poor families were not only deprived of an education but also had to contribute their labor to support the family, even helping their brothers stay in school. Things began to change in 1911; women demanded more education. Prior to the adoption of the Constitution in 1947, which guaranteed everyone a free education, many parents still favored their sons' education. Articles

159 and 160 of the Constitution proclaim that all Chinese citizens between the ages of 6 and 12 shall have a free education regardless of sex, creed, religion, and/or race. During the past decade, literacy among women in Taiwan has risen from 9.8% to 83.6%, compared to that of men which rose from 90% to 94.5%.[6] Such a jump is attributed to the educational policy adopted by the government which includes literacy classes for adults in the countryside. Besides the availability of adult education and free education for school age children from the government, social stability and economic growth have also fostered parents' changing attitudes towards girls' education. Instead of taking advantage of a daughter's financial contributions to the family, they have become less reluctant to send their daughters to school.

The figures in Tables 9-13 clearly indicate the rapid growth of women's education at all levels of formal education. For example, Table 9 shows that elementary school age girls and boys have the same chance for education. It is interesting to note that Table 13 reveals that a higher percentage of girls than boys want higher education. No longer are they much affected by the traditional belief that ignorance is a woman's virtue. Yet, the potential for growth is greatest in overseas graduate studies, for the fewest women are there. There are four reasons for this. First, even today in China it is not socially acceptable for a man to marry a woman with a higher education than his own. Thus education reduces potential marriage partners for women. As a result, many intelligent young women simply avoid pursuing graduate studies abroad. Secondly, the separation from parents required by graduate studies may not only worry the parents but also their college-graduate daughters, who have either been protected or are just afraid of facing a foreign country alone. Thirdly, the son's education still receives priority. With limited resources, parents have to limit the number of children they send abroad for expensive studies. The traditional discrimination against daughters often unconsciously dictates parents' decision as to which of their children will receive educational opportunities. Age is another factor. The age range among the male students who study abroad is wider than among the females. Men can postpone their marriage in order to earn money for their education. Yet, a couple of years of employment, followed by graduate studies, will lessen a girl's chances for marriage. The fear of becoming instantly past-prime time for marriage is still shared by many young women. The decline in male students studying abroad as shown in Table 13 may be due to the increasing availability of graduate studies in Taiwan. As a result, women studying abroad have even less choices of marital partners.

Table 9*
Percentage of School Children to School Age Children

Year	% Boys	% Girls
1951	93.44%	68.58%
1961	97.54%	94.32%
1971	98.26%	97.77%
1980	99.70%	99.67%

Table 10*
**Percentage of Elementary School Graduates Entering
Junior High School**

Year	% Boys	% Girls
1951		
1961		
1971	89.34%	72.70%
1980	98.87%	93.39%

Table 11*
**Percentage of Junior High Graduates Entering
Senior Secondary Schools**

Year	% Boys	% Girls
1967	81.09%	76.28%
1970	91.52%	87.88%
1975	69.24%	64.28%
1980	63.30%	61.44%

*Source: Ministry of Education, *Educational Statistics of the Republic of China* (Taipei, Taiwan: Ministry of Education, R.O.C., 1980).

Table 12*
Percntage of Senior High School Graduates Entering
Universities, Colleges, and Junior Colleges

Year	% Men	%Women
1967	64.71%	83.81%
1970	62.15%	87.36%
1975	77.40%	80.70%
1980	74.80%	85.80%

Table 13*
Chinese Students Studying Abroad for Advanced Studies

Year	No. of Men	% Men	No. of Women	% Women
1950	132	61%	85	39%
1960	497	77%	146	23%
1970	1351	66%	705	34%
1980	3424	59%	2377	41%

Although women have been given more educational opportunities than ever, they still cannot escape from certain societal "restrictions". Society still expects women to be in the "right" fields: those which presumably fit women's "innate traits". Minor courses in secondary schools, such as homemaking, handicrafts, and first aid for girls, and industrial arts, carpentry, and electronic wiring for boys, reflects such social expectations. Later, when women choose their majors in college they are evidently influenced by their friends and relatives to enter areas considered suitable for them. Table 14 shows the number of students who took the 1978 Annual College Entrance Examination in four major areas: science and engineering, liberal arts and human sciences, biology and medical studies, and business and industrial management.

Girls tend to choose and concentrate their efforts in one area: liberal arts and human sciences. Consequently, upon their graduation, their employment in sciences and industry is limited. Since the Republic of China has been experiencing an economic boom and industrial growth, the liberal arts graduates eventually have to switch to other fields that are in

*Source: Ministry of Education, *ibid.*

Table 14*
**Registration of the Area of Study by Sex for the
College Entrance Examination of 1978**

Area of Study	% Men	% Women
Science & Engineering	93.24%	6.76%
Liberal Arts & Human Sciences	29.15%	70.85%
Biology & Medical Sciences	69.16%	30.84%
Business & Industry Mangement (including law schools)	64.22%	35.78%

demand or become unemployed. Most female graduates take the latter alternative and devote their life to marriage and family, making futile efforts to obtain a higher education. Actually, each year only about 30 to 35 percent of the registered contestants pass the examination and enter colleges. No wonder a newspaper recently praised the fact that more boys were accepted for higher education than girls. Girls, the paper pointed out, tend to stay home after graduation, making their education a waste of taxpayers' money.[8]

Table 15**
Sex Ratio of Students at Each Educational Level During 1980-1981

Type of Education	% Male	% Female
Elementary schools	51.4%	48.1%
Junior high schools	52.6%	47.4%
Senior high schools	56.1%	43.9%
Vocational high schools	49.7%	50.3%
Junior Colleges	59.5%	40.5%
Universities	62.1%	37.9%
Teacher Education:		
Junior colleges	38.2%	61.8%
Normal universities	41.4%	58.6%
Supplementary schools:		
Junior high schools	36.8%	63.8%
Vocational schools	44.4%	55.6%

*Source: *Report on the Annual College Entrance Examination of 1978* (Taipei, Taiwan: Taiwan Normal University, 1979).

**Source: Provided by the Ministry of Education to the author during a personal visit in June, 1981.

Another educational difference found between boys and girls is the type of school that they enroll in. Table 15 (p. 211) illustrates more females than males are enrolled in vocational schools, normal schools, and supplementary schools, further perpetuating the traditional sex roles of men and women through sexually stereotyped curricula. In universities, which require both financial resources and academic achievement, women are the minority. It remains unclear whether this is due more to traditional views held by parents or to the general social expectations that a woman needs only a high school education to fulfill her proper role as a wife and mother. Broadening women's potential career fields and extending the years of education for larger numbers of women are the challenges for the government and the people, both men and women.

C. *Industrialization and Women in the Labor Force*

Industrialization and economic prosperity in Taiwan which began with the gradual reduction of U.S. economic aid in the 1960s gave a booster to women's employment. Since the government has adopted a more liberal economic policy to attract foreign investors and to encourage trade with foreign countries, including those which have no diplomatic relations with the Republic of China. Employment opportunities in industry and commerce thus follow economic expansion. Owing to environmental restrictions, most of the new manufacturing establishments are in light industry, such as textile, plastics, electronics, and import-export. To minimize the cost of their products, manufacturers take full advantage of cheap female labor in Taiwan. Many elementary and junior high school graduates have suddenly poured into the labor force.

Two additional reasons have spurred women to enter the job market. Their increasing education has promoted women's self-esteem and self-confidence. At least some well-educated women have become interested in searching for satisfaction beyond the confines of their own household. The desire to enjoy material goods which mark the advanced countries has also spread to the people of Taiwan through the mass media. Eager to enjoy a higher standard of living, women have become interested in joining the labor force.

Table 16*
Employed Persons by Sex (1958-1980)
(Unit: in Thousands)

Year	Male		Female	
1958	2,485	78.22%	692	21.78%
1963	2,839	78.53%	776	21.47%
1971	3,224	68.47%	1,494	31.53%
1972	3,338	67.46%	1,610	32.54%
1973	3,486	65.44%	1,841	34.56%
1974	3,672	66.93%	1,814	33.07%
1975	3,740	67.74%	1,781	32.26%
1976	3,856	68.09%	1,807	31.91%
1977	4,039	67.86%	1,913	32.14%
1978	4,179	67.10%	2,049	32.90%
1979	3,743	65.86%	1,941	34.14%
1980	4,156	65.58%	2,181	34.42%

Women's participation in the labor force has swelled since 1958 (Table 16). The peak of women's employment came in 1973, when the economic growth rate slowed. A saturated job market meant limited employment opportunities which generated greater competition between men and women, and women were often elbowed out of the way. When a job opening attracts equally qualified male and female applicants, the man will most likely obtain the position because it is believed his need is greater since he has to support his family, revealing once again the traditional role expectation of men in family finances.

Facing such fixed job openings, women must either seek advanced learning abroad or additional on-the-job training to improve their skills in order to compete with men. Table 13 (p. 210) shows that the percentage of female students going abroad for graduate studies has increased in the past decade. Those women who remain in Taiwan have also demonstrated occupational progress. More women than before have entered professional, technical, administrative and managerial

*Source: Directorate-General of Budget, Accounting, and Statistics, *Yearbook of Laborer Statistics* (Taipei, Taiwan: Executive Yuan, R.O.C., 1958-1960).

areas (Table 17). Concurrently, the number of female clerical and service workers has declined. Table 17 reveals that women are better trained and tend to shift from non- or semi-skilled jobs to skilled or professional positions. Although women's employment opportunities are still restricted due to sexual preferences held by employers, women have gradually improved the quality of their job performance.

There are some characteristics of the female labor force, which includes 46.7% of the able-bodied women of 15 years and over, compared with 82.4% of the men. The most popular reason given for women's unemployment is their household responsibilities (Ministry of the Interior, 1980). Table 18 indicates that more than half of the employed women are under the age of thirty. The percentage of working women decreases as their age increases, suggesting some truth in the popular idea that women's employment tends to terminate once they marry and have children. Men's employment activity, on the other hand, spreads out pretty evenly between their twenties and fifties. The rate for women suggests that women are less choosy than men since their wages will most likely be either a supplementary income for their family or pocket money for those unmarried.

In spite of the increasing number of employed women, women still encounter a variety of challenges in the job market. Society's notions about women's traditional role still play an important part in women's employment, not only in the matter of whether they work or not, but also in the kind of job. Career choices for women are generally restricted (Wei, 1975; Lu, 1977b). Because their college training is frequently influenced by the social norms indicated earlier in Table 14, female graduates are concentrated in the fields of teaching, nursing, accounting, typing, and bookkeeping. Other well-paid and prestigious areas are seldom open to women. Married women face unique problems. Among the economically inactive female population in 1979, 77.32% claimed to be full-time housewives and 17.79% said that they were students. The notion that women's place is in the home still seems to be prevalent. Even the professionally successful women interviewed by the author felt similarly and placed their family above their careers (Yao, 1981). On the other hand, male employers, especially in private indus-

Table 17*
Employed Persons by Occupation & Sex
(Total equals 100%)

Occup. Year	Prof. & Tech. related		Admin & Mgmt		Clerical & Relat.		Sales Workers		Service Workers		Agri/Fishermen & Hunters		Productive & related jobs	
	M	F	M	F	M	F	M	F	M	F	M	F	M	F
1971	65.13	34.87	91.16	08.86	66.35	33.65	65.92	35.08	54.30	45.70	66.16	33.84	72.80	27.20
1972	65.35	34.65	92.86	07.14	64.69	35.31	66.83	33.17	52.33	47.67	65.06	34.95	72.39	27.61
1973	67.35	32.65	93.60	06.40	59.83	40.17	63.19	36.81	50.07	49.33	64.18	35.92	68.86	31.14
1974	68.05	31.95	92.78	07.22	60.61	39.39	65.72	34.28	54.85	45.15	64.47	35.53	71.31	28.69
1975	65.44	34.56	91.74	08.26	60.21	39.79	67.46	32.54	60.26	39.74	65.35	34.65	71.76	28.24
1976	65.08	34.92	92.31	07.69	58.57	41.43	68.46	31.54	62.22	37.78	67.66	32.34	70.41	29.59
1977	64.95	35.05	90.24	09.76	55.33	44.67	67.55	32.45	61.22	39.78	67.75	32.25	70.85	29.25
1978	62.81	37.19	90.91	09.09	58.70	41.30	66.67	33.33	60.67	39.24	69.71	30.23	69.09	30.91
1979	62.85	37.14	92.10	07.90	54.06	45.94	63.25	36.75	56.00	44.00	69.24	30.76	68.84	31.16
1980	62.96	37.04	80.95	19.05	73.55	26.44	62.28	37.71	60.55	39.55	63.15	36.85	64.00	36.00

Source: Directorate-General of Budget, Accounting & Statistics, *Yearbook of Laborer Statistics* (Taipei, Taiwan: Executive Yuan, R.O.C., 1971-1980).

Table 18*
Age & Employment in 1979

Age Group	Male (100%)	Female (100%)
15-19	5	14
20-24	9	23
25-29	18	22
30-34	13	15
35-39	12	11
40-44	9.5	7
45-49	10.0	4
50-54	10.5	3
55-59	7.5	1
60-64	4	0.5
above 65	1	0

Table 19**
*Women's Educational Attainment & Employment
as Compared with Men's in 1979*
(over 15 years of age)

Educational level	Male (100%)	Female (100%)
Illiterate	4.2	12
Self-educated	2.2	2
Primary school	30.3	35.5
Junior high school	15.2	12
Senior high school	14.4	11
Vocational	10.6	12.5
Junior College	7.7	7.4
College & Graduate School	15.4	7.6

*Source: Directorate-General of Budget, Accounting & Statistics, *ibid.*
**Source: Directorate-General of Budget, Accounting & Statistics, *Monthly Bulletin of Labor Statistics* (Taipei, Taiwan: Executive Yuan, R.O.C., March, 1979).

Table 20*
Unemployment by Sex & Educational Attainment
1979

Educational Level	Male	Female
Total 85 (in thousands)	52	33
Illiterate	1	0
Primary School	13	9
Junior High	13	6
Senior High	8	4
Vocational	10	9
Junior College	4	3
College & Graduate School	2	2

try, remain reluctant to hire women who might either be un-
ambitious or quit after marriage or childbirth. Even when
they hire women, employers tend to place them in sex-related positions.

"Equal pay for equal work" has been the government
policy implemented for civil service. Rank determines re-
numeration, and both male and female workers receive the
same salary for the same position. However, a sexual bias
appears in considerations for promotion (Wei, 1975; Lu,
1977a; and, Yao, 1981). Men get a better chance than
women. Very few women are in managerial positions. Even
today no leading newspaper has a female chief editor, no
public university has a female president, and the cabinet has
no female minister. Private industry does not pay equally for
equal work. Female workers not only receive less pay from
employers but also are laid off first during an economic down
turn or recession. Greater discrepancies between male and
female wages are found among Japanese-owned factories
(Wei, 1975). The lower pay and less frequent hiring of
women reflects society's attitude toward women's com-
petency and their traditional role in the family. For example,
among the 462 publicly recognized outstanding industrialists,
only four were women (Wei, 1975).

Source: *Ibid.*

Another critical problem encountered by many employed mothers is childcare. The fact that fewer mothers than single women are employed (Directorate-General of Budget, Accounting and Statistics, 1979) explains the high demand for childcare facilities for a potential female working force. Unlike the Communist Party on the Mainland, the National Government pays very little attention to the special problems of working or prospective working mothers who have pre-school children. Although in the decade between 1969 and 1979, the total number of nurseries increased more than three times, over 95% were privately operated (Ministry of the Interior, 1980). A majority of the employed women have to rely on relatives and baby sitters in the neighborhood (Table 21). To encourage women to enter the labor force, childcare facilities must be provided. As the size of the family shrinks and mobility becomes greater, employed women will have less chance of getting help from their relatives.

D. Women's Role in Society

Chinese women are no longer confined to the household. With better educational and employment opportunities women are not only more visible occupationally, but also gaining respect as a result of their performance. In order to prove that they are not inferior to men in knowledge and ability they have to work twice as hard (Yao, 1981). Many of their superiors still have reservations about women's ability and potential. Nevertheless, some women have overcome these barriers and achieved a great deal in various areas. Their contribution to the society can be discussed in the following three areas.

Chinese women have played a vital role in education because teaching has been considered the most suitable career for women (Lu, 1977a). The association of women and teaching can be traced back to the early stage of the women's movement in China, when education was considered the medicine for curing women's ignorance and liberating them from traditional thinking. Educated female leaders founded schools for girls to transmit western knowledge and values to them. In higher education, female students dominated the areas of liberal arts and education. These female college

Table 21*

Childcare for Employed Women

Type of Childcare

Type of Occupation	Child age Children	Cared for by relatives	Babysitter	Day-Care Center	Family Child-care	Other
Employers	68.60	25.12	04.68	00.00	01.60	00.00
Self-employed	77.83	20.42	01.20	00.00	00.55	00.00
Helping family business (no pay)	75.26	23.52	00.70	00.13	00.34	00.05
Employees	55.10	34.79	04.28	00.44	05.15	00.24
Professional & Technical	14.35	52.88	13.52	01.83	16.75	00.72
Administrative & Management	33.01	45.47	21.52	00.00	00.00	00.00
Clerical	21.66	51.96	12.30	01.23	12.85	00.00
Sales Personnel	80.57	16.62	01.91	00.17	00.60	00.13
Service Worker	75.83	19.99	01.91	00.00	02.27	00.00
Productive & related operator	72.92	25.14	00.79	00.06	00.87	00.22

*Source: Directorate-General of Budget, Accounting & Statistics, *Report on the Relationship between Family Fertility and Employment in Taiwan Area* (Taipei, Taiwan: Executive Yuan, R.O.C., 1980).

graduates later played an important role in journalism, literature, politics, and education, directly and indirectly influencing many more young women. Because of this historical tie, many women have been most successful in education. For example, female principals have headed a renowned female high school in Taipei, Taiwan, the First Girls' High School. The first female deputy minister of education, Ms. Y.C. Wang, orchestrated the extension of free compulsory education from six to nine years. Table 22 shows the distribution of female teachers at all levels.

Table 22*
Educators at All Levels by Sex During 1979-1980

Educational Level	Total	Male	Female
Universities, colleges, & junior colleges	16,129 (100%)	11,784 (73%)	4,345 (27%)
Secondary schools	13,035 (100%)	8,194 (63%)	4,841 (37%)
Junior high schools	43,647 (100%)	21,644 (49%)	22,003 (51%)
Elementary Schools	69,207 (100%)	34,544 (50%)	34,663 (50%)
Kindergarten	6,275 (100%)	103 (1.6%)	6,172 (98.4%)

A higher percentage of female teachers concentrate in the lower grades and men in the higher levels. Such sexual distinction suggests that women have less education than men and have been perceived as kinder, gentler, and more patient caretakers and mentors for younger children. On the other hand, male teachers are considered more suitable to higher level students who need disciplinarians and scholars to reach their educational goals.

*Source: Ministry of Education, *Educational Statistics of the Republic of China* (Taipei, Taiwan: Ministry of Education, R.O.C., 1980).

In spite of the large number of female teachers, however, women are not well represented in school administrative positions. The higher the level, the fewer female administrators are found (Lu, 1977a; and, Yao, 1981). Up to the present, no four year college has had a female president, and no school has a female dean. Such imbalance is more conspicuous among public schools and universities than privately operated schools, because the government assigns the administrators for the public schools.

Since the beginning of the women's movement, mass media, like eduation, has attracted many intelligent women. Numerous novelists, writers, and news reporters have displayed their talents through their published works. The association between radio broadcasting and women started before World War II. By 1965, four-fifths of the broadcasters in Taiwan were women (Chang, 1966). During the past two decades, the rapidly growing television broadcasting industry in Taiwan has opened its door wider for women in this field, and they now work as news reporters, writers, producers, directors, art designers, singers, actresses, and entertainers. Altogether, by 1976, women constituted 13% of the total employees in the field of broadcasting.[9] Like their sisters in television, female newspaper reporters are usually assigned to cover cultural, social, or educational events. However, a very popular sports reporter, Ms. Su Yu-chen, broke the tradition and carved out a splendid career in the 1960s. She traveled extensively with various national athletic teams to international championships throughout the world. Since then, many other young female reporters have followed in her footsteps into areas formerly closed to women.

Despite the growing number of female reporters in television, radio, and newspapers, which are owned and/or monitored by the government, women enjoy little administrative power. They are still subordinate to male superiors who have greater authority in decision making (Wei, 1975; and, Lu, 1977a). Opportunities for promotion also favor males (Yao, 1981). Yet, a slightly different situation exists in most private publishing businesses. Female publishers and managers are not uncommon. Writers for these companies are predominately women and are highly admired by readers. Most women's magazines, however, have a very narrow scope and deal mainly with domestic affairs and women' role in the family. Among the 58 women's periodicals collected by the National Central Library in 1979, only 28 touched topics beyond the family sphere. The rest of them focus on housekeeping, cooking, sewing, fashion, cosmetics, and interior decorating.

Unlike the fields of education and mass media, women are less active in politics. The close tie between the women's movement and the revolution in 1911, did little to promote women's political consciousness and advancement in the following decades. Young women in Taiwan today are even less aggressive than their early 20th-century predecessors in the pursuit of equal rights (Wolf, 1974; and, Lu, 1977a). Lu (1977a) reports women have shown less concern about politics then men: 30% of the male voters were interested in politics, while only 13% of the female voters expressed such an interest. The low level of female involvement in politics is reflected in their membership in political parties: where 12.9% of the eligible women joined, compared to 31.4% of the eligible men. More than 70% of the surveyed males indicated that they would vote, while only 65.6% of the women had such a commitment. This result is inconsistent with the actual figures provided by the Ministry of the Interior as shown in Table 23. Although women have become more interested in elections since 1969, men still dominate politics, a pattern reminiscent of the conventional notion that men should handle outside business while women should be domestically oriented.

This deep-rooted attitude not only affects women's participation in voting, but also in seeking election to public office. Table 24 shows that although the number of female representatives has been increasing over the years, very few women run for public office. The 10% of electoral seats reserved for women prescribed by the 1947 Constitution is no longer necessary. Female candidates win more than 10% of the seats at all levels of government; 15.35% of the members of the National Assembly are women; 13.21% of the Legislative Yuan are women; and, 22.03% of the Central Yuan are women (Ministry of the Interior, 1980). Nevertheless, women obviously need more representation in politics to match women's progress in education and overall employment.

Table 23*

Election of Vacancies & Additional Members of Congress by Voters' Sex Ratio

Types and Years	% Male Voters	% Female Voters
1. Delegates of National Assembly		
in 1969: Taiwan Province	81.9%	18.1%
Taipei Municipal	58.9%	41.1%
2. Additional Delegates of the National Assembly in 1973	53.8%	46.2%
3. Additional members of Legislators in 1973	53.9%	46.1%
4. Additional members of Legislators in 1975	53.4%	46.6%

The Kuomintang (KMT) has played a vital role in elections and political appointments, especially at the national level. Most of the elected officials are nominated and supported by the Party, including female candidates. Yet, the Party has not gone beyond the guidelines stipulated by the Constitution, which guarantees 10% of the seats for women. Consequently, some female candidates left the KMT and campaigned independently. If the Party had used its influence in favor of female candidates, women's political status could have been higher. Again, women hold even fewer appointed positions than elected ones. Up to the present, only one woman, Ms. Y.C. Wang, once served as the Deputy Minister of Education. Even well-educated women have not been able to avoid completely being stereotyped as fragile, emotional, and indecisive by high-ranking policy makers. Without confidence from the top level, women continue having difficulty breaking through their traditional

*Source: Department of Civil Affairs, Ministry of the Interior (Taipei, Taiwan: Ministry of the Interior, R.O.C., 1981).

Table 24*
Elected Public Officers by Sex from 1950-1981

Types of Election	Year	Men	Women
Elections of Prefectual & City Councils in Taiwan	1950	745	69
	1952	786	74
	1954	834	94
	1958	924	101
	1961	834	95
	1964	784	123
	1968	724	123
	1973	731	119
	1977	736	121
Elections of Taipei Municipal Assembly	1969	41	7
	1973	42	7
	1977	43	8
	1981	44	7
Election of Taiwan Provincial Assembly	1951	128	12
	1954	92	18
	1957	96	22
	1960	108	18
	1963	123	14
	1968	110	19
	1973	100	21
	1977	102	23
	1981	67	10

stereotypes. Moreover, the emphasis on motherhood by the government has further restrained women's involvement in political activities.

Of course, Chinese women's role in today's society is not restricted to the above-mentioned fields. Nowadays, women's outstanding performances can be seen in many areas. The research study conducted in Taiwan (Yao, 1981) examines women's successful experiences in different areas. Despite their professional success, however, women still labor under some of the cultural disadvantages which have grown from the traditional personal and social expectations of a Chinese woman.

*Source: *ibid.*.

E. The Family Role of Women

The family role of Chinese women has geared to the social background of China which was an agriculture-oriented society for thousands of years. Since manpower was the major means of crop production and field cultivation, extended families were needed. The role of women in the family was two-fold. First, they were considered domestic humanpower to be utilized for household chores, and they were available to labor in the fields (women from poor families toiled with their babies tied to their backs as they helped in the field). Secondly, Chinese women were expected to produce as many offspring, preferably male, as possible. In general, Chinese women assumed the entire responsibility for running the home while their husbands assumed the role of breadwinner working outside the house. Because women were considered inferior, morally pure, physically weaker than men, and intellectually naive, it was believed that they only deserved a subordinate position. Social norms dictated that they be submissive to their parents, husbands, and their adult sons. The industrialization of Taiwan since the late 1960s, and the accompanying economic boon have little influence on women's traditional role and value system. They continue to bear strong social pressure, even though they gained equal legal rights nearly half a century ago. Under many circumstances women have no other choice but to conform to traditional expectations for women. For example, marriage is still considered a necessary step for females. Young women receive greater pressure than young men to marry. The marital prospects of their daughters is a genuine concern of most parents.

Basically speaking, there are three types of marriage practiced in Taiwan: arranged or matched, romantic, and a combination of both. Arranged or matched marriages have nearly vanished in the urban areas and among the younger generation, but they are still found among the older or rural people. A survey of 980 women conducted by Lu (1978), indicates that 50% of the couples younger than 34 years of age enjoy a romantic marriage; 40% of them had been introduced to one another by mutual friends of both families and had a dating period prior to marriage (known as a combination marriage); only 10% were arranged marriages. On the other hand, 50% of the sample of couples over 35 years of age had combination marriages. It is evident that arranged marriage has been gradually fading out while romantic marriage is becoming more popular.

Likewise, today's marital ceremony in Taiwan has been modified. In China it was once the custom that wedding feasts be arranged at the expense of the groom's family. His family also sent gifts, such as money, gold, and jewelry to the bride's home. To insure higher esteem for the bride, her family was obligated to top the amount given by the groom's family by stretching its financial resources to the limit. The more she brought with her from her family, the more favorable her status was in her husband's family. Wedding feasts and dowries were symbols of socioeconomic status. With educational betterment, contemporary Chinese women have gradually abandoned the custom of bringing a dowry to a marriage. Influenced by westernization, they consider wedding feasts and dowries old fashioned; such practices are also discouraged by the government. Any monetary exchange between the two families is often denounced by the romantic couple as a business deal.

In terms of marital status, women can basically be classified into four groups: full-time housewives, employed wives, divorced women, and single women. With the increasing number of employed wives (33% of the total labor force), the family role as perceived by women has become less restrictive because of increased contacts outside the home. According to the results of several studies (Chang, 1974; Lu, 1978; Yao, 1981; and, Yao, 1982), the family role of married women can be discussed with respect to four major aspects: (1) status at home, (2) role expectation, (3) division of household affairs/labor, and (4) dominance and family integration.

The status of women at home has not changed significantly from their traditionally subordinate position in the wife-husband relationship. More than three-fourths of a group of women studied believed that the husband should be considered the head of the family, to be respected by all family members (Chang, 1974; and, Lu, 1978). These wives were willing to make concessions when their own preferences were disapproved by their husbands. Yao (1981) found that the successful career women she studied had struggled under the strong influence and constraint of their husbands. Issues of job transfer, promotion, salary increase, and any professional growth were considered only after obtaining their husband's consent, being unwilling to hurt their husband's ego or self-esteem. Since they gave top priority to husband and children, many of these women abandoned promising opportunities for career advancement in order to keep peace within their families.

While social favoritism of males is pervasive in Chinese society, Lu (1978) has found that not all women are unhappy with their subordinate role. Twenty-seven percent of the college-educated women, fifteen percent of junior high school graduates, and seven percent of the women with no education reported that they were satisfied to be women. Apparently a woman's degree of preference for her own sex is inversely proportional to her level of education. Seventy percent of the same sample believed that women are qualified for the presidency; thus it appears that Chinese women, in a society that greatly favors male development, manage to have a positive self-image and are confident of their abilities.

An interesting finding is that many urban wives exert strong control over living expenses (Chang, 1974; and, Lu, 1978). This concurs with the fact that most middle-class Chinese husbands hand over their pay checks to their wives who take care of the details of the family budget. However, managing their husband's pay checks does not mean that the wives have any higher decision-making status at home. Any major purchase involving a large sum of money still requires the husband's consent. Also, an investment decision is generally the husband's (Yao, 1982).

Role expectations for women are formed by immense social pressures. Influenced by their traditional family status, most of the women in several studies (Chang, 1974; Robins & Cheng, 1977; Lu, 1978; and, Yao, 1981) dutifully tried to fulfill their role at home. They counted their blessings by keeping house, taking care of the children, and serving their husbands. These women were willing to sacrifice personal interests and ambitions for the sake of their families; "home, sweet home" was the ultimate goal of the majority of the women studied. Whether employed or not, women obviously play an important domestic role. Regardless of their professional achievements, working mothers are expected to maintain comfortable homes for their families. If a successful career woman fails in her role as a wife and mother, she is likely to be criticized by the public as incompetent. Very often a broken marriage or delinquent child will ruin a woman's career. A working wife essentially plays a dual role—that of housekeeper and employee. In order to live up to social standards and expectations, a career woman must be a "superwoman" who works extremely hard to play this dual role efficiently. She will probably be accused of ignoring her husband and children if she fails to keep up with the standards set for full-time housewives. With the increasing shortage of domestic maids, it will be even harder for young career women than for their predecessors to play both roles at home and in the job market.

Division of labor between husbands and wives in the household has gradually changed in Taiwan. The results of a recent study by Yao (1982) with a heterogeneous sample of topic indicate an increasing amount of chores shared by both husband and wife. Because of better education and employment opportunities, Chinese women nowadays have become more competent and independent in dealing with various situations outside the home. They no longer rely on their husbands for calling repairmen, making doctor's appointments, talking with their children's school teachers, shopping for food and household items, and even mailing a package. Having changed from an agricultural, production unit, to an urban, consuming unit, the family requires more interaction with the outside world. Women cannot be confined at home to fulfill their obligations like their predecessors centuries ago; they must venture outside their homes and face new challenges. With the diminishing supply of maids, men are sharing more of the household responsibilities, especially babysitting and dishwashing (Yao, 1982). Lu (1978) found that more than half of the selected unemployed women under 30 and over 60 years of age expected their husbands to help with the household chores. Those women under 30 who have young children and older women who may be physically limited in their ability to handle all household tasks, may need a helping hand from their husbands. However, women in rural areas still tend to maintain their traditional role in domestic affairs (Wolf, 1974; Robins & Cheng, 1977), preferring that their husbands have little to do with household work. It is believed that this attitude is related to the amount of education a woman has received and her degree of exposure to the outside world (Chang, 1974).

The role of the husband in family integration has been fading away. The unity of the traditional family used to be determined by the head of the family—the husband. He had absolute authority in decision making in every aspect from child discipline to property management. The wife had little voice in any issue; even her own emotional needs were often overlooked. With the increasing percentage of romantic marriages, women have begun to play a more equal role in the family unit, eroding male dominance. In a study of urban women (Chang, 1974), 95% of the sample believed there was a balance of dominance of power between husbands and wives. The areas of decision making and patterns of allocating power in the urban Taiwan family can be found in Chang's paper (1974). Based on these samples, it appears that the husband-executive model no longer applies to urban marriages.

Marriage often generates problems for employed women although the number of employed women has risen substantially since the late 1960s; only 18.2% of married women are employed in Taiwan (Directorate-General of Budget, Accounting & Statistics, 1979). The salaries of working women are considered supplemental income for most families (Chang, 1974; Lu, 1978). The Chinese husband, with higher education than his wife, is still expected to be the sole bread winner of the family (Lu, 1978).

One of the major problems encountered by the working mother is the lack of childcare. Domestic maids do not assist in this area as they did twenty years ago. The government has not actively addressed the problem of inadequate childcare, which becomes progressively worse with the increasing number of working mothers. Legislation implemented in 1973, only specified standards and requirements for childcare facilities (Bureau of Social Welfare, 1979). There are two basic types of childcare available to working mothers—public and private. By the end of 1977, there were 531 nurseries in urban areas, accommodating over 50,000 children (five years old and under) of working women from low-income families. Nurseries for farm families were established in 1955 with the financial assistance of UNICEF. There were 85,093 children benefitted in 2,351 nurseries by the end of 1977. Unfortunately, UNICEF resources were discontinued in that same year and the project shrank to sixteen centers (ten in urban areas and six in rural) for 8,787 children. While the number of public government-run childcare centers has been diminishing, the number of private nurseries has emerged rapidly since 1968. There were only 177 private nurseries for 16,947 youngsters in 1968. As of June, 1979, 651 private nurseries have been established to serve 63,236 preschoolers (Ministry of the Interior, 1980). In addition to the facilities for childcare, personnel training also presents a problem for working mothers. Qualified teachers for and workers with preschool children are in great demand. The problem of adequately staffing childcare centers can only be solved through an educational process which, unfortunately, takes time to accomplish and may create a significant lag in supply and demand. For some young working mothers an alternative to this childcare problem is to leave the children in their grandparents' care. Other young mothers may be discouraged from seeking employment due to the lack of childcare. Therefore, a majority (80%) of studied married women with young children preferred to stay home and fulfill their child-rearing responsibilities (Chang, 1974).

Due to the population explosion, for over two decades the government has implemented various types of family planning programs. The Health Department of the Provincial Government provides different kinds of free contraceptives to women in rural areas. Urban wives tend to use birth control methods voluntarily. Messages spring from billboards in urban areas encouraging husbands to get vasectomies. This interesting phenomenon may imply that urban husbands are more open-minded and willing to have vasectomies than those in rural areas. Thus, rural wives and urban husbands play a vital role in birth control. The birth rate in 1976 was 2.59% compared to 4.66% in 1952. As a result the size of the average household has declined from 6.08 persons in 1946, to 5.3 persons in 1975 (Research, Development and

Evaluation Committee, 1977).

Even though family size is shrinking, automation in housekeeping is shortening the time spent on household responsibilities, and many educational opportunities are open to women—still, over 80% of married Chinese women remain at home (Directorate-General of Budget, Accounting & Statistics, 1980). This probably reflects the priority these women place on family as influenced by the traditional role expectation. Years of child rearing and housekeeping make them less confident and less ambitious when it comes to seeking employment or to be reeducated. By the time their children have grown up they suddenly feel impotent and useless at home as well as in the job market. With more leisure time available than ever before, housewives appear to have few outlets for spending this time. Unfortunately, adult or continuous education is not popular in Taiwan; thus, women in middle adulthood generally do not return to school for advanced studies or to embark on a new career. Consequently the most popular leisure activities of Chinese women in Taiwan are window shopping, novel reading, and watching television. Only a very small percentage of them (0.5%) are involved in volunteer work in the community (Lu, 1978). In some cases wives are expected to help their self-employed husbands take care of such tasks as bookkeeping, tending the shop, and other clerical work. Some middle and upper-middle class women indulge themselves in a gambling game known as *Machiang*, which consumes much time and money. How to use their spare time constructively is the major challenge facing today's Chinese housewives.

Aside from the problems caused by surplus time and energy, Chinese housewives are also confronted with the same kinds of emotional shock experienced by women in other advanced nations. The crises faced by these housewives seem to be caused by the imbalance between a rapidly changing society and the slowly growing progressive attitude of women toward their family role. Industrialization and urbanization have augmented the two major cultural shocks of social isolation and lack of spiritual support from the family. As a result of urbanization, less and less space is available for each housing unit. The crowded housing situation inhibits social interaction and encourages anonymity in the neighborhood. The fast-paced lifestyle observed in an industrial society leaves little time for human interaction. Moral support from the family was once a source of confidence and comfort during crises, particularly for those women who had few social contacts outside the home.

However, kinship has been diluted by urban lifestyles and the decline of the extended family. According to Chang (1974) and Lu (1978), only 20-22% of married women lived with in-laws, while the rest had nuclear families. Friction between the two generations under one roof is not a welcome topic to be discussed, even on the anonymous questionnaire on Lu's survey (1978)—50% of the sample did not respond to this question. As far as married daughters' interaction with their own families is concerned, 73% of those under 25 years of age, 38% of those over 45, and 17% of those over 55 had regular visits to their parents' homes. These results indicate that the ties with the wife's family tend to diminish with age.

Although people in Taiwan still hold the notion that marriage is a necessary step in life, the age of marriage is being delayed (Table 25) resulting in more and more single persons. Between 1960 and 1974 the number of married women in the 20-39 year old age bracket had steadily decreased to 2.2% of the total population of married women. In contrast, the percentage of married women over the age of 40 had increased 3.9% (Chai, 1977). Such trends reflect the tendency for people to postpone marriage or even remain single. There was an increase in the singles population of all ages, both sexes, between 1946 and 1979, from 32.4% to 41.6% for males, and 23.5% to 31.11% for females (Table 26). Based upon the observations and analysis by Hsiao (1977) four factors appear to contribute to the increase of single women. First, younger women set higher standards than men for selection of their mates. Second, young women are overly concerned about both the financial condition and physical height of their prospective spouse. Third, well educated young men who are short in stature are less popular but will eventually marry. Finally, young men in isolated or male-dominated working environments are not as active in seeking dates as are young women whose marital perspective is tied to their age. Consequently, a less sought after young man has more opportunities than overly-selective women to get married, once he decides to settle for a less educated or less attractive woman. The above-mentioned factors reflect two basic public attitudes toward marriage. First, there is the traditional idea that the husband should be superior to the wife; such thought still dominates the thinking of young women. As a result, well educated young women have a harder time finding superior males to marry. Also, "romanticism" exaggerated by movies, television, and books inflate the false hope that every young woman will eventually fall in love with the ideal man. An activist in the women's movement has suggested that society should no longer discourage women from marrying younger husbands or men with less education than themselves; women need more freedom to make their own choices (Lu, 1978).

The fact that women are delaying marriage implies that the concepts of individualism and independence have germinated in their minds. Today's females are not as enthusiastic about marriage and motherhood as their predecessors. Industrialization and growing employment opportunities enable them to become financially and, presumably, psychologically, independent. Employed women tend to pay less attention to traditional teachings because their satisfaction comes mainly from their occupation. Meanwhile, homosexuality among young women is beginning to appear among this younger generation; social gatherings and formation of female clubs are not at all unusual (Kuang, 1977). Society is concerned about this trend, but cannot offer any solution to worried parents who strongly desire that their daughters marry.

Parental reinforcement of both the sanctity of marriage and a sense of responsibility for the younger generation are considered the key factors in maintaining the marital bond. Additionally, Chinese women possess a fairly traditional attitude toward marriage in that they tend to tolerate circumstances which could contribute to marital discord (such as a husband's extramarital affair, mental mistreatment, and physical abuse). However, marital stability does not necessarily imply that women are completely content with their marriages. On the contrary, two studies (Lu, 1978 ; and, Robins & Cheng, 1977) indicate that most women were not sure they would marry the same spouse again if the choice were given. Concerning attitudes toward divorce, Lu (1978) found the younger women in her sample having a more liberal viewpoint than older women. When asked what they would do if their friends were considering divorce, 57% of those younger than 24 years old indicated that they would try to reconcile both parties, while 32% felt it depended on the particular situation. Seventy-eight percent of the sample over 45 years of age indicated that they would try to help their friends save the marriage, while only 12% would take steps according to the situation.

Women whose marriages end in divorce are few in Taiwan. The divorce rate has increased insignificantly over the past three decades, from .47% in 1946, to .90% in 1974 (Robins & Gheng, 1977; and, Chai, 1977). Insignificant as this percentage may seem, translated into numerical terms it indicates that approximately 90,000 women are divorcees. Among the total number of divorcees, 55.9% are initiated by males, 44.1% by females (Ch'ai, 1977). A divorce woman usually resumes her single life possessing only her personal belongings; contrary to the spirit of the law, her husband retains custody of the children and the house. She must re-establish interpersonal relationships and seek employment for herself. Such harsh reality may have discouraged many women from seeking divorce.

Since Chinese husbands are usually older than their wives, and since women outlive men, there is a higher percentage of widowed women over 50 than men (Table 26). Remarriage for widows is not as socially acceptable as it is for widowers. Because of the traditional notion of chastity for women, it is still considered disgraceful for a widow with grown children to remarry, particularly if the new spouse is younger. However, the latest statistics show that the rate of widowhood is decreasing (Table 26) and the remarriage rate among women is 16.1% compared to 33.2% of men (Ministry of the Interior, 1980).

Besides the increasing number of single women, other subgroups within the female population—factory workers, farm women, bar girls, and prostitutes—are emerging from their dormant status. Women from these groups possess different value systems, lifestyles, and levels of education than the majority of women (Chu, *et al.*, 1976). As a result of industrialization and the extension of free education, many junior high school female graduates went into light industry, especially textiles, electronics, and plastics factories. Since most factories provide room and board for their workers, these young girls prefer to stay away from the supervision of parents or other adults, and enjoy the freedom of activities outside their homes. The boring work day routine generates a strong desire for excitement after work. Their newly experienced independence and naivety give rise to excessive dating, and problems such as unwanted pregnancies arise in the factory compounds. Their low level of education, coupled with the developmental characteristics of adolescence, create confusion about their behavior and values. These girls become easily bewildered when trying to solve problems or make decisions. This group of maturing young women need desperately to have organized leisure activities and readily available, competent counseling services.

Farm women are usually older than the above-mentioned factory workers. In general, their attitudes and beliefs are more conservative than those of urban women (Wolf, 1972, Chu, *et al.*, 1976). Although like all other women they are entitled to nine years of free education, they usually drop out of junior high school to labor in the fields. They experience a monotonous life full of hard work and a minimal standard of living. Home economics extension workers can help them improve their physical environment and housekeeping techniques, but cannot change their value system. Most of the time the family role of women on the farms is similar to that of women in history. Battered farm wives are not uncommon (Chu, *et al.*, 1976). They are victims of the traditional norm of female submissiveness.

Contrary to the farm women, bar girls and prostitutes encounter a different living environment. Most of them (72.5%) are escapees from poverty or from a traditional family setting (Lu, 1977b; Chu, *et al.*, 1976). Others include those who lost their virginity to boy friends or by rape. Their educational level varies according to their family background and motive for this type of work. Most of them are still influenced by traditional moral standards, and so have low self-esteem. Their "job identity" has an undesirable negative impact upon their potential marriage even when they are given the opportunity. The feelings of guilt associated with their work cannot be easily erased; consequently, their low-self-esteem is usually irreversible.

Society takes a passive view of these women. They must fight their way through life on their own. The social welfare system in Taiwan, as compared to other advanced nations, is in the primary developmental stage. All benefits are designed mainly for the majority, both female and male, without taking exceptional groups of female citizens into consideration. The special needs of today's women, including childcare facilities, homes for battered wives or unmarried mothers, abortion clinics, etc., have not been met by implemented governmental policies. Most of the welfare policies focus on labor benefits, employment, vocational training, housing development, and medical care, needs of those people who are recognized and accepted by the social norms.

In conclusion, Chinese married women are facing the challenges of both the traditional role expectation in the family and their changing legal and social statuses in an industrialized country. A majority of these housewives are not aware of the advancement of the women's movement with regard to legal rights. Their potential resources, including educational training, are not fully utilized, simply because of the restrictions of the traditional role expectations at home. Even working women are no exception; they must assume a dual role in order to pursue employment opportunities. Regardless of marital status, educational level, or geographical location, Chinese women have a long way to go before freeing themselves completely from the bondage of the traditional role. Legal rights provided by the constitution serve only as a foundation for women's advancement in society. Women have to enhance their self-image and their attitude toward their role in life in order to build upon the foundation of equal rights.

F. A Comparison of Women in Taiwan & Mainland China

Comparing the different experiences of Chinese women in Taiwan and in Mainland China is a difficult task. They live in societies of different ethnic composition, geographic location, political ideology, economic system, and social structure. Not taking these elements into consideration would invalidate any comparison. To determine the intricate relationships among these elements and their impact on the women's movement, however, would require another book. The following comparison merely serves as a general overview of women's experience under the two regimes.

Perhaps the most fundamental difference between the women in Mainland China and in Taiwan is the attitude and perception of their role in society which the political climate sanctions. Since part of the Communist revolutionary ideology is to liberate women from traditional bondage, women are encouraged to question and protest their traditional role. Divorce no longer stigmatizes a woman as an unfit human being. The burden and pressure of being a good daughter-in-law and supportive, self-sacrificing wife and mother no longer weigh on her. Instead, she is expected to live up to her potential by contributing her share to the economic growth and socialistic construction of the country. To meet the working mother's needs, employers and the government have taken the responsibility of providing good childcare facilities, eliminating one of the biggest worries of the working mother. Thus, women in Mainland China are not only encouraged, but pressured to work outside the home, and by so doing have gained economic power and independence.

On the other hand, women in Taiwan, even with the provision of legal rights, are encouraged to play an important role in family life, including maintaining good relationships with kinfolk. Although educational and employment opportunities are equally open to both sexes, women often find that the education they receive does not directly provide either personal satisfaction or job training. Because of the influence of traditional roles imposed on women, and/or the demand of the employers, many women quit their jobs after marriage or childbirth. Proportionately speaking, a lower percentage of women with young children are employed outside the home (Directorate-General of Budget, Accounting & Statistics, 1980). Moreover, the Women's Committee of the KMT has recently initiated a campaign to revive the traditional view of family life which includes the notion that being a good wife and mother is a woman's best way of making her contribution to society and the nation. The government's attitude also keeps the number of working mothers from growing as rapidly as on the Mainland. Additionally, shortages of childcare programs, public and private, slows the growth of the female labor force.

Another immediately obvious difference is the governmental role relating to women's issues. The Communist government takes an active role in women's changing lives while the KMT government is less active in engineering the changes in women's traditional role. To the KMT, pressuring women to participate in the labor force and abandon their "natural gifts" for homemaking is a form of exploitation of women.

In Mainland China, the government is able to translate Communist ideology concerning women into effective policy through political networks that reach down to the individuals through the organizations of communes and street committees. Thus the government not only implements the marriage law but also makes sure that women participate in political meetings and skill-training programs. Thus women, like men, are given the opportunity to work in the field and in other traditionally male jobs such as tractor drivers and pilots. Older women also prove their usefulness by working in nurseries. Counseling and guidance for marital problems can be obtained from local political and productive units. Often the intervention of these units resolves domestic strife resulting from women's non-traditional attitudes. Criticism from other organization members and self-criticism also helps change attitudes and facilitates women's new role. Because of the political and productive network, women's sense of belonging extends beyond the confines of the home; her concerns involve the community and her satisfaction can be drawn from there.

Unlike the Communist government which in the beginning of the women's movement encouraged women to speak out against their bitter past, the KMT has merely rallied women to contribute their time and effort to the unity of the nation. The KMT has not encouraged women to speak publicly of their distressing experiences and express their resentment toward husband and parents-in-law who mistreated them. This lack of training in public speech and leadership contributes to women's insensitivity to politics in Taiwan. The ten percent of legislative seats reserved for women is perhaps the only incentive for political involvement of women in the government. Since the Northern Expedition in the late 1920s, the issue of women's legal rights has been on the agenda of legislatures and constitutional conventions. Yet the implementation of the legal codes to insure equal rights for women has been frustrated by people's traditional values. Very often in Taiwan, today, the Marriage Law is not enforced by the government, and decisions of judges still reflect the traditional mode of family life practiced by the general public.

Meanwhile, women in Taiwan receive public praise for being full-time housewives, but enjoy no such support for working outside the home, even though many are forced to do so for financial reasons. Unlike women in Mainland China, they are not encouraged by governmental policies to be wage earners. Non-working, middle-class mothers have the freedom to arrange their leisure time around activities which involve no interaction with the outside world and may make no contribution to the nation. Thus, they become isolated and incapable socially and politically. Fortunately, the major women's organizations administered by the government have tried to attract more women to work voluntarily for various organizational projects. Women's occupational choices in Mainland China are to a greater extent influenced and determined by the current governmental policy and priority.

Although educational opportunities are equally given to boys and girls in both Mainland China and Taiwan, the method for reaching the goal is different. In Taiwan, as they reach their teens, school children are steered to different subjects: girls to homemaking and nursing, and boys to mechanical and industrial training. Later, social norms and parental attitudes influence most girls to pursue a college education in liberal arts and human sciences while boys are directed toward sciences and engineering. Such sex distinction in career choices is much less evident in Mainland China.

The self-image of women in Taiwan is strongly influenced by the advertisements and mass media which depict women as sex objects. Women spend a great deal of money and effort on clothes and make-up. Dieting and cosmetic surgery are practically unheard of in Mainland China, but are quite common in Taiwan. Admiration of popular female

240

singers and actresses is a social phenomenon among the young people, both enhancing and degrading women at the same time. While profit-making singers and actresses serve as a role model for youngsters showing women's financial strength, the women's image as sex objects for men's pleasure also permeates among people.

Conclusion

Based on my personal visit to Mainland China and fragmentary reports from there which has recently undergone drastic political changes, I conclude that the differences found in the lives and value systems between these two groups of Chinese women during the past decades essentially reflect the differences of political ideology. Mainland China has focused on socialist reconstruction and Taiwan on maintaining a more traditional and conservative social structure. Whether the present trend will continue is subject to future political shifts and emphasis of both parties. However, it is certain that overall, Chinese women's status in family and society has improved. The oppression of women is definitely a matter of historical record.

The author: **Esther Lee S. Yao**

NOTES

[1] Taiwan Committee on Promotion of Women's Status, *Ten-year plan to promote women's status in the Republic of China* (Taipei, Taiwan: Ministry of Interior Affairs, 1968), pp. 48-50.

[2] Information given to the author by the Ministry of the Interior in 1979

[3] P'i Yi-shu, *Chinese Women's Movement* (Taipei, Taiwan: United Women Publishers 1973), pp. 129-130.

[4]*Ibid.*, pp. 116-125.

[5]Information given to the author by the Ministry of the Interior in 1979.

[6]*Encyclopaedia Britannica*, I, p. 727

[7]Ministry of the Interior, *Demographic Fact Book* (Taipei, Taiwan: Ministry of the Interior; December 1980), p. 112.

[8]"More males than females," *China Times* (July 29, 1979).

[9]Information provided to the author by the Ministry of the Interior, 1976

242

Bibliography

Andors, Phyllis. *The ongoing revolution in women's liberation in the People's Republic of China* (New York: Far East Reporter, 1979).

Ayscough, Florence. *Chinese women: yesterday and today* (Boston: Houghton Mifflin Company, 1937).

Brandt, Conrad, Benjamin Schwartz, and John Fairbank. *A documentary history of Chinese communism* (Cambridge, Massachusetts: Harvard University Press, 1959).

Bureau of Social Welfare. *Introduction to Chinese welfare systems* (Taipei, Taiwan: Ministry of the Interior, Republic of China, 1979).

Ch'ai, Sung-lin, "Marriage made in Taiwan," in *Taiwan Bank Quarterly* XXVIII.1 (1977).

Chang, Hsiao-chun, "A study of urban housewives' role in modern society," in *Bulletin of the Institute of Ethnology* No. 37 (1974).

Chang, Min. *Women in Taiwan in the past twenty years* (Taipei, Taiwan: Women's Writers League Association, 1966).

Chao, Feng-chieh *Legal position of Chinese women* (Estimated published in 1928; reprinted in Taipei, Taiwan: Shih Huo Publishing Company, 1973).

Ch'en, Ku-yuan. *History of Chinese marriage* (Estimated published in 1926; reprinted in Taipei, Taiwan: Commerce Publishing Company, 1975).

Ch'en, Kung-po. *The Communist movement in China* (New York: Columbia University Press, 1960).

Ch'en, Tung-yuan. *History of the life of Chinese women* (Estimated published in 1926; reprinted in Taipei, Taiwan: Commerce Publishing Company, 1977).

Chesneaux, Jean. *The Chinese Labor movement, 1919-1927* (Palo Alto, California: Stanford University Press, 1968).

Chesneaux, Jean, Marianne Bastid, and Marie-Claire Bergere. *China from the Opium Wars to the 1911 Revolution* (New York: Pantheon Books, 1976).

Chia, Shen, "Examination of women's footbinding in China," in *Geographical and historical report* III.3 (October, 1924).

Chiang, Nan, "Political arena: women rivaling men," in *Times Weekly* (December 11, 1977).

Chiang, Yung-chien, "Hu Han-ming's philosophy and the Chinese Women's movement," in *Journal of Shih Huo* VIII.7 (October, 1978).

Chin, Aili S. "Mainland China," in Rahael Patai's *Women in the modern world* (New York: Free Press, 1967).

Chin, Aili S., "Family relations in modern Chinese fiction," in *Family and kinship in Chinese society*, edited by Maurice Freedman (Palo Alto, California: Stanford University Press, 1970).

Chiu, Chiu-wen, "Women in education," *Weekly Times* (December 11, 1977).

Committee of Concerned Asian Scholars. *China: inside the People's Republic* (New York: Bantam, 1976).

Chu, Min, Yeh-ch'in Lo and An-an Liu, *Their labors and their tears* (Taipei, Taiwan: Pioneer Publisher, 1976).

Ch'uan, Han-cheng, "Women wage earners in the Sung Dynasty," in *Journal of Shih Huo* I.9 (April, 1935).

Creel, Harrlee Glessner, *The birth of China* (New York: John Day Publishing Company, 1954).

Crespigny, Rafede, "The harem of Emperor Huan: A study of court politics in the Latter Han," in *Far Eastern history* XII (1975).

Croll, Elizabeth, *The Women's movement in China* (2d ed.; London: Anglo-Chinese Educational Institute, 1976).

Croll, Elizabeth, *Feminism and socialism in China* (London: Routledge and Kegan Paul, 1978).

Croll, Elizabeth, "Rural China: segregation to solidarity," in *Women united, women divided* by Patricia Caplan and Janet M. Bujra (Indianapolis, Indiana: Indiana University Press, 1979).

Crooks, Isabel and David Crooks, *Revolution in a Chinese village* (London: Routledge and Kegan Paul, 1959).

Davin, Delia, *Woman-work: women and the Party in Revolutionary*

244

China (Oxford, England: Clarendon Press, 1976).

de Bary, William Theodore. *Sources of Chinese tradition* (New York: Columbia University Press, 1960).

Directorate-General of Budget, Accounting & Statistics. *Monthly bulletin of labor statistics, Republic of China* (Taipei, Taiwan: Executive Yuan of the Republic of China, 1978-1979).

Directorate-General of Budget, Accounting & Statistics. *Report on the relationships between female fertility and employment in the Taiwan area* (Taipei, Taiwan: Executive Yuan of the Republic of China, 1980).

Document of the Women's movement in the liberated areas of China (Shanghai, 1949).

Doolittle Justus. *Social life of the Chinese* (London: Sampson Low, Son and Martson, 1868).

Ebernard, Wolfram. *A history of China* (Los Angeles: University of California Press 1977).

Emerson, John Philip. *Sex, age and level of skill of non-agricultural labor force of Mainland China* (Washington, D.C.: Foreign Demographic Analysis Division, Bureau of Census, 1965).

Emerson, John Philip. *Employment in Mainland China: problems and prospects* (New York: Praeger, 1968).

Executive Yuan of the Republic of China. *National Statistics, 1972-77* (Taipei, Taiwan: Executive Yuan of the Republic of China, 1978).

Fang, Fu-an. *Chinese labor* (London: P.S. King & Son, Ltd., 1931).

Fawdry, Marguerite. *Chinese childhood* (New York: Barron's, 1977).

Fitzgerald, C.P. *China* (New York: Frederick Praeger, Inc., 1958).

Fitzgerald, C.P. *The Empress Wu* (Vancouver, British Columbia: University of British Columbia Press, 1968).

Fong, Stanley L.M., "Sex roles in the modern fabric of China," in *Sex roles in changing society*, edited by Georgene H. Seward and Robert C. Williamson (New York: Random House, 1970).

Forman H. *Changing China* (New York: Crown Publishing Company, 1948).

245

Fu, Le-ch'eng, "Women's lives in the T'ang Dynasty,' in *Shih-huo Magazine* IV.1 & 2 (May, 1974).

"Further liberated women's labor capacity," *People's Daily* (June 2, 1958).

Granet, Marcel. *Chinese civilization* (London: Kegan Paul, Trench, Trubner and Company, 1930).

Gross, Susan Hill and Marjorie Wall Bingham. *Women in traditional China* (Hudson, Wisconsin: GEM Publications, Inc., 1980).

Hibbert, Christopher. *The dragon wakes: China and the West, 1793-1911* (New York: Harper & Row, 1970).

Hibbert, Eloise Talcott. *Embroidered gauze: portraits of famous Chinese ladies* (London: John Lane, 1938).

Holmgren, Jennifer, "Empress Dowager Ling of the Northern Wei and the Touba Sinicization question," *Far Eastern history* XVIII (1978).

Hong, Yuan, "Li Ch'ing-ch'ao—an eleventh century woman poet," *Women of China* (September, 1980).

Hou, Chi-ming, "Man-power, employment, and unemployment," in *Economic trends in Communist China*, edited by Alexander Eckstein, *et al.* (Chicago: Aldine, 1968).

Hsiao, Kao-ho, "Marital problems among young people—an analysis based on the marriage advertisement," *Journal of College* (May, 1977).

Hsin Chung-kuo hun-yin wen-ti (Marriage problems in New China) 1949.

Hsu-Balzer, Eileen, Richard J. Balzer, and Francis L.K. Hsu. *China day by day* (New Haven, Connecticut: Yale University Press, 1974).

Hsu, Cho-yun, "Women's responsibilities in antiquity based on the *Rites of Chou*," in *Mainland Magazine* VIII.7 (April, 1954).

Hsu, Tien-hsiao. *New history of Chinese women* (originally published in Shaghai, by Shen Chou Publishing Company, 1913; reprinted in Taipei, Taiwan: Shih Huo Publishing Company, 1978).

Jen, Ta-jung, "Archaeological search of matriarchy in Chinese antiquity," *East Magazine* XXXII.1 (January, 1935).

Johnson, Kay Ann, "Women in China: problems of sex inequality and socioeconomic change," in *Beyond intellectual sexism: a new woman, a new reality*, edited by Joan I. Roberts (New York: David McKay Company, 1976).

Kao, Mai, "The development of shrines of chastity in China " *Eastern Magazine* (March, 1935).

Kao, Mai, "Historical review of Chinese prostitution," in *Readings in Chinese women's history*, edited by Pao Chia-lin (Taipei, Taiwan: Mu T'ung Publishing Company, 1979).

Kessen, William, ed. *Childhood in China* (New Haven, Connecticut: Yale University Press, 1975).

Klein, Donald W. and Anne B. Clark. *Geographic dictionary of Chinese Communism, 1921-65* (Cambridge, Massachusetts: Harvard University Press, 1971).

Kuang, Tai . *The diary of a divorced woman* (Taipei, Taiwan: Time Newspaper Publishers, 1977).

Lang, Olga. *Chinese family and society* (New Haven, Connecticut: Yale University Press, 1946; reprinted in New York: Archon Books, 1968).

Legge, James *The Sacred Books of the East* vols. 4, 27, 28 (Oxford, England: Clarendon Press, 1885).

Levy, Howard. *Harem favorites of an illustrious celestrial* (Taipei, Taiwan: Chung Tai Printing, 1958).

Levy, Howard. *Chinese footbinding* (New York: Walton Rawis, 1966).

Lewis, Ida Belle. *The education of girls in China* (New York: Columbia University Press, 1919).

Li, Ch'ia-fu . *Chinese ancient women* (Taipei, Taiwan: Li Min Publishing Company, 1978a).

Li, Ch'ia-fu. *Lives of ancient Chinese women* (Taipei, Taiwan: Li Min Publishing Company, 1978b).

Li, Ch'ang-nien, "Female infanticide and inequality of two sexes in China," *Eastern Magazine* (June, 1935).

Li, Yu-ning and Yu-fa Chang, eds. *Documents on the Feminist Movement in modern China* (Taipei, Taiwan: Biographical Literature Publishing Company, 1975).

Lin, Y.T. *My country and my people* (New York: Reynal & Hitchcock, 1935).

Liu, Liang-ch'un. *A study on Chinese women's legal status* (Taipei, Taiwan: Commerce Publishing Company, 1977).

Liu, Mao-shu, "Champion of the Chinese Women's movement," *Women of China* (March & April, 1980).

Liu, Nai-he, "China's first woman historian," *Women of China* (April, 1980).

Liu, Tzu-ch'ing. *Critical biographies of famous women in Chinese history* (Taipei, Taiwan: Li Min Publishing Company, 1978).

Lu, Hsiu-lien. *New feminist* (Taipei, Taiwan: Pioneer Publisher, 1977).

Lu, Hsui-lien. *Where to go from New Feminist* (Taipei, Taiwan: Pioneer Publisher, 1977).

Ma, Kuang-chu. *Chinese folktales* (Kao Hsiang, Taiwan: Kuang Ming Publishing Company, 1979).

Mandel, William M. *Soviet women* (New York: Anchor Press, 1975).

Mao, Tse-tung, "Socialist upsurge in the countryside," quoted in *Peking Review* (November 11, 1964).

Ministry of Education. *Educational statistics of the Republic of China* (Taipei, Taiwan: R.O.C., 1980).

Ministry of the Interior. *Introduction to social welfare in Taiwan* (Taipei, Taiwan: R.O.C., 1978).

Ministry of the Interior. *Statistical abstract of the Interior of the Republic of China* (Taipei, Taiwan: R.O.C., 1978).

Ministry of the Interior. *1979 Taiwan-Fukien Demographic fact-book, Republic of China* (Taipei, Taiwan: R.O.C., 1980).

Ministry of Justice. *Revision on Civil Laws on the Family* (Taipei, Taiwan: R.O.C., 1979).

Mou, Hsun, "Kung Yang's evidence of matriarchy in the Spring and Autumn period," *Hsin Ya Hsueh Po* I.1 (August, 1966).

Myrdal, Jan and Gun Kessle. *China: the revolution continued* (New York: Vintage, 1970).

248

Nieh, Chung-ch'i, "The historical change on women's remarriage," in *Readings in Chinese women's history*, edited by Pao Chia-lin (Taipei, Taiwan: Mu T'ung Publishing Company, 1979).

Orleans, Leo A. *Professional manpower and education in Communist China* (Washington, D.C.: U.S. Government Printing Office, 1961).

Orleans, Leo A., "Communist Chinese education," in *An economic profile of Mainland China* by the Joint Economic Committee of the United States Congress (Washington, D.C.: U.S. Government Printing Office, 1967).

Orleans, Leo A., "China's science and technology," in *People's Republic of China: an economic assessment* by the Joint Ecomic Committee of the United States Congress (Washington: D.C.: U.S. Government Printing Office, 1972).

Pao, Chia-lin, ed. *Readings in Chinese women's history* (Taipei, Taiwan: Mu T'ung Publishing Company 1979).

Patai, Raphael. *Women in the modern world* (New York: Free Press, 1967).

P'i, Yi-shu. *Chinese Women's movement* (Taipei, Taiwan: United Women Publishers, 1973).

Pott, F.I. Hawks. *A sketch of Chinese history* (Shanghai: Kelly and Walsh, 1903).

"Report of the Writing Group of the Communist Provincial Committee," *Red Flag* (February 1, 1971).

Research Development and Evaluation Commission. *Introduction to administration* (Taipei, Taiwan: Executive Yuan of the Republic of China, 1977).

Richman, Barry. *Industrial society in Communist China* (New York: Random House, 1969).

Robins, Lisa Dale and Carol Cheng, "Women's perceptions of their roles in Taiwan area studies," in *Asian studies* I.1 (June, 1977).

Roberts, Joan I., ed. *Beyond intellectual sexism: a new woman a new reality* (New York: David McKay, 1976).

Ross, Edward A. *The changing Chinese* (New York: Century, 1920).

Russell, Maud. *Chinese women: liberated* (New York: Far East Reporter; 2d. ed., 1979).

Safford, A C. *Typical women of China* (London: Kelly Walsh, Ltd., 1899).

Salaff, Janet, "Institutionalized motivation for fertility limitation in China," *Population studies* XXVI.2 (July, 1972).

Shafer, Edward H. *Ancient China* (New York: Time-Life Books, 1967).

Shih, Vincent Y.E. *The Taiping ideology* (Seattle: University of Washington Press, 1967).

Shu, Jiong. *The most famous beauty of China* (New York: D. Appleton and Company, 1924).

Sidel, Ruth. *Women and child-care in China: a firsthand report* (Baltimore: Penguin, 1972).

Snow, E. *Red Star over China* (New York: Grove Publishing Company, 1968).

Swann, Nancy Lee. *Pan Ch'ao: foremost scholar of China* (New York: Century Company, 1932).

The Committee on Promotion of Women's Status. *Ten-Year Plan to promote women's status in the Republic of China* (Taipei, Taiwan: Ministry of the Interior of the Republic of China, 1968).

Taiwan Normal University. *Final report on the college entrance examination of 1978* (Taipei, Taiwan: Taiwan Normal University Press, 1979).

Taiwan Provincial Labor Force Study and Research Institute. *Quarterly reports on the labor force survey in Taiwan* (Taipei, Taiwan: The Executive Yuan of the Republic of China, 1971-1979).

Townsend, James R. *The People's Republic of China: a basic book* (New York: The China Council of the Asian Society, 1979).

Ts'ai, Hsien-jung, "The beginning of polygany in China," *Journal of New Social Science* I.2 (1934).

Tung, Chia-tsun, "Research on widows from Han Dynasty to Sung Dynasty," *Historical literature of Central University* III.2 (1937).

Waley, Arthur, trans. *Shih Ching (The Book of Songs)* (Boston: Houghton, 1937).

Wang, Li-shing, "Women in the arts and literature," *Weekly Times* (December 11, 1977).

Wei, Fu-jen. *Life and compassion* (Taipei, Taiwan: Yuen Lin Publishing Company, 1975).

Weitz, Shirley. *Sex roles* (New York: Oxford University Press, 1977).

Wilburn, C. Martin, "The influence of the past; how the early years helped to shape the future of the Chinese Communist Party," in *Party leadership and revolutionary power in China*, edited by John Wilson Lewis (Cambridge, England: Cambridge University Press, 1970).

Wilhelm, Richard. *A short history of Chinese civilization* (New York: Kennikat Press, 1970).

Wilhelm, Richard. *I Ching (Book of Changes)*, translated by Cary F. Baynes (New York: Pantheon Books, 1950).

Wittfogel, Karl and Feng Jiasheng. *History of Chinese society* (Philadelphia: American Philosophical Society, 1949).

Wolf, Margery. *Women and the family in rural Taiwan* (Palo Alto, California: Stanford University Press, 1972).

Wolf, Margery, "Chinese women: old skills in a new context," in *Women, culture and society*, edited by M.Z. Rosaldo and L. Lamphere (Palo Alto, California: Stanford University Press, 1974).

"Women can prop up half of heaven," *Kuoming Daily* (January 14, 1974).

Women's Department. *Our work* (Taipei, Taiwan: Central Committee of Kuomingtang, 1976).

Women's Department. *Readings on Mme. Chiang's Collection of speechs* (Taipei, Taiwan: Central Committee of Kuomingtang, 1979).

Wu, K.C. *The Chinese heritage* (New York: Crown Publishers, 1982).

Yang, C.K. *Chinese Communist society: the family and the village* (Cambridge, Massachusetts: M.I.T. Press, 1965).

Yang, Lian-sheng, "Female rulers in Imperial China," *Harvard Journal of Asiatic Studies* XXIII (1960).

Yang, Martin. *A Chinese village: Taiton, Shantung Province* (New York: Columbia University Press, 1945).

Yao, Esther S. Lee, "Successful professional women in Taiwan," *Cornell Journal of Social Relations* XVI.1 (1981).

Yao, Esther S. Lee, "Variables for household division of labor as revealed by Chinese women in Taiwan," (mss.; scheduled for 1983 publication).

Young, Marilyn. *Women in China* (Ann Arbor, Michigan: The University of Michigan, Center for Chinese Studies, 1973).

Yu, Li-hua. *New Chinese women* (Hong Kong: the Seventies Magazine Publisher, 1977).

252

INDEX

*denotes women.

256

258

260